The author has certainly done his homework. I should know
... I am that homework.

Paul McDermott

Mesmerising. It made me feel I was really there. Hang on ...
I really was there.

Richard Fidler

Amazing! This guy can really spell.

Tim Ferguson

You'll be hearing from my lawyer.

C.P. Mellor

He doesn't really have a lawyer ...

Samantha Kelly

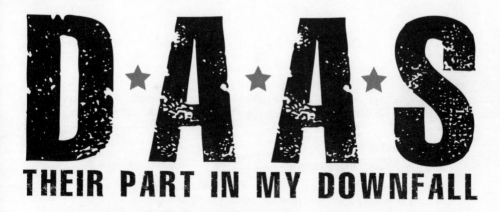

D·A·A·S

THEIR PART IN MY DOWNFALL

How I survived life on the road with the
DOUG ANTHONY ALL-STARS

★ PAUL LIVINGSTON ★

ALLEN&UNWIN
SYDNEY·MELBOURNE·AUCKLAND·LONDON

First published in 2016

Allen & Unwin
83 Alexander Street
Crows Nest NSW 2065
Australia
Phone: (61 2) 8425 0100
Email: info@allenandunwin.com
Web: www.allenandunwin.com

Cataloguing-in-Publication details are available
from the National Library of Australia
www.trove.nla.gov.au

ISBN 978 1 76029 076 4

Set in 12.25/18 pt Chaparral Pro by Bookhouse, Sydney
Printed and bound in Australia by Griffin Press

10 9 8 7 6 5 4 3 2 1

To the ever-stoppable Ted Robinson

CONTENTS

MOVEMENT III

MOVEMENT IV

PREFACE

Foolery, sir, does walk about the orb
like the sun; it shines everywhere.

SHAKESPEARE, *TWELFTH NIGHT*, ACT 3, SCENE 1

The subtitle of this book is an allusion to the first of Spike
Milligan's war memoirs, *Adolf Hitler: My Part in His Downfall*. It
was on seeing Spike perform in 1984 that a germ hatched in my
brain: the idea that I might have it in me to stand onstage in
front of a roomful of strangers and attempt to entertain them.
I had formerly presumed comedy was about telling jokes, yet
in this two-and-a-half-hour performance there were no setups
and no punchlines. Spike Milligan was simply funny for funny's
sake. I swiftly set about writing no jokes with no setups and
no punchlines. That was the easy part. I had no inkling of
what was to come: the years on the road, homelessness, near
alcoholism and those bemused audiences who are perhaps still
waiting for the punchline – yet their response was enough

to keep me not writing jokes for them for the best part of three decades.

It is my wish to avoid the panegyrical in what follows. Stand-up comedy is widely perceived among thespians to be the lowest of arts, and it is my intention to prove this premise true. Shakespeare knew a thing or two about comedy. *Twelfth Night* is full of low comedy, thus turning low comedy into high art. 'Better a witty fool, than a foolish wit,' sayeth the witty fool in Act 1, Scene 5. Using the bard as my yardstick, I set to thirty years ago in an attempt to spin comic yarns of the finest silk. When I boasted of this to a low comedic companion she said, 'Silk is secreted from the spinnerets of a lowly grub.' I was certainly put in my place, or cocoon as the case may have been. I even had to look up 'spinnerets' in the same way that you reached for the dictionary to locate 'panegyrical'.

INTRODUCTION

Get your facts first, then you can
distort them as you please.

MARK TWAIN

My first memory of the Doug Anthony All-Stars is a hot
summer afternoon during the Adelaide Fringe Festival of 1986.
I had procured a pie floater from a famous pie stand. The pie
floater is perhaps the most impractical takeaway snack ever
invented by an Australian. A meat pie, face down, submerged in
a lagoon of pea soup. I was sitting in Rundle Mall in blistering
heat, gravy dripping into my lap, when three boys leapt into
view. The first thing I recall is the smell – a rank, sour stench
of sweat and denim. The agitated anatomic manoeuvrings of
these pungent gents only served to spread their combined fetor.
They were young, ebullient, whiffy and loud.

My instant dislike of D.A.A.S. stemmed from my yearning
at that time to punch above my intellectual station. I stated

publicly, on my A4 flyer, that I didn't perform comedy; I advertised myself instead as 'a phrenic yet frenetic comic monologist' in the hope of enticing the higher browed to my as-yet-not-so-well-attended (only two stars in the *Adelaide Advertiser*) solo excursions during the festival. My arty ire was further aroused when a crowd of over a hundred soon gathered to enjoy the antics of these three young Festes. Entertainment? 'How uncool,' thought I, wallowing in aesthetic prejudice, yet something compelled me to endure their antics.

On the surface here was a trio of pretty boys singing trite ditties in three-part harmonies. The sweet songs were a form of enticement. No sooner do you take a step into their world than they attack like a rabid pack of spider monkeys. They clambered over their audience, scavenging handbags, wallets, neckties and small children.

D.A.A.S. worked hard that afternoon. We were a tough audience. It was Adelaide, it was festival time, and the city was teeming with arts festival tossers fresh out of a matinee performance of Samuel Beckett's *Endgame* followed by a discussion on po-mo sub-patriarchialist narratives (believe me, I was there). But even as pretentious a mob as this was no match for the Doug Anthony All-Stars. Like willing payers in a sadomasochistic dungeon, they were tied down, whipped and asking for more from their youthful dominatricksters. I maintained a fair impression of disdainful aloofness, until a certain spider monkey attempted to lap up the remains of my pie floater. It's hard to remain cool with Paul McDermott burrowing into your groin in the cold light of a very hot day.

A short time later, Paul McDermott, Richard Fidler and Tim Ferguson introduced themselves to me. They had witnessed my monologue and were impressed. Suddenly, I was enamoured with them. Flattery got them everywhere. I was nothing if not young and fickle, and I was about to take the plunge from high art to low, from monologist to stand-up comedian.

What did impress me upon first encountering the Doug Anthony All-Stars was their shallowness. They had 'the appearance of knowledge', a trope I had been employing in my own comic monologues in the guise of my alter ego, Flacco, an improbable comic creation who somehow attained the status of minor celebrity in Australia by bathing in the glow of the limelight cast by giants like D.A.A.S. Flacco was a fragile creature who flickered for a moment and died, again and again and again. Despite my best efforts, Flacco has proven to be akin to the proverbial vegetarian turd, seemingly unflushable. He has had so many bites of the cherry that these days he's just gnawing at the pit. After a determined decade-long battle to loosen the Flacco shackle, I am presently resigned to embracing this altered ego that has followed me for over a quarter of a century. That aka has opened many doors (and slammed quite a few in my face), both personally and professionally.

Early on, I learned that you need only a pithy quote and a dropped name to convey a sense of sagacity. Clive James described one of Hitler's most demonic gifts as 'the con-man's knack of making himself seem profoundly steeped in any subject just by the fluency with which he could learn a list of facts and reel them off to the susceptible ear of a worshipping disciple'. Flacco recklessly paraphrased Foucault, Descartes and Sartre, and was immediately embraced by the few. Meanwhile D.A.A.S. were tossing off similar names and attracting the attention of a wider audience through incessant busking. It takes a lot of gall in the mall to throw in a highbrow curved ball – for example, this verse from one of their more popular tunes, 'Broad Lic Nic':

> We took the whacks from Kerouacs
> And dusty Dostoyevskys
> And when all was said and done
> Booze was all that was left me
> For all the world's great thinkers
> Are all a load of pus
> And if you ask how Zarathustra spoke
> He spake thus!

The boys quickly dragged things back to the gutter in the chorus:

> Drink, drink, drink
> Drink until you're drunk
> Drink until you can't stand up
> Till you're roly-poly stunk
> Till your bladder bursts
> Till you throw a fit to curse
> Till they lift you up still comatose
> And slamdance in the hearse

I would describe my recruitment into the current incarnation of D.A.A.S. as a kidnapping for which I'm being paid a handsome ransom. After bathing in the reflected glory of Tim Ferguson, Paul McDermott and Richard Fidler throughout those heady years of the late eighties and into the early nineties, crossing continents and international date lines, I now find myself (a self happily enjoying retirement in the comfort that obscurity brings) treading the boards once more with two of the original members of D.A.A.S. on a reunion course which threatens to land us back where it all began in 1989: Edinburgh.

It is with heels dug tight into the earth that I endure a tour that has so far taken in all Australian states, revisiting theatres stormed by D.A.A.S. more than twenty years ago. Well past our collective primes, a seam seems to have been struck as an ageing recalcitrant bald man, a feisty host who refuses to believe he is not still a teenager and a man in a wheelchair who refuses to take sitting down lying down weave their rusty magic upon sell-out crowds. It is my intention here to document the horror, the glory, the egos and the strife of life on the road, then and now. The highs and the lows this travelling court jester continues to endure while supporting Australia's most fearless comedy export, who for a moment had the world (or at least Great Britain) at their feet. At their peak D.A.A.S. teetered on greatness, and I teetered with them, until that teeter was sabotaged by a complaint known primarily by its initials, MS: multiple sclerosis.

As a fly on the pungent walls of D.A.A.S. dressing-rooms across the globe, I have had ample opportunity to probe the depths and the shallows of these men. The vexing problem is that in all seriousness I cannot remember the finer details of my own life. Modern science is showing that my own, your own, anyone's own memories are not at all reliable. My diary notes scratched down in those early, brain-addled hours of my youth are almost indecipherable. So in the interests of fair play I have drawn on not just my own memories, but picked the brains of a select few who were there – fans, friends and foes.

These are the confessions of a reluctant farceur, a terminally introverted working-class boy, former animator, stand-up comedian, actor on film and television who, in 2016, finds himself on the road supporting the last remnants of the Doug Anthony All-Stars. The whole sorry mess reads like a soap opera. To convey this tale, I have chosen to present what follows in the format of a choral symphony with elements of light opera. The choral structure lends itself to a group experience, at times perfectly harmonious, at times hideously atonal, the four movements in this instance performed by a highly strung quartet.

MOVEMENT I

Allegro fugato (from the Latin *alacrem*, lively, cheerful, brisk, gay)

THE PLAYERS

PAUL McDERMOTT: Early twenties, lawless, malodorous, velvet-voiced, not at all tall.

TIM FERGUSON: Elegant, dapper, comely, winsome, not at all short.

RICHARD FIDLER: The guitarist.

PAUL 'FLACCO' LIVINGSTON: Not the guitarist.

CAMERON P. MELLOR: Hanger-on.

MINOR PLAYERS: Shady tour managers, illegal-substance enablers, assorted comedic wannabes, gonnabes and neverwillbes.

LOCATION

The world.

TIME

Late 1980s–early 1990s.

TOMORROW THE WORLD . . .

Stand-up comedy is a sad, cruel and ugly world,
a twilight zone of retarded personalities and
megalomaniacal dreamers . . . like myself.
PAUL LIVINGSTON, 1989

I'd worked in toilets before. Kitchens, restrooms and back
alleys often serve as makeshift dressing-rooms for comedians
breaking into the game. Huddled in a cupboard, awaiting your
introduction, listening to an audience either irritated to the
point of violence by the act you are to follow or completely
sated with laughter, the comedy bar is set too high or too low.
There are only two possible outcomes for a stand-up comedian:
you either kill, or you die. My alter ego, Flacco, a fast-talking,
Eastern European concoction, more props and puns than talent,
kicked off his solo career in a small club in Canberra in 1985.
Cafe Jax had no dressing-room. It had a storeroom. But no
toilet. I had a full bladder. As Richard Fidler once told me, 'The

great benefit of being a man is that the world is your urinal.' Richard remembers being with Paul McDermott in Venice when he pissed into the Grand Canal. And then later in New York City when he pissed into the John Lennon Strawberry Fields memorial garden in Central Park. With no national monument to soil, I located a crate containing glass flagons of moselle. I poured out a portion of the sweet wine and added my own bitter extraction. I often wonder who received the first taste – sweet, sickly, yet with just a hint of bitterness and a long lingering finish. The next day the *Canberra Times* described Flacco as 'an undernourished Garry McDonald'. Perhaps this was intended as a slur, but I was delighted to be mentioned in the same sentence as one of my comedy heroes in my first review.

Four years and several hundred dressing-rooms later, on Friday, 11 August 1989, I found myself huddled next to Mark Trevorrow (aka Bob Downe), who shared the dressing cubicle next to mine in the boys' toilets in back of the school hall of George Heriot's School in Edinburgh, Scotland. Bob Downe and Flacco were the support acts in a show called *Love Frenzy*. Founded in the seventeenth century, George Heriot's School was dedicated to the care and education of 'fatherless bairns'. Tonight, in this twentieth century, it was the location for the opening night's performance by Australia's bad boys of comedy, the Doug Anthony All-Stars. Bob Downe was the host for the evening and the warm-up act was Flacco.

The expansive school cafeteria was the All-Stars' allocated dressing-room. Meanwhile the boys' toilets would serve as backstage accommodation for their lower-billed companions. Mark Trevorrow, a known quantity in Edinburgh after storming the Fringe the previous year, remains a part of the Fringe furniture to this day. As performing furniture goes, Mark would be the Eames Lounge Chair and Ottoman in a room full of plastic bar stools. Flacco, however, was something out of *The Cabinet of Dr Caligari*, and in August 1989 he was a Fringe virgin.

Paul McDermott, Timothy Ferguson and Richard Fidler were the hardest-working act on the Fringe. When not onstage they busked incessantly around the city, constantly adding to their already considerable audience. Back home D.A.A.S. were gaining a national audience through regular appearances on *Tuesday Night Live: The Big Gig* on ABC TV. But here in the United Kingdom they were already ahead of the game, and as Bob Downe and Flacco prepared for death or dishonour in the restrooms of George Heriot's School, outside a stream of fans snaked around the building.

Opening night was a full house, five hundred plus, setting a familiar pattern for the three-week season. Mark Trevorrow had etched himself into the Australian entertainment landscape via cabaret duo The Globos in the early eighties before emerging as Bob Downe, the Prince of Polyester. Mark and I had worked together in the past but were to become far more familiar to each other on this trip. We had been relegated to the smoking section of our Thai Airways flight, surrounded by a rowdy cluster of sublimely ugly Australians who mercifully vacated the aircraft in Bangkok, leaving us to passively smoke in peace until we reached London. Mark recalls the horror.

Oh, my giddy aunt, it was the nightmare flight from hell. We were both recovering from horrendous flus and they mistakenly put us in smoking! We were seated one row behind a bulkhead, which in those days Aussies would turn into a pop-up bar, lounge, card game and nightclub of the air. They drank the bar dry, smoked their heads off, and it was just abject misery for us all the way to Bangkok. I particularly remember one slatternly girl standing in the aisle right next to me, watching the game, smoking, and she casually moved my hand out of the way to use my ashtray! That's when I snapped. We couldn't believe our luck when the Aussies departed in BKK and were replaced by civilised Brits on their way home from hols.

The Bloomsbury Theatre in central London was the venue for our pre-Edinburgh warm-up show and Flacco's first appearance outside Australia. The northern hemisphere was new to me; I'd never known jet lag and never stood beneath such oppressively low, grey skies. The Bloomsbury seated close to six hundred and boasted actual dressing-rooms for the cast. Mark and I had no need to share a toilet in this theatre, but we did share a bed. During their sorties across the British Isles, D.A.A.S. attracted a posse of dedicated followers who appeared happy to endure a troupe of Australians gatecrashing their compact abodes. Mark, Paul McDermott and I were staying in North London in the home of Rachel Tackley, an angel of a woman who would go on to be, among other illustrious postings, the director of English Touring Theatre, one of England's foremost theatre companies. The three of us shared one room and one double bed between us. Or a futon, as Paul McDermott reminds me – in a slightly ungrateful tone, if you ask me.

> A rag, a canvas calico rag, an old thing you wrap up and sit on as a couch and fold it out to be a double bed. It was myself that ended up enduring a totally sleepless night between the two of you and your male needs as you rolled backwards and forwards in your happy dreams. I was stuck there. It was horrible.

We tried every combination on that bed, but it was Mark's impressive snoring that earned him the total futon while McDermott and myself shared a floorboard. Paul also reminded me of a certain incident the next morning. The English were not big on showering, and my feeling was that this particular shower, a rare item in an English dwelling at the time, had not been used in some time. Paul McDermott remembers it well.

> An English shower was just a trickle of water. And we all had twenty-minute showers, full flow, splashing water all over the place. I remember sitting in the kitchen and looking up at what was a bubble of something, and I could hear Mark upstairs in the shower, singing away, having a great time. The ceiling was sagging, so I picked up a knife and just prodded it, and water flooded the kitchen. We had an Australian shower in an English bathroom, with disastrous results.

While Paul puzzled over the deluge from the ceiling, the jigsaw puzzle of my professional life began to fall into place. Doors of opportunity were opening. Friendships were forged, some more readily than others. It was around this time I first met Cameron P. Mellor, a young antipodean traveller and D.A.A.S. disciple. If D.A.A.S. were Jesus of Nazareth, Cameron P. Mellor would have been a little-mentioned semi-healed leper. And in my opinion, an intrusion. I took an instant dislike to the man. Little did we know what the future held for us, that the second decade of the coming century would find us merrily travelling the world, touring with those same All-Stars who brought us together. But here in London at the end of the eighties, the foot we got off on was entirely the wrong one.

Cameron P. Mellor spent the major part of 1989 in the USA interviewing indie bands for Melbourne's 3RRR radio. Cameron was pure rock 'n' roll. Comedy was the last thing on his mind. C.P. Mellor was a cool guy with a voice like warm syrup. His first meeting with Paul McDermott would initiate a major tangent in young Mr Mellor's life. His flatmate in Melbourne was allegedly going out with Paul McDermott. After six months of hearing about this boy and never laying eyes on him, Mellor was beginning to doubt his existence.

I thought, 'Am I ever going to meet this guy?' And then one morning I woke up and there was this thing in my kitchen. It was half nude and had dreadlocked hair and there was this odour that was quite confronting. He had these Coke-bottle glasses that would have to have been an inch and a half thick, and he kind of looked at me and I heard this voice in my head go, 'That's it? This is him? This is the guy? The boyfriend?'

The real trouble started for Cameron when McDermott urged him to call if he happened to be in London later that year. Unfortunately for Cameron, in August 1989, en route from New York, he did make that call, and from that moment on Cameron P. Mellor's cool thawed somewhat, but there were still plenty of cold shoulders to rub against. On McDermott's insistence, he was to share a floor with McDermott, Richard Fidler, Tim Ferguson and Mark Trevorrow in the home of Rachel Tackley, much to her chagrin. A picnic was organised in Hyde Park, to break the ice so to speak. Cameron ended up sharing a ride with Rachel.

> It was a little Vauxhall, very cute little retro car. She was still having trouble speaking to me because I was yet another colonist taking up floor space in her very small house.

On the way they picked up a friend of Rachel's who was harbouring yet another Australian on her own floor. This woman lived in a South Kensington terrace with a roomy, upmarket kind of a floor. I should know – I was the only Australian sleeping on it, having been ejected from Rachel's floor some time earlier. I felt territorial, having found such luxuriant boards to rest on, far from McDermott's foul pong and Trevorrow's snoring, and I was nervous about the intrusion of another denizen from the southern hemisphere who looked to me like a young Tom Petty crossed with Peter Frampton and the lead singer from Cheap Trick. I was not immediately impressed when I slid into the back seat beside Mr Mellor, and our conversation had more pauses than a Pinter play.

London, noon, late eighties. Interior of a very cute retro Vauxhall. After a long pause followed by an even longer pause, Mr Mellor turns to Mr Livingston.

MELLOR: Hi . . .

Pause.

MELLOR: How are you going?

Longer pause. Livingston turns, stares at Mellor, turns away again.

MELLOR: *(thinks: Who the fuck is this guy?)*

Stony silence as Livingston continues to stare out of the car window.

MELLOR: *(thinks: I've got to say something.)*

Pause.

MELLOR: *(plucking up courage)* So . . . what brings you to the UK?

Pause with stony silence until . . .

LIVINGSTON: Edinburgh Festival.

Pause.

MELLOR: Oh.

Pause. Livingston stares straight ahead.

MELLOR: Are you a journalist?

Stony silence.

LIVINGSTON: *(straight face, no emotion)* I'm a comedian.

Pause.

THE END

I think we should hear the rest from Cameron's own lips; there'll be fewer pauses that way.

> At that point I thought, 'Fuck this.' So I started staring out the window. There has never been a more incongruous situation in my life than staring at your head with the words coming out of it, 'I'm a comedian . . .' And I'm thinking to myself, 'Well, if this is fucking comedy, am I in for a wild ride or what!' You hated me . . . You definitely hated me.

Hate isn't a term I would use. I simply had a fondness for pauses.

The Bloomsbury swiftly sold out. There were expats in the audience but mostly locals, a testament to the growing popularity of D.A.A.S. in the UK. I have no memory of my performance on the night. A note scrawled in my travel diary is ambiguous. I noted that I started well and ended well. This might indicate a decent effort or perhaps that the bulk of my performance fell short. Mark Trevorrow remembers the shock of just how warm and accepting the London audiences were:

> Real pinch-yourself stuff. Not to mention the thrill of watching everyone else on the bill do just as well.

I also noted that Robert Stigwood's accountant came back-stage to congratulate us. For some reason I must have been impressed. I have to admit, I hadn't met many accountants. Another mysterious note scrawled in my diary stated, '3rd

August 89 – Lunch with Prince Edward.' Odd. How could I forget having lunch with the Earl of Wessex?

The train from London's Kings Cross station to Edinburgh's Waverley station took five hours. A mere stone's throw in comparison with Australian interstate train journeys. Edinburgh's lumpy terrain and cobblestone streets impressed me, and the apartment I shared with Mark at the foot of Edinburgh Castle had a fully functional shower. (The English habit of hopping in a bath first thing in the morning left me cold, and wrinkly, and generally in need of a shower.) But it was Edinburgh's antiquity that overwhelmed me. While little can compare to the inconceivable ancientness of the Australian terra, to be surrounded by this more recent, human-made ancient history was affecting. The shock of the old. Richard Fidler remembers the shock of the old fondly.

> I have quite magical memories of that . . . If you live in a country like Australia where the built environment is not very old at all, to be in a place like Edinburgh, it feels like a deep relief in a funny sort of way, it's like all the fairy stories you've been told as a child . . . In these kind of liminal cities you feel that if you stepped around a wrong corner you'd encounter a golem.

I was new to the old, but the Golem-like Flacco had long embraced it; he was firmly in his Elizabethan period at this stage. Standing alone in my cubicle at George Heriot's School, awaiting my first exposure to the Edinburgh D.A.A.S. faithful, I oozed daunt. Nervous? I was petrified. I was in Scotland, perched on a toilet bowl, wearing white pancake, black lipstick, a lick of hair welded to my forehead in the shape of a question mark, the remaining strands gelled into spikes (bearing in mind most of my hair fell out at the age of seventeen, leaving me with a fast-diminishing horizon of locks surrounding my dominant bald pate), an Elizabethan puffy shirt and vest, black tights and – probably not my best idea, in retrospect – a 'kilt' made from the pelt of a child's teddy bear fashioned into the shape of a dead cat, plus an assortment of props including a garden hose and a dead rat. What on earth was I thinking? And how did I get all this through customs at Heathrow? 'May I see your bag, sir? Right then: dead cat, lipstick, mascara, hair gel, a dead rat and only fifty pounds to your name? Thank you, sir, straight through.' (This was more than a decade before 9/11.)

Ever the optimist, Mark Trevorrow burst out of his cubicle and onto the stage. He had the crowd singing along to Gloria Gaynor's 'I Will Survive' in no time. The line between Mark and his stage persona Bob Downe has always been a fine one. The main traits Bob and Mark share are unabashed confidence and self-belief. Their relationship is one of mutual admiration, support and unbridled audacity. In this age of non-gender-specific couplings I'd love to see Bob and Mark tie the knot. A marriage made in heathen.

By covering my civilian self in props and make-up, coupled with a ridiculous rapid-fire pseudo Eastern European accent, I did my utmost to hide my true self from the audience. My onstage and offstage personas have never really hit it off, so it was fortunate that Flacco did not share my misgivings as, unperturbed, he leapt off the blocks and onto the stage with all the gusto of a creature totally oblivious to the dangers before him, a fairy penguin among the orcas.

On a good night everything gels, there is no thinking ahead to try to locate the next line or lamenting the slow death of the previous gag. 'In the zone' is the term generally applied. I felt nowhere near the zone as Flacco exited the stage and morphed into me. I had no idea what had taken place out there. After Flacco's fervent few minutes of fame, Bob Downe took the stage and introduced D.A.A.S. The change in gear was electrifying. This was not mere appreciation, it was devotion, and the trio milked the devout for the next hour. Three rabid yet surprisingly cute lads from Australia, with the voices of angels and tongues of Satan, attacked, full frontal and unrelenting, for over an hour. The crowd demanded more. Alas, D.A.A.S. had left the building; they were off to despoil the late-night postshow venues scattered throughout Edinburgh. D.A.A.S. never slept. And it paid off.

On the whole the All-Stars received glowing reviews, as did Bob Downe. Flacco's were mixed, although my comedic eclat was boosted by a headline review in *The Guardian*. Carol Sarler, my new favourite British citizen, began the review: 'I went back just to be sure, for superlatives can be dangerous things. As in: the single most innovative act I have seen on the fringe for years is Flacco.' The Dundee *Courier* described Flacco as the Salvador Dali of comedy. The *Fringe Review* called him 'a cross between Franz Kafka and Daffy Duck'. Nevertheless, it remained a battle each night; reviewers and the general public do not necessarily see eye to eye, and the Scottish public did not necessarily have a discerning one, but they did have an eye for any weakness. Should a crack appear in a performer's veneer, the locals went for the jugular, or the juggler, or, in my case, a juggler of words. Which is why I declined to try my luck at any of the late-night comedy spots on offer.

By nature a reticent soul, I recoil from adventure, but the All-Stars relished the attention, to the point of facing the equivalent of a comedy firing squad by daring to perform at Edinburgh's legendary Fringe Club, known affectionately after 10 pm as the Bear Pit. Cameron P. Mellor was in the Pit the night the Dougs declared war.

> They played the Fringe Club – that's where all the locals would go because it only cost a couple of pounds to get in. Spending six or seven quid on a show is not something a local is going to do. They go to the Bear Pit and they see ten acts do short spots, and of course it's a sport for the locals to destroy acts. If you are even remotely unsure about your material they will destroy you, and it's probably where the Dougs impressed me the most because they stood up to that crowd. That is where the Dougs were truly at their best.

Cameron described their set as incendiary. Tables and ashtrays flew, McDermott scampered up into the balcony and attacked a local, trapping the sizeable Scot in a headlock. After taming the beasts they sang some lovely, sweet songs. Victory in the Pit.

I stayed well away from the comedy front lines, preferring to don civilian attire and soak up the offerings of Edinburgh's comedy royalty: Jo Brand, Michael Redmond, the inexpressible genius of Jerry Sadowitz, the uneasy charm of Earl Okin (Old Horny Mouth), Arnold Brown, Arthur Smith and Fay Presto, to name a few. Although barely past the age of forty, Arnold and Michael were considered grand old men of Edinburgh. At the age of thirty-three, I was not far behind them. I never imagined that twenty-seven years hence I would be lured back to the Fringe, supporting the same act that launched me into Edinburgh obscurity.

The choice of Bob Downe as supporting cast for D.A.A.S. was a no-brainer. Mark Trevorrow was a proven Fringe quantity and his unrelenting barrage of pure razzamatazz was hard to resist; it set up an evening of offbeat, energetic but ever-so-slightly-unnerving fun. But why D.A.A.S. chose Flacco – a renowned Australian room-divider of a performer with a cult following of about thirteen – remains mystifying. Timothy Dorcen Langbene Ferguson agreed to shed a little light on the conundrum.

> We were all very excited because we were under the impression that Flacco would give us credibility; to us, he had the appearance of art. We thought that having Flacco with us would be a square-peg, round-hole scenario.

But who was the peg and who was the hole? I've got a pretty good idea, and I still have the scars. It is true, Flacco had the veneer of artiness and credibility, and these young men saw right through that guise to the hapless lowbrow clown beneath. So they dragged me halfway across the planet to test their waters each night. And then to pit Flacco against Bob Downe?

> Bob Downe was right at the other end of entertainment. It's all entertainment with Bob Downe, that's the beginning and the end of Bob, and you have Flacco down the other end of the pool doing something other than entertaining. So we were just covering our own bases.

> Covering their arses was closer to the point, according to Richard Fidler.

> We loved the strangeness of both acts, it seemed to frame what we did really well in a kind of a context that made us look more interesting . . . we started getting all these teenage girl fans and part of our thinking maybe was that we wanted to still remain firmly in the fringe comedy camp rather than the pop star camp. It seemed like a perfect eruption of filth and strangeness and glam.

So D.A.A.S. hired a bald man in make-up and a kilt, and a camp guy singing sixties pop tunes to make them appear less attractive to their fans? Whatever that mix was, it most certainly wasn't pretty.

Another local up-and-comer who shared the stage as support act for D.A.A.S. in those Edinburgh years would later become the creator one of Britain's beloved characters, the Pub

Landlord. In 2007 Al Murray was voted the sixteenth-greatest stand-up comic on Channel 4's *100 Greatest Stand-Ups*. The future sixteenth-greatest comic first sighted D.A.A.S. at the Edinburgh Fringe in 1988, the year the All-Stars were nominated for the coveted Edinburgh Perrier Comedy Award. Al was touring with a kids' show.

> I remember one of the girls in our group coming in and going: 'We have got to go and see these guys. I saw them busking today and we've got to go.' She fancied them, so she was driven there by that. I remember they were in a room upstairs at the Gilded Balloon, and I've never been in a room where the audience has been so excited in anticipation, and then the performers had delivered on that over and above everyone's expectations.

Al was used to taboos being either shunned or baulked at by the Greater British populace. In the UK, taboos were taboo:

> . . . and then the Dougs came on and it was like, they didn't give a fuck. But they had a go at everyone and so it didn't feel one-sided; it was a complete revelation . . . I saw them at the Fringe Club climbing the walls, Paul and Tim climbing the scenery, or the architecture of the room. English stand-up at that time was very political, but in one direction. It was still post-punk so you didn't 'put on a show', comics dressed drably, they didn't dress like psychedelic conquistadors or whatever . . . So that was my first impression of them. My first encounter with them was

basically completely fucking mind-blowing. They were big news and like nothing else at all.

Another up-and-comer who first encountered D.A.A.S while working the street in Edinburgh in '88 went on to become the third-greatest stand-up comic on Channel 4's *100 Greatest Stand-Ups* of 2007. Eddie Izzard was impressed, and just a little jealous.

It was exciting stuff they were doing, the vocal harmonies and the look, it just worked and I thought, 'Wow, that is amazing.' I was kind of pissed off . . . why can't I be three people and do that? I just thought it was annoyingly good. [D.A.A.S.] were getting so much traction and people were really excited about it and I was still just struggling away. They just came in like a thunderbolt and took off. It was like they walked in the door and just got the top table. There is something about going to Edinburgh and just taking over and it occasionally happens . . . but my first Edinburgh was 1981. My second was 1982. My third Edinburgh was 1983. My fourth Edinburgh was '85. My fifth Edinburgh was 1986 . . . I just went on and on and I didn't get nominated [for the Perrier Award] until 1991. Whereas their arrival was perfect, blew everything apart.

The All-Stars and Eddie hit it off immediately, whereas for Al Murray their first meeting was less amiable.

One year the student group that I was involved with got conned into playing at [late-night show] Late'n'Live and

I remember them heckling, you know, and thinking, 'Oh, brilliant, the Dougs are in and they've seen my stuff – but, shut the fuck up!'

Tim Ferguson remembers seeing Al that night.

He came out in front of this slovenly grimy thug-headed bunch of cocks, this handsome young man in a beautiful tuxedo, and he did his firearms impersonations. And the crowd were their usual rambunctious, argumentative selves, but Al just kept going . . . The thing that struck me about Al was that there was no place anywhere in all of creativity to find a comparison to this thing I was watching, and I said, 'Boys, boys, boys – we have to have Al Murray.' People can say, 'I was expecting a guy called Kevin in a flannelette shirt to come out and say, "Hey, how the fuck are youse? Where are you from?"' And instead Al Murray comes on and says, 'The Walther PPK, first developed in 1894, two chambers . . .' He just made me laugh.

Not long after being abused and misused by the Dougs (it's an initiation we all have to suffer for the privilege of sharing the limelight with D.A.A.S.), Al scored the much coveted D.A.A.S. support spot in London in 1990.

Being on before them, to have a bite of that excitement, was a seriously cool thing. You've got to do well; you've got to raise your game and all that. I remember it being a really long show because in Edinburgh you don't see them do any longer than an hour, and I always got the sense that there was a lot more of them to see. So being able to sit back and watch the show for an hour and a half, two hours was, again, mind-blowing. And the breadth of its conception was really good too.

One of Al's most enduring memories was the atmosphere surrounding those three men. Especially at close quarters.

The thing about the Dougs is they do stink. I was doing a Comedy Zone show in 1991 and we had to share a dressing-room. They were on before us, and so you've got the thing of us all turning up and getting ready and then they'd come in sweating and stinking, and they'd get changed and there'd be these disgusting costumes hanging on the door and in a tiny change room in the cabaret bar in The Pleasance; it was really squalid in there. And I remember Paul going, 'Yeah, yeah, we wear these costumes till they fall apart,' and you're thinking, 'You know, you don't have to.' It was horrible. But then again, the thing they had onstage was commitment, so I suppose wearing stinking disgusting clothes is all about that.

Eddie Izzard too found it hard to ignore the stench of D.A.A.S.

You have to look visually interesting if you are doing the street. They had that. I know in the end, their costumes, you could never clean them so they actually had a problem washing them and they could sort of stand up by themselves. But they looked great and it just fucking worked.

D.A.A.S. generously donated those costumes to the Performing Arts Collection in Victoria with the specific orders, 'Never to be cleaned.' It is rumoured that the current uniforms on display are not the originals. They have allegedly long been destroyed after it was thought they would threaten the entire collection. I also have it on good authority that one of the keepers of these original clothes voiced an urgent desire to wash the costumes and copped an abusive phone call from Paul McDermott. Yet this person remains a fan to this day. D.A.A.S. fans are loyal, if nothing else. (I know of another woman who was served a restraining order to keep well away from Mr McDermott. She had the document framed and it now holds pride of place in this middle-aged woman's home.)

Eau de D.A.A.S. had less effect on veteran Australian comedian and renowned stirrer of shit Rod Quantock, who premiered his *Bus Show* in Edinburgh. This encompassed the use of a bus as the venue, on a journey of improvised tourism for the benefit of passengers who doubled as audience.

> I was spending six hours a day on the road working out where to go, and then two hours a night doing it, and I might have only seen one show, and it wouldn't have been them.

Rod's mobile show sold out within two days. The main obstacle for Rod was finding a public space or building that was not being used as a venue, a mission near impossible in Edinburgh at festival time.

Everything was a venue. So in terms of my bus trip I'd go to the Seventh-day Adventist hall to show people Seventh-day Adventists at work, but instead we'd find some European theatre group doing *Hamlet* in Russian, and what's funny about that? But I got sick at the end of it and I had to stay another five days and I saw Edinburgh as it was outside of festival time, and it was Geelong.

Rod was doing so well he failed to notice anyone else's success. Frank Woodley, late of Lano and Woodley, was in Edinburgh in 1989 with comedy trio the Found Objects. He was aware of something in the air:

There was a sense the Dougs were playing a five-hundred-seat venue and selling it out every night and that they were kind of the talk of the town.

Melbourne comedy stalwart and nabob of bon mots Greg Fleet made his Edinburgh debut in 1990 and to him the scent of D.A.A.S. was evident.

They must have had a big impact the year before. I think in some ways we benefited from their success as I happened to be doing a show with two other guys called *Three Blokes and Their Jokes*. We'd been there a couple of days and noticed that people were really interested that we were Australian and it seemed to be a really good thing, so we got a rubber stamp made saying 'Australian Export' and stamped every fucking poster and every flyer. And I think it made a huge difference to the numbers we got and the interest.

The All-Stars had first ventured to Edinburgh in 1987 against the advice of their management, who told them: 'It's a big world out there, there are thousands of acts at the Edinburgh Festival, and you boys will get swallowed up, no-one will notice you, so just stay here and make money.' This advice was obviously beneficial to management, who were not keen on their star attraction eloping into global stardom and paying their fifteen per cent to an entirely different agency. But the boys had a dream, as Paul McDermott recalls.

> Richard was quite extraordinary actually. He was the one who organised it, all credit to him. He managed to get on to The Pleasance [a prime Edinburgh venue] and secured us the last slot at midnight, for the last week. No-one else would want it in a pink fit. It was available and we snaffled it.

Richard Fidler had never been overseas before, but a bullet was there to be bit.

> That was terribly romantic. I wrote a letter, because you had to write letters then, to Christopher Richardson, the manager [of The Pleasance], who wrote back and said, 'As it turns out someone has dropped out and we'd be very interested in having you.' So I made a long-distance phone call to Britain in the dead of night and had this strange sort of stilted conversation, 'We'd like to come and use your venue

in Edinburgh, over.' Christopher was an absolute English gent who looked like someone who had been kicked out of the Tory party, tweed jacket, very posh accent, leather patches on his elbows, and just a beautiful, wonderful man who really loved alternative comedy. So we went off on this shoestring and arrived there and almost immediately things fell into place.

The boys had hit gold. Christopher Richardson has been dubbed the Godfather to the Fringe. They packed their bags. What they didn't pack was money, or any idea of accommodation. Just three boys and their airfares. Paul McDermott recalls his first footsteps on Scottish soil with glee.

When we arrived in Edinburgh, Richard had one of the first bags in the world that had wheels on it. And as we got off the train there was a group of punks who basically just followed Richard out of the station barking like dogs. They were real dyed-in-the-wool Scottish punks, with the mohawks and the tartan – they were nasty pieces of work – and Tim and I got to shoulder our packs and walk behind him and just laugh.

It would seem the group dynamic offstage was very close to that of onstage: two rakish waifs and the hapless third party, the butt of their jokes.

The first thing we did was busk. You are there with the Chilean pipe orchestras and really weird people, confronting and wonderful and bizarre, a fellow with a wooden clotheshorse holding a Girl Guide book on etiquette from 1959 screaming, 'Give me money!' We put the guitar case out and said, 'We are basically homeless, we don't know what we are doing, can anyone put us up for the night?' And thanks to the extraordinary generosity of the Scottish people we ended up with three names and addresses in the guitar case as well as a paltry amount of coins, but we had somewhere to stay if we wanted it.

The All-Stars arrived just before the beginning of the three-week festival and during that first week a group had dropped out of the Cabaret Room at The Pleasance and D.A.A.S. were asked if they would like the midday spot. The first day they played to the staff and crew, but with ceaseless busking and spots at the notorious Bear Pit they swiftly managed to secure an audience. By the third day the shows were sold out. The second week another group dropped out, and this time the 3 pm slot was up for grabs. Sold out again. The third week, the slot that Richard had booked, sold out from day one until the end. In the meantime they'd been making money on the street, doing unscheduled gigs across the festival, and by the end of that first festival they had made many friends and fans and, most remarkable of all, a profit. Paul McDermott recalls the climax of their adventure.

On that very last night, in the shadow of Arthur's Seat, I noticed all these people carrying stage sets; they were busting up all the sets from the shows. So I said, 'Where is all that going?' They said they were taking it outside, behind the chapel that we were performing in, and they were going to burn it.

The All-Stars show came down around 1 am, so Paul asked if they might like to start burning it around that time.

So we took our audience out that night to a bonfire – it was a brilliant way to end the festival – and we asked people to release themselves of the burdens that society places on them.

It was at this point that Nigel, a friend and cohort of D.A.A.S., took out what appeared to be a credit card (in fact it was a student ID card), which he claimed he owed a lot of money on, and threw it on the fire.

This then got everyone stepping up to the fire and making confessions about what they didn't want in their life anymore. It was quite a purge. I was running across the flames, I made it through once, but then, being a cocky little fellow, thought I could do it twice, but the second time I actually fell into the fire. I moved quick in those days though. I'd be dead now. That was a real adventure.

The All-Stars had taken the challenge, lived the dream, did it all off their own bat and managed to float to the very top of a rather daunting pile of performers after only their first crack at the Edinburgh Fringe.

Another curious entry appears in my tour diary for Tuesday, 15 August 1989: 'Dougs and Bob met Prince Edward, who asked about the man in the headless coat [Flacco]. He had recognised Paul at the cafe in London.'

I prodded Paul McDermott for any recollections.

We were all playing the Bloomsbury in London, and we were at a table at a place called Kettner's and I think at the time Prince Edward was dabbling in the arts, and he just happened to be at another table. I was on the side facing Prince Edward, and he kept looking over. We'd later discover that it was because he had seen us on [British television music and comedy show] *Friday Night Live* and liked what we did, but at the time I just kept thinking, 'My god, that guy has got very blue eyes.' Immediately Mark Trevorrow demanded that I swap seats with him, then made eyes at the royal for the rest of the meal. His day was made.

But we didn't meet him there. We did meet him at Heriot-Watt University in Edinburgh. It was a charity night, a royal performance, and Edward was the royal in attendance. Ronnie Corbett was on, and the cast of *Brideshead Revisited*, and ourselves. I remember arriving and the venue, which was normally filled with kids who were performing in *Joseph and the Amazing Technicolor Dreamcoat*, was empty. Well, I say empty, but there were these three big tall fellows, all wearing tuxedos, and there was one fellow standing leaning against the wall in the corner, and

there were ladies in taffeta frocks. I was a bit panicked.
I'd just come in off the Edinburgh streets, I was wearing
some sort of weird floppy hat, almost a wimple, I was
drenched, cold and grumpy – which was my usual state –
and then I arrived in the room and I was just concerned
that I was running late getting to the dressing-room to
get my gear on for the show. But these big fellows in the
tuxedos shepherded me over to a corner of the room,
saying, 'You have to come and meet this fellow.' I said,
'What's this bullshit?' I was quite gruff, I had no idea I
was talking to Edward, when he started saying, 'I was
charmed by your performance, absolutely wonderful!' I'm
going, 'Yeah, right, mate, but I've got to get to the dressing-room.' But I kept looking at him, thinking, 'Where
have I seen those blue eyes before?' It only occurred to
me upstairs, when I saw doe-eyed Richard going, 'Oh my
god, did you get to meet Edward?' Then it clicked: 'That's
it, royal command performance tonight,' and my brain put
two and two together.

Tim too had little time for formalities in the presence of a
prince and harangued Edward from the stage with a tongue-
lashing on the subject of the IRA. Richard's approach to royalty
was far more benign.

He's quite a tiny thing. Exquisite. He was really nervous
around us. He thought we were about to monster him I
think. He was very nice about it all and seemed to be a
bit of a fan.

I met no members of the royal family, but I was a little doe-eyed to learn that Edward had asked about the man in the headless coat (even though, logically, all coats are headless).

The Bulletin dubbed *Love Frenzy* the biggest show of the 1989 Edinburgh Fringe. D.A.A.S. were moving swiftly up the ladder in that part of the planet and I thought maybe I was too. Post-Edinburgh I returned to London to try my hand at the King's Head, arguably the best comedy room in Britain at the time. After changing into my work clothes somewhere between the kitchen and the toilet I wandered onstage, the stage being an area of cleared carpet in the pub. The reception was lukewarm to say the least. My glowing *Guardian* review had given me false hope, and after the King's Head gig it was clear I was not destined to take this town by storm in any great hurry.

But I had other irons in the fire. On 7 September I was booked to appear at the Crocodile Club in Brighton, supporting the legendary Malcolm Hardee with that fine Irish gentleman Sean Hughes on emceeing duty and Flacco warming up the room. I was apprehensive about sharing a stage and dressing quarters with Malcolm. His reputation for audacious acts of sabotage preceded him. In Edinburgh I witnessed not only Malcolm's famous enormous testicles at close quarters but a brazen stunt where, after some not-so-flattering reviews, he and Arthur Smith concocted a glowing five-star review of Malcolm's Fringe show and somehow contrived to get it printed in *The Scotsman*, attributed to that newspaper's most acclaimed theatre critic. I warmed to Malcolm somewhat as a result, since this same critic had slammed Flacco's performance.

The Brighton natives were friendly, and ever-so-slightly arty and highbrow. Just how I like them. The cool reserve of the pompous is preferable to the deathly quiet of the confused commoner. And Malcolm, to my surprise and great relief, was supportive and charming. On 2 February 2005, a few days after being reported missing, Malcolm Hardee was found six metres below the surface of the Thames clutching a beer bottle in his right hand. It's what he would have wanted: he died doing what he really loved.

Meanwhile, half a world away, *Big Gig* producer Ted Robinson secured a deal for a D.A.A.S. television series. Mark Trevorrow and I were invited to participate. After making my way home via New York and Los Angeles I was penniless, but it didn't matter – for better or worse I had dipped a toe into the deep end of the international comedy pool. Mind you, it didn't take long to settle back into the kiddie-sized self-inflatable pool of Australian light entertainment.

HOME IS WHERE THE ART IS

I believe entertainment can aspire to
be art, and can become art, but if you
set out to make art you're an idiot.
STEVE MARTIN

The taxi ride from Fitzroy to Elsternwick puzzled me for a time.
Each morning a different driver greeted me with a knowing
smirk whenever I announced my destination. This smirk was
typically followed by a conversation along these lines:

'Going to work, are we?'

'As a matter of fact I am.'

'Wish I had a "job" like yours.' (nudge, wink)

Having by this stage appeared on national television all of
half a dozen times, I could only presume that the taxi drivers
of Melbourne were huge fans of small-screen comedy. It was
only after one driver asked about the women I worked with that
things became clearer. For some reason they didn't seem all

The All-Stars busk on The Mound, Edinburgh '89. *Dave Taranto*

The Scots respond with coins, food, insults and the odd infant. *Dave Taranto*

D.A.A.S. tame the Gaelic beasts in the Bear Pit. *Dave Taranto*

From sheepish animator to kilted clown.

'What on earth was I thinking?' Paul Livingston as Flacco, *The Big Gig*, 1989.

McDermott and Livingston. Strange men in a strange land. Edinburgh '89.
Rachel Tackley

Bob Downe toasting
himself backstage,
August '89. *Paul Livingston*

D.A.A.S. enjoying the sweet smell of international success . . . but no-one was enjoying the smell of their costumes. *Graham Macindoe*

MEAN FIDDLER PRESENTS

READING '92

AUGUST BANK HOLIDAY WEEKEND

FRI 28TH AUGUST
FROM 2PM

THE WONDERSTUFF
THE CHARLATANS
PUBLIC IMAGE LIMITED
PJ HARVEY
MEGA CITY FOUR
THE MILLTOWN BROTHERS
FATIMA MANSIONS
REDD KROSS

SAT 29TH AUGUST
FROM MIDDAY

PUBLIC ENEMY
RIDE
MANIC STREET PREACHERS
THE FARM
SMASHING PUMPKINS
ROLLINS BAND
THOUSAND YARD STARE
BUFFALO TOM
THERAPY?

SUN 30TH AUGUST
FROM MIDDAY

NIRVANA
NICK CAVE
MUDHONEY
TEENAGE FANCLUB
L7
PAVEMENT
SCREAMING TREES
THE MELVINS

SESSION TENT

LEVITATION
CARDIACS
CRACKER
LUNACHICKS
THE GOD MACHINE
COP SHOOT COP
LEATHERFACE
SOME HAVE FINS
HAIR AND SKIN TRADING CO
DF 118
SWEET JESUS

BAD II
SUEDE
SUNSCREEM
SULTANS OF PING FC
THE HEARTHROBS
FINITRIBE
SHONEN KNIFE
SPIT FIRE
THE STAIRS
URGE OVERKILL
SENSITIZE
TABITHA ZU

ROCKINGBIRDS
ROLLING REVUE
CATHERINE WHEEL
EAT
DR PHIBES AND THE HOUSE OF WAX
EQUATIONS
REVOLVER
SCORPIO RISING
PELE · EUGENIUS
POWER OF DREAMS
25TH OF MAY
POPS COOL LOVE

COMEDY TENT

FRANK SIDEBOTTOM
BRIGHTON BOTTLE ORCHESTRA
HUGH LENNON
MARK LAMARR
DOON
LOGAN MURRAY
WOODY BOP MUDDY
AL MURRAY
HARRY HILL

THE DOUG ANTHONY ALLSTARS
MARK HURST
TOMMY COCKLES
RUBBER BISHOPS
UNCO-ORDINATED JUGGLERS ASSOCIATION
JAMES MACABRE
BOB MILLS NOEL JAMES
BOB DOWNES

FRANK SKINNER
JOHN HEGLEY
CHRIS LYNAM
SIMON GODLEY
CHRIS & GEORGE
CHRIS LUBY
FELIX
GAYLE TUESDAY
ANDRE VINCENT

INFORMATION LINE:
081 963 0797
No extra charge

THREE DAY TICKET AVAILABLE IN ADVANCE AT £49

BILL SUBJECT TO CHANGE
ARTISTS NOT IN ORDER OF APPEARANCE

THE DOUG ANTHONY ALLSTARS ★ ★

UNIVERSAL THEATRE JUNE 29 TO JULY 22 WED TO SAT

SPECIAL GUESTS BOB DOWNE & FLACCO

$18/$14 PLUS BOOKING FEE PHONE 419 3777 OR BASS

An actor prepares . . . for the worst. Adelaide '88.

'I woke up and there was this thing in my kitchen . . .' Cameron P. Mellor, Melbourne, '88.

Without the aid of fermented beverages, C.P. Mellor and P.J. Livingston did not see eye to eye at first sight. *Peter Milne*

CHEESESHOP
CHRISTMAS SHOW

Book Now it will be
sold out, everybody
funny including our
very special guest
FLACCO

PRINCE PATRICK HOTEL   Wednesday 12th Dec
135 Victoria Parade Collingwood 9419-4197 9pm $15 & $13

COMEDY
THURSDAYS

THE CONCORDE
MADEIRA DRIVE
BRIGHTON

CROCODILE

THURS 7th SEPT
FLACCO
MALCOLM HARDEE
HENRY NORMAL
TRACEY BROS.
Sean Hughes comperes

THURS 14th SEPT
CALYPSO TWINS
JOHN MALONEY
ANDY SMART
Sean Hughes comperes

THURS 21st SEPT
TONY ALLEN
KEVIN DAY
Pete McCarthy comperes

THURS 28th SEPT
AN EVENING WITH
THEATRESPORTS

9.00PM
£3.50/£3.00
LATE BAR

ASSISTED BY SOUTH EAST ARTS

flacco

is

FLYSPECK
ON THE PIECRUST OF ETERNITY

ASSEMBLY ROOMS
SUPPER ROOM
12 MIDNIGHT

AUGUST 14 - SEPTEMBER 5
(EXCEPT SUN 23, MON 24)
BOX OFFICE - TEL 031 226 2428

The single most innovative cabaret act I have seen on the fringe for years -The Guardian
Almost beyond description...the Salvador Dali of Comedy -The Dundee Courier

Flacco and Livingston kiss curl and make up, *D.A.A.S. Kapital*, '91.

The 'unsexiest comedian alive' meets his polar opposite in Timothy Ferguson.

Michael 'Psycho Bob' Petroni in the *D.A.A.S. Kapital* cross-dressing-room, '91.

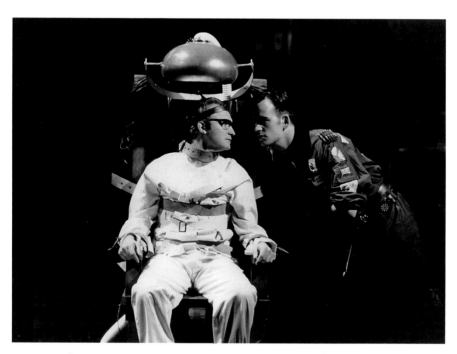

Psycho Bob and Tim share an intimate moment . . .

In Peril Films in association with Morgan Productions and the Harold Park Hotel presents...

For One Night Only

A DODGY FILM FUNDRAISER!

You can WIN! A cameo role in the yet to be named Morgan/Petroni blockbuster!

FEATURING LIVE ON STAGE...

FLACCO
...in a rare appearance!

- Mr Sandman
- Gretel Killeen
- The BOOFTAS

- Psycho Bob
- Warwick Irwin
- Rhonda Shelling
- Kitty Flanagan
- Johnny Goodman
& many more...

- Compered by Peter Berner -

$10 Bargain!

8PM Wed 17th November
The Harold Park Hotel
115 Wigram Rd
Glebe 692 0564

The gig that catapulted Michael Petroni out of Harold Park and into the Hollywood Hills.

The All-Stars on the set of *The Big Gig*, where the boys made their mark on a nation that is still trying to remove the stain.

The *D.A.A.S. Kapital* Klan – Psycho Bob, Richard, Paul, Tim, Khym Lam and Flacco.

Mr McDermott shows off his feather boa constrictor.

Hair today, gone tomorrow. Four Flaccos and an Edward Robinson.

that interested in hearing about the exploits of Wendy Harmer, Jean Kittson or Denise Scott. After a month working on the newly commissioned D.A.A.S. sitcom I was made aware that the ABC offices on Horne Street, Elsternwick, were next door to an infamous Melbourne establishment, the Daily Planet. I had noticed the building's facade; it was hard to miss with a bas-relief globe of the world broadcasting the building's global location. I thought it was a contemporary design studio or a glossy magazine's headquarters. As it turned out, the Planet was one of the more popular Melbourne brothels. Instantly those innocent early morning conversations took on another meaning.

'You like to start early, eh?'

'I find it helps.'

'Can't do any harm.'

'I get a bit exhausted by midday . . .'

'I'll bet you do.'

'Some people think it's glamorous but they don't realise the effort we put into it.'

'You work forty hours a week?'

'Sometimes more. And there's plenty of homework . . .'

'You da man, Floppo . . .'

'Flacco.'

It also explained the impressive diligence shown by Mr Paul McDermott, who was always the first to arrive and the last to leave. His desk, parked in a dark corner, had a delightful outlook directly above the comings and goings of the hindquarters of the Daily Planet. Perhaps this explains the titles of the seven episodes in that first series: 'Lust', 'Avarice', 'Envy', 'Gluttony', 'Sloth', 'Pride' and 'Anger'.

The title of the series, *D.A.A.S. Kapital*, a mocking reference to *Das Kapital*, Karl Marx's seminal nineteenth-century manifesto highlighting capitalism's exploitation of labour, was a joke that flew directly over the heads of many an All-Stars devotee. In this instance, the exploitation was of the audience's gullibility, and any capital was to be deposited directly into the D.A.A.S. coffers. The philosophy of D.A.A.S. was closer to that of Groucho than Karl. The series was powered by the three cylinders of gall, confidence and folly, and steered by our fearless mentor, Ted Robinson, and a ragtag crew of his own making.

Edward T. Robinson is a man who has dined out on stories of dining out with the likes of Peter Allen, Liza Minnelli, Bette Midler, David Bowie, Harry Nilsson, Ringo Starr, Tina Turner and Salvador and Gala Dali. But it has been on these Australian shores that Ted has left his stubborn stain.

The first TV I got to work on was *The Aunty Jack Show*, which was a hell of a way to start. There were two or three directors in any half-hour show. There were location film shoots, and if you were on location in those days you went out and shot with film, and because I had a bit of a film background from commercials, I started off shooting film on location and I ended up in the chair in the studio. Which was one of the most terrifying things I ever did, getting on top of all that technology – it was like being on the flight deck of an aircraft carrier. Of course, everyone is babbling the whole time and just learning to concentrate on your part of it almost blew my brain. I just wanted to scream 'Shut the fuck up' to everyone! But they were all doing their own job. In those days it was like being in a crowded restaurant and trying to direct.

I was a teenager when *The Aunty Jack Show* went to air, and the show was a revelation. I had enjoyed the Monty Python TV series, which gave me a taste for no-punchline, obscure comedy, but with *Aunty Jack* it struck me that we could do it right here, in my home town. It seeded something within my swiftly balding pate, and all the while Ted Robinson was in there behind the scenes, learning the ropes.

That's where I really learned some of the first lessons about comedy. Grahame Bond and Rory O'Donoghue were very funny men, but you mustn't ever rehearse with them, because they would be funny the first time they did it, and they'd have to rehearse it a second time, and they'd realise that people weren't laughing as much, so they'd change it to keep the crew laughing. By the time we got to shoot the fucking thing it bore no resemblance to the original, and made no sense unless you knew where it had departed from. Some people thought it was deliberately surreal, but it was just people disappearing up their own clackers.

Over five decades Ted Robinson has championed the under-lings of entertainment, nurtured them until they pecked the hand that fed them, then flew the nest to soar Icarus-like into the searing heat of stardom, some dropping to the pavement, never to be heard from again, some still flapping their tattered wings and losing altitude with every passing year. Show business. It's a cruel world.

As a lifelong sufferer of what is now referred to in medical circles as selective mutism, the business of show may seem like an odd career choice for me. SM symptoms usually begin in early childhood and can spill over into adulthood – or senior citizenship in my case.

> Selective mutism (SM) is an anxiety disorder in which a person who is normally capable of speech does not speak in specific situations or to specific people. Selective mutism usually co-exists with shyness or social anxiety. People with selective mutism stay silent even when the consequences of their silence include shame, social ostracism or even punishment.
>
> Wikipedia

Thanks to SM, I did not possess the wherewithal to fight my own fights. Selective mutants like myself need the likes of a Ted Robinson to go into the ring on our behalves. Ted has gone more than a few rounds with many a blinkered television executive on my behalf. There have been some spectacular wins and more than a few losses, but Ted has never left my corner. Now that I've beaten the life out of that metaphor, let's move on . . .

Not far from the nefarious mind of McDermott, Michael Petroni and I shared a desk at *D.A.A.S. Kapital* headquarters. Michael was to play the role of Psycho Bob. It was a brave act, and finely honed. There was a dark humour to Bob's psychopathic rants. While the rest of the cast were playing for laughs, Petroni immersed himself in the role, just like a real actor. I had known Michael for some time and we had become firm friends. We first met in a dole office in Sydney in 1988. We knew of each other through the only venue we could find work in at that time, the Harold Park Hotel in Glebe. Gigs were scarce and I was supplementing my comedy income with the dole, or vice versa. Michael held a Bachelor of Arts with an honours degree in psychology but had decided on the life of an actor. Hence the dole office scenario.

In what almost seems like life imitating art, Michael eventually left Australia to become an American citizen, a screenwriter and director of renown, carving out a unique niche in the Hollywood film industry without once storming a McDonald's with a .44 Magnum or assassinating the famous. But I digress; Michael's tale is one of boundless success, achievement and veneration. So let's get back to the All-Stars.

Michael and I were fed snippets of the themes for each episode, and our mission was to weave our plotlines through the main script. So we wrote whatever we wanted, and attached it to the scripts. This was free jazz comedy writing. To say Australia wasn't ready for it is perhaps an understatement. *We* weren't ready it. I'm still not ready for it. One accusation levelled at the show was the intrusion of highly audible and frequently manic canned laugher dominating the episodes. This is incorrect. The laughter wasn't canned. It came from the throats of the D.A.A.S. fans, who lined up in the late afternoon at the ABC's Gordon Street studios every week to worship at the altar of D.A.A.S. They would not be muzzled. No volume level could contain them. They were full-voiced, excitable, fanatical and still up for more at 12.30 am, when the show usually wrapped.

The first episode of *D.A.A.S. Kapital* went to air on 1 April 1991. When it comes to the media, honeymoon periods don't last too long in Australia. The All-Stars bypassed the honeymoon period and went straight to divorce. By the time *D.A.A.S. Kapital* premiered they had been adored, chewed up and spat out by the press. Which seems fair enough, since the press had been seduced, chewed up and spat upon by the All-Stars. As Tim Ferguson has said, 'Even now it is hard to find a fact about the All-Stars that is not contestable.' The boys were always available for a chat, but truth was a maxim they avoided at all costs. And hell hath no fury like the media spurned.

The irony was that D.A.A.S. truly were on the verge of stardom in Britain. But no-one in the Australian media believed them. The boys had cried wolf once too often. The local media turned its back on the D.A.A.S. affront. They weren't the first to slip one by the odd journo. In 1975 Rod Quantock was interviewed for *Vogue* magazine.

I told her that I'd been to Paris to study mime at L'École Internationale de Théâtre Jacques Lecoq, but on my first morning I was hungover, in a rush, and I fell down the stairs and broke my leg. I couldn't do mime, so instead I ended up studying the cello at L'École de Bow Arte. She printed it all. And about every ten years I'm interviewed by somebody who's done some proper research and they say, 'Why don't you play the cello in your show?'

One reviewer, who shall remain nameless because no name was attached to the review, hurled vitriol at the All-Stars and the *D.A.A.S. Kapital* series, yet in the same article proved to be completely taken in by their tall tale of being too busy to play the Joker's henchmen in *Batman Returns* after their much self-publicised role in the first film, as Jack Nicholson's henchmen, allegedly ended up on the cutting-room floor. The reviewer hoped that another *D.A.A.S. Kapital* series might suffer the same fate. The last laugh is the longest and the sweetest but, overall, *D.A.A.S. Kapital* was shunned, demeaned and frowned upon by the critics. So the ABC agreed to a second series.

Ted Robinson remembers there being a bit of disenchantment over the first series of *D.A.A.S. Kapital* within the corridors of ABC power.

I saw the Dougs in Edinburgh and said, 'Look, we've got a small possibility of a second series. But we've got to come up with some new thoughts and twists so I can go back and say, "Hey, here's the new improved version."' And the only thing we came up with – because I think we started drinking – was 'Let's make it in space rather than in a submarine.'

Back home, at one of the regular program meetings at the ABC, the conversation went something like this:

> TED: I want to talk about another series of *D.A.A.S. Kapital*.
> *Deep silence in the room.*
> MICHAEL SHRIMPTON (the man in charge of television): The first series was a little bit soft . . .
> TED: Oh yeah, but it takes everything a series or two to find its way, and there'll be quite a few changes.
> MICHAEL: What's going to change?
> TED: Well, instead of being in a submarine at the bottom of the ocean . . . *(thinks: Fuck, how do I do this? Everyone's looking at me)* . . . this one's in space.
> *Pause.*
> MICHAEL: Oh, that sounds good.

Deal done. Series two commissioned. These days, Ted is philosophical.

> You learn your job on the second series, which is the sad thing about today, because there's sort of nowhere left to fail – if you don't get it right, you know, in the first minute, you're dead.

You have to learn somewhere, and Ted gained a great deal from working with Frank Ward, the executive producer of *The Big Gig*.

> Even though I was a dreadful younger man and didn't appreciate a lot of what he had to offer, he was amazing. Frank was real old showbiz; he'd been a Tivoli straight

man for all the great comedians of the world for seventeen years. And every day he had an anecdote and I'd think, 'Oh fuck, boring Frank and his anecdotes,' but I realised pretty soon that every anecdote was a lesson that I've carried with me for most of my life. So that's what he did: that old Tivoli hoofer became a straight man and then went into telly.

Television executives with a hands-on knowledge of show business are all but extinct these days.

Despite D.A.A.S. alienating themselves from every media outlet in Australia, in another hemisphere Geoff Posner firmly believed in them. By 1991 Posner was already an acclaimed director of television comedy in Britain, with episodes of *The Young Ones*, *Black Adder* and *The Lenny Henry Show* under his belt. Geoff was keen to exploit the talents of D.A.A.S. and offered them a BBC television special, a taster, an entrée into the iconic realm of BBC comedy.

For reasons known only to D.A.A.S., they insisted I make the journey with them. Was it the old ploy of hiring a mediocre warm-up guy to throw their brilliance into heightened relief? (Call me paranoid if you like, everyone else does. All of them. All the time . . .) Whatever their reasons, on a grey London morning on 28 August 1991, I was to be found jet-lagged, wandering into the BBC Television Centre in West London, past framed photos of Pete and Dud, The Goodies, Benny Hill,

Frankie Howerd, Eric Morecambe, both of the Ronnies and all of the Pythons on my way to a rehearsal of the Doug Anthony All-Stars BBC 2 special, *Love*. Tim Ferguson too felt something move in those hallowed halls of the BBC.

> Just to be in those dressing-rooms where Ronnie Barker and Ronnie Corbett had been farting . . .

The boys were on a good wicket with Mr Posner. The world and their oyster were encroaching on each other. Just keep a cool head and do the work. The first element we had to control was the urge to giggle while the master worked. Geoff had a very professional attitude, and we just weren't used to that. He had a habit of circling the talent as they rehearsed, one eye closed, the other framing each shot. During a scene he would suddenly click his fingers, indicating, 'Cut!', startling the performers and inducing laugher, at first. We soon learned not to laugh while attempting to be hilarious in front of this man. His technique was off-putting yet at the same time so impressively virtuosic.

The BBC studio, while no different to any other in appearance, was intimidating. We were standing in comedy's Abbey Road, on lino trod by the greats. Flacco was still enjoying his Elizabethan phase, and the BBC wardrobe, a hangar of a space, was overflowing with puffy shirts and codpieces. Under the cool right eye of Geoff Posner, we gave our all, took our bows, and returned to Australia before the special was screened.

After a whirlwind week in London rubbing shoulders with framed photos of the famous, we were back in Elsternwick for series two of *D.A.A.S. Kapital*. The clicking fingers of Geoff Posner were replaced by the incessant pacing of Ted Robinson – or Chief Dark Cloud as Steve 'The Sandman' Abbott once dubbed him. Ted wore a frown more omnipresent than Peter FitzSimons's bandana – or, more to the point, a frown wore Ted Robinson, who sheltered beneath it. We cowered before it. Ted's frown overbit his brow and yearned to meet his jaw. Perhaps this is why Paul McDermott dubbed him the Predator.

Ted's approval was registered via a simple utterance, the singular 'ha!'. Ted shunned the plural 'ha ha'. He pooh-poohed it. Or, rather, he poohed it. The problem for the uninitiated was that it was quite easy to mistake impending fury for impending *ha!* On the surface, the frown that rimmed the volcano gave no hint of what lay beneath. Mostly Ted was dormant. This man could hold his lava. But if by chance you overstepped Ted's furrowed rim, an eruption was never far from the surface. Much slag had been spilled onto the floor of that studio during the making of the first series. And old Krakatoa was ready to blow again.

Ted was no mere Posneresque finger-snapper. When Ted snapped, it was more akin to a Venus flytrap, the trigger hairs on his overhanging brow clamping down on its prey. In the main, the trigger for those trigger hairs was the behaviour of Paul McDermott, who delighted in locating a sensitive button on the Predator and pushing and pushing and pushing until the hair triggers triggered and the only way to free our trapped companion was to administer the antidote – that is, to bait the Predator with amusing material. No easy feat. Eventually one of our team would throw the correct comedic worm, and at the cry of the singular *ha!* the shaken victim would fall to the floor. Were this not the case, and no *ha!* was forthcoming, the prey was leeched upon for around ten days, by which time it was reduced to a mere husk. The most important thing to remember if you found yourself enmeshed in the murky mucilage of Ted Robinson's ire was to stay calm, for if the prey were to struggle, the trap would close and digestion would begin in earnest.

Ted was a man you wanted on your side, doing your dirty work. For instance, talking television executives into hiring you. Not a job for the faint-hearted. One of Australia's finest comedy programs almost came to a close after the first episode thanks to the judgement of those in positions of power and authority. *The Norman Gunston Show* was under fire from within right up until the impossible happened: people began watching the show. Impressive ratings cause these otherwise nameless, faceless executives to swoop on the chance to take the credit when a show becomes popular through no fault of their own. These accidental successes generally mean the headless chickens in question are given free range on their next project. This is the point where the emperors' and empresses' new clothes begin to wear thin. The late Eric Sykes described heads of light entertainment at the BBC as a 'disappointing bunch of trainee bureaucrats with a limited knowledge of what makes people laugh'. That was over fifty years ago. There has to date been no apparent evolutionary growth in the mentality of the species. Great comedy shows happen in spite of, not because of, those who hold the purse strings. Ted Robinson had his fingers in that purse for a short while, making Tim Ferguson wary on first encountering the Predator.

> To me he was just some guy from a gigantic, faceless organisation with whom we would never have any contact. It turns out he was the last man to hold the role that should still exist at the ABC, which is to be able to see it and commission it, to literally be the commissioning editor as opposed to just an opinionist along the way. I'm sure the current head of comedy would love to have that power. Instead, he or she has got to answer to some committee of drama writers.

There is a condition known as the Dunning–Kruger effect. Symptoms include:

- failing to recognise one's own lack of skill
- failing to recognise the extent of one's inadequacy
- failing to recognise genuine skill in others

You'll find the Dunning–Kruger effect infecting many in positions of power and influence, but it is particularly virulent among the light heads of entertainment. Sorry, heads of light entertainment. Their lack of vision is spectacular. The lack of a sense of humour is compulsory.

Ted Robinson was a rare exception to the rule. Beneath a veneer of soft-spoken equanimity there lurked a demon fuelled by white-faced fury, which showed itself in extreme circumstances – for instance, when said Predator has painstakingly secured a second series of a TV show after going the full fifteen rounds with assorted television executives, only to be confronted with a team of players, some of whom were hungover, some of whom were drunk and some of whom were irritatingly ambivalent, but none of whom had any sign of a script forty-eight hours out from shooting episode one of series two in front of a live studio audience. That's enough to rouse the carpels of any hot-sapped angiosperm.

Ted managed to contain himself until the final episode of *D.A.A.S. Kapital*, fittingly titled 'Patience'. The episode was to end with D.A.A.S.'s version of the Mad Hatter's tea party from *Alice's Adventures in Wonderland*. I was playing the March Hare, because I didn't have – wait for it – much hair. To add to Ted's woes, there were guests in the studio that day observing the rehearsal, a small group of gentlemen from Japan who would bear witness to the latest eruption of Mt Robinson. When Ted fumes, it's internal, you can't smell the fumes, therefore you can't predict when he's about to blow. McDermott held the match, and was doing his best to strike it as he sat at the head of the table, the Mad Hatter himself.

Ted Robinson has fond memories of the day he strangled the bejesus out of Paul McDermott.

Paul was very good at storing up little pieces of information, and you should never give him any, because one
day he will find a way to use them against you. And I'd
been struck by something I'd read, the hypothesis that
every animal, including humans, had more or less the

same number of heartbeats in their life. So a mouse whose heart beats at two hundred beats a minute might only last three months, or however long a mouse lives, but an elephant whose heart beats at twenty beats per minute might last for one hundred years or more. And so I told Paul this story, and I felt quite touched by that possibility, even if it was not true. And then you were all sitting at the Mad Hatter's table chatting and I suddenly heard this arsehole riffing on the hypothesis I'd related to him, but rather than heartbeats he'd replaced it with menstrual cycles. I knew that he knew that I was listening, and I felt I therefore had to respond to it. It was a joke that only he and I would get, but he was having a little dig at the same time, so I came running down the spiral staircase and then, as often happened, everyone stopped what they were doing and were watching to see what was going to happen next. And I thought, 'I've made this great entrance, but what the fuck do I do now?' And the only thing I could think of was that, well, it was my studio and my set and I just kept running and dived and swept everything off the table. But it did take Paul by surprise, because he thought he was quite safe with the table between the two of us. I got him by the throat and we slid off the end. It was a good moment of theatre. But those were days when you could be stupid and you could do things like that. I think if I were to do something like that today in a studio, I'd have to report to occupational health and safety and explain myself.

Being caught in the headlights of an oncoming director is a memory Paul also finds hard to suppress. He remembers Ted waxing lyrical earlier in the day with his relative heartbeat theory.

> Ted spoke of this in such glowing and reverential terms it was almost like it pointed to a deeper and more wondrous truth for him. There was a fragility about it and it made him vulnerable, which is an area I really like in people, their vulnerability, because that can be exploited. I was just sitting back in my chair, a smile on my face at having provoked the bull, so I wasn't prepared for when he actually launched himself up onto the riser, over the table and clamped both his giant man paws around my neck. The whole chair, myself and Ted on top of me went flying backwards. It was just when he got to my neck that I had a spike of worry.

The Venus flytrap is found in bogs and wet savannas, it tolerates fire and depends on periodic burning to suppress competition. I defy anyone to find a better description of your common-or-garden-variety television producer/director.

Edward 'Dionaea muscipula' Robinson was not the only rare life form cohabiting within that little hothouse beside a whorehouse in Elsternwick. Timothy Ferguson blossomed into the slender Larkspur, a tall 'Black Knight' delphinium. Tim was no wallflower; he preferred full sun and was generally low maintenance, although to this day he does attract the odd hummingbird. Tim put down his roots and we gladly supplied his nutrients, although he would occasionally require fertilisation. The hummingbirds took care of that. Mind you, he did snap easily in high winds.

Young Richard Fidler was more your boab. Richard carried all the sustenance he needed in his swollen trunk, enough life-giving supplies to get him through the rigours of the Australian cultural desert regions. Like most boabs, Richard often had the appearance of being upside down with his roots in the air. This was an illusion, for this antipodean *Adansonia* harboured a well-adapted hidden root system and, as time has proved, when all the other plants around him withered and dried up, Richard was able to sit it out and wait for the life-giving rains to come. And come they did. Apparently his growth rings fade away as his trunk ages, but his genus has been known to live for more than two thousand years, and that's a lot of conversations . . .

Paul McDermott is the Brood Parasite, a born manipulator who, somehow, through charm or promised favour, manages to wiggle its way under your skin, feeding off your creative nutrients before claiming them as its own. The McDermott is a cross between the brown-headed cowbird and the great spotted cuckoo. Never needing a nest of his own, he contents himself with foraging in the nests of others, and willingly produces more of his kind. By deploying an ingenious form of creative cuckoldry, he would swap his immature egg for one of yours, leaving you to inadvertently hatch his germ of an idea which, once hatched, would be reclaimed by the brooding parasite sitting in the corner taking in the backdoor activities of the Daily Planet. And I wouldn't be at all surprised if he left a few eggs in our neighbour's nest.

While Tim spent his time looking adorable all year round and McDermott was busy spreading his seed, Richard was sensibly soaking up all the nutrients he would need to survive the coming decades. And my role in all of this? I drew sustenance from Richard's trunk, occasionally watered Tim and was the perfect host to McDermott's creative hatchlings – all the while keeping well clear of the sinister cilia of Ted Robinson.

You can see why I love these people.

A STREETCAR NAMED A TRAM

Drama, death, tragedy – everybody
has these. But with humour you've
got all these, and the antidote.

ERIC SYKES

According to Hubble's law, universes don't have centres; everything is relative. This was particularly true if you lived in Melbourne in the latter quarter of the twentieth century and happened to be a comedian. Melbourne was the self-proclaimed centre of the comedy universe. For good reason. In the 1980s the universal comedy centre was the Last Laugh in Smith Street, Collingwood. The Laugh boasted a main stage and a smaller venue, Le Joke, a room that became my personal black hole of comedy. I died there, twice. While I could barely make out the few faces from the stage, I could hear them breathing, just. I might have been working in a Buddhist monastery such was the profound silence. Over two nights, only one lone voice, perhaps the most punishing heckle I've ever received. It wasn't technically a heckle, just a quiet voice pleading, 'But it's Friday night?' After that I let the Last Laugh have the last laugh and headed down the road to the Prince Patrick Hotel in Collingwood, where the nascent Flacco was welcomed with open minds.

Heckling was of another order at the Prince Patrick (or 'The Pat' to its patrons). Flacco's most memorable heckle was from an earnest but somewhat inebriated young woman in the front row who continually rose to her feet and shouted, 'Comedy is for the people!' Flacco's comeback line was, 'Then why won't you let them listen to it?' I was pretty happy with that when it sprang into my mind – four days later. Sometimes the muse is tardy.

Heckles come in all shapes and sizes. There is the friendly fire, where a punter who is obviously enjoying the show throws one in the ring. These are relatively harmless, depending on the amount of alcohol said heckler has consumed. Then there's the more biting salvo, usually fired from the mouth of a self-appointed critic, more often than not from a patron with delusions of stand-up. Then there's the googly: hard to pick and coming out of nowhere, these can stun. Al Murray copped a googly from the front row of a show when he was first working up his Pub Landlord character. Jongleurs in North London was the venue, and Al was doing okay until one citizen decided to make a contribution.

I heard this woman at the front go, 'He's got the wrong shoes on.' And I thought, 'Fuck, she's right – they *are* the wrong shoes for this act,' and I still had ten minutes to go so I spent ten minutes trying to get through my stuff thinking, 'These are the wrong shoes, I've got the wrong fucking shoes on. What an idiot! I mean, I like these shoes but they're not right.'

And that's the heckle that sticks.

Jongleurs was also the venue for the All-Stars' preview of an upcoming West End season at the Duke of York Theatre. The lads had always killed at Jongleurs and they were feeling quite cocky. Not long after they hit the stage and started in on their new 'killer routines' the laughter petered out and morphed into angry grumbling. As they left the stage and wandered through the audience on their way to the bar, Richard was overheard pondering why this audience might hate them so much when a woman fired back, 'Because you were shit!' Now that is one cruel heckle, and in retrospect Richard agrees.

We were definitely shit. We stood in the bar after the show whining to Arthur Smith, who said, 'It's alright lads, we all get nights like this.' We were really hurt, these rough tough guys who were supposed to be the hard men of comedy, we were so wounded. I think we got booed.

Duly humbled and chastened, the boys promptly got their act together for what became a sell-out West End season, but for some, the wounds never heal. While supporting the All-Stars in the guise of Psycho Bob, Michael Petroni recalls walking out on stage in front of a D.A.A.S. audience to the sound of his own footsteps and the feeble voice of one fan: 'Oh no. Not Bob . . .'

Another googly hits the stumps. Back to the change room, Bob.

It took a brave promoter to hire Flacco. Larry Buttrose, who ran Comics in the Park at Sydney's Harold Park Hotel, took a chance. Sydney audiences demanded to be won over. They made you sweat. To score a spot at Sydney's premier venue, the Comedy Store, you needed skill, discipline and actual jokes – three qualities I had neglected to hone. I steered clear of the Store. I was bundled into the 'alternative comedy' camp – a curious turn of phrase, for logic would say the alternative to comedy might be self-indulgent, left-field unconventional flap-doodle. Now that, I could deliver. At the Harold Park Hotel the audience was discerning, intelligent and, on a good night, impressively intoxicated. Intoxicated enough to swallow my bewildering hodgepodge of flapdoodlery.

Mark Trevorrow admits that the Harold Park Hotel literally changed his life.

Entirely and completely. My cabaret group The Globos had bitten the dust and I was back in journalism, my showbiz dreams in ashes. Larry didn't have a regular host to call on and he suggested that I might like to try hosting as Bob Downe. I was horrified and terrified, with absolutely no interest in being a solo comic, but luckily he talked me into it, and in January 1987 I went solo, and the rest is hysteria. The first couple of hosting gigs went amazingly well. Then, of course, as happens to all new comics, I fell into a hole and was completely shithouse – I mean real flopsweat stuff, with the audience smelling blood – for the next few months. Larry, bless him, stuck with me through it all.

As with the Harold Park Hotel, at Melbourne's Prince Patrick performers were encouraged to go out on a limb, snap it, crash to the ground, then have another shot. You could stretch your legs and your flapdoodle. That is, unless they discovered your dirty secret – that you were actually from Sydney. This is the unforgivable sin. Melburnians harbour a deep-seated aversion to the harbour citizens. Sydnesians, for their part, remain on the whole oblivious. Perhaps that's what Melburnians find so infuriating. Rod Quantock recalls his first close encounter with Flacco.

The first time I saw Flacco was at the Prince Pat, covered in fur and bones and sticks and God knows what. You were the first Sydney comic I ever liked – because you weren't a Sydney comic in my eyes. I just thought it was absolutely extraordinary and it was so completely different to anything else going on. What attracts me to comedians is their brains. I like comedians who think about things they do and Flacco and The Sandman . . . I remember seeing a thing you did at the Opera House. You each had a bottle of wine, sitting on a bench, and I thought that was one of the great comedy double acts of history. It was just incredible.

High praise from the master for not one but two Sydney comedians. Melbourne far outshines Sydney in documenting and celebrating its own history. Sydney moves in the moment; what's done is done. In Sydney, you simply had to be there.

In the eighties other comic fledglings were also learning the ropes at those twin towers of alternative comedy. The Harold Park Hotel, under the proprietorship of Mark Morgan and family, was propagating the likes of Vince Sorrenti, Sandy 'Austen Tayshus' Gutman, Bob Downe, Jimeoin, George Smilovici and famously, one night, Robin Williams. Williams had a habit of crashing the odd comedy venue when he was in town. One memorable Monday night in the mid-eighties he did just that at the Harold Park Hotel. I was offered a support spot on the night. Larry Buttrose urged me repeatedly to come along, even though I'd declined the opportunity to perform. I couldn't understand the fuss. I mean, I enjoyed listening to Robyn Williams, host of the ABC's *Science Show*, and I knew he had a soft spot for comedy, having appeared with the Pythons once or twice. Still, what's funny about science? It can't even decide on a centre of the universe. Yet for months people were raving about how great the gig was. 'You should have been there,' they tell me to this day. It took a long time for the penny to drop. Regrets? Oh, I've had a few.

Both The Pat and The Park paid around fifty dollars a spot, but there were perks. The Prince Patrick allowed its comedy workers to remain in the venue after hours, with slippery nipples on tap until sunrise. The nipples were not so slippery at the Harold Park, but you could always take your fee and attempt to double it over the road at the Harold Park Paceway. I'd use my fee from a gig in one city to pay for the twelve-hour overnight rail trip to the other. I'd arrive, red-eyed and hungover, at Melbourne's Flinders Street station, where it was a short wander down to the Royal Botanic Gardens to get some sleep before heading off to The Pat. Occasionally, post-performance, someone would offer a bed or a floor. But with slippery nipples on offer until dawn I rarely needed one.

Cameron P. Mellor's first brush with D.A.A.S. live was at the Prince Patrick Hotel.

> It was the infamous night when the great man Ted Robinson was talent-spotting and I remember thinking, 'Well, I'll be nice to the flatmate's boyfriend and go and see his show.'

Cameron had zero expectations. The half-naked, half-blind creature he had previously met in his kitchen, whom we all now know and love as Paul McDermott, had not convinced Cameron that therein lay a comedy warrior of significant proportions. Cameron rehearsed his post-show speech.

> I thought I'd see the show and at the end I'd go, 'Oh, that was really good, Paul.' Then the Dougs came out and I remember him walking onto the stage and then just stepping straight onto the tables, and glasses and ashtrays and shit went flying everywhere and he started hacking into some punter about their dress sense or hairstyle, really laying into them, and it woke me up. I was not expecting what came that night. I loved it. There was talk in the room

of a new TV comedy show happening, and with Ted in the room, the rest is history. Ted's an amazing man, incredibly courageous. Any man that can actually go, 'I'm going to do a live comedy show that has no delay whatsoever, and I'm going to hire these guys to be one of the flagship acts' – that's a brave man, and *The Big Gig* was a fantastic show that, even if you were brave enough to try it, they wouldn't let you do today. The world we live in is very beige.

Ted's expectations that night at The Pat were no higher than Cameron's.

I'd seen them possibly on breakfast TV somewhere, and it was abominable, whatever it was, but my interest was piqued when I went to the Prince Patrick to see them and they were terrific, instantly. I was in Melbourne putting together the pilot for *The Big Gig* and I think that very night I went backstage and said, 'Do you want to be in a TV show?' It was that quick. And I think they thought, 'Oh yeah, bullshit.'

A good reason to give your all at every opportunity is the fact that you never really know who is in the room, no matter the size of the audience or the scale of the venue. Richard recalls an exuberant Ted Robinson on that occasion. Exuberant as a newt.

Ted has a great poker face, but by the end of the night he was pissed and he had such a good time and he laughed so much, and he embraced us all and told us how much he loved the show, and I do remember him saying after he'd seen our parody of *Jesus Christ Superstar* with the crucifixion scene . . . 'and that *Jesus Christ Superstar*' . . . We were thinking, 'Oh he's going to tell us we can't do it . . .' He said, 'We'll keep that for Easter.'

Ted's first sighting of Flacco prompted a mixed response. *Comédien provocateur* Geoff Kelso invited Ted to the Trade Union Club in Sydney to see 'this guy you'll really like'.

And it was Flacco. And he was right, I liked Flacco, but I think on that night I thought there was absolutely no way this kind of an act would ever get on TV. But then I saw Flacco working with the Dougs and it made perfect sense. What I liked about it that time was the fact that it was a multilayered thing and it was quite a theatrical conceit, but it was really surreal and so it had lots of elements about it that I really liked embodied in this one creation. I looked at the things we might do, and yeah, okay, Flacco could come and do a spot. But clearly in the broader world which I arrived at with *D.A.A.S. Kapital*, and a bit in *The Big Gig*, certainly with the things you did with Bob, Flacco was kind of an everyman because he could be anything anywhere in any situation. He could adopt any persona within that role.

Another tireless champion of up-and-coming comedians at that time was David Angelo Taranto, who ran the comedy room at the Prince Patrick Hotel. After he forgave me for having been born in Sydney, I acquired a friend of unswerving loyalty, a promoter of my flapdoodling and a place to sleep. Dave was a professional nurturer. He took us all under his wing. I had plenty of company under that wing, including Anthony Morgan, Mark Little, Greg Fleet, Lynda Gibson, Judith Lucy, Bob Franklin, Rachel Berger and Lano and Woodley, to name a few.

Greg Fleet remembers the eclectic nature of comedy performance in those years.

> I'd done The Pat once or twice. It was Fringe Comedy night, and there were guys with dogs – the guy's act was him and his dog, and the dog would worry a thong. It would just go off at a thong. So I would think that's normal. And I think the Dougs were on, Corky and the Juice Pigs, double acts, quadruple acts, you know, seven people on stage, not talking, it was all very normal. In fact, weirdly enough, stand-up seemed to be in the minority.

For a couple of decades Dave hosted a radio show called *The Cheese Shop*, first on 3PBS and then 3RRR. We all had a play in that sandbox, along with many major players from international parallel comedy universes, including Steven Wright, Emo Philips, Lee Evans, Terry Jones, Lenny Henry, Jo Brand, Bobcat Goldthwait, Alan Davies, Jenny Eclair and Ardal O'Hanlon. Dave Taranto was the David Attenborough of comedy's natural histrionics, meticulously documenting every detail. His knowledge of contemporary comedy was encyclopaedic and his dedication an inspiration, but his waterbed was faulty. Dave allowed me access to his boudoir while he was overseas collecting interviews in Edinburgh. To cut an uncomfortable and embarrassing story short, the waterbed exploded, raining through the bare floorboards to the unit below. They were not happy. I was quite moist. End of story.

Janet McLeod, the fairy godmother of Melbourne comedy, was Dave's trusted sidekick at the time, playing a major role behind the scenes introducing acts to Dave, who then introduced them to a broader public. She met Dave in 1989 after a stint in community radio in Ballarat. Janet was amazed at how little effort was needed to draw a crowd at the Prince Pat, even in those days before social media. Words travelling by mouth. Verbal communication. Who would have thought? Janet recalls that at The Pat there was a better gender balance of performers and audience alike. Lynda Gibson, Judith Lucy, Sue-Ann Post, Rachel Berger, Miss Itchy and Corinne Grant were just a few who shared the tiny stage at The Pat.

In the most pernicious of cosmic jokes, Dave Taranto left the centre of this comedy universe on 12 December 1999 at the age of forty-one. Our personal champion and historian had left the building before us. We were speechless, wingless and stunned. The gap left by Dave was larger than the one between his front teeth. Hundreds filled a park near his Yarraville home for the funeral. The crowd consisted of everyone from upstarts like Dave Hughes and Adam Hills to old hands John Clarke and Rod Quantock. Thirty years of Australian comedy gathered together and no one was laughing.

There was a story Dave loved to tell about a night at The Pat when Flacco took a mid-performance detour to referee a street fight. It went something like this.

The owners of The Pat (be they Pete or Paul or Chris or John, depending on the era) were always protective of their performers. They were aware Flacco was a fragile entity, and when a couple of pre-loaded blow-ins decided to heckle, they took umbrage. It is part and parcel of the game to deal with heckling; indeed there is nothing like a great comeback to unify the audience and ensure ownership of the room. In this instance Flacco was outnumbered as the two took to attacking everything from his hairstyle to his gender choices. Flacco waited patiently for the opportunity to 'come back'. His moment didn't materialise on this occasion as his protective employers attempted to eject the pair from the venue. With a radio microphone attached to his lapel, Flacco was not restricted to the stage, so he wandered offstage to the back of the room to investigate the ruckus. Both owners and the quite sizeable male hecklers were deep in mutual insult combined with some furious shirtfronting. Flacco danced around the impending melee like Daffy Duck in the role of a wrestling referee, drawing laughs from the audience but adding fuel to the fire.

Inevitably, punches began to fly, and this ball of fists and foul language rolled out the door and out of sight of the audience as the owners and the intruders took their fight to the laneway behind the pub. Flacco stayed with the action, commentating all the way, much to the delight of the audience, who sat staring at an empty stage. I received a rare standing ovation when I re-entered the venue. The owners were not amused, just mostly bruised. Dave Taranto could not stop laughing.

Dave was a large gentleman, with a legacy to match. There's been a lot of water under the bed since Dave left, and if homeopathy were real, there'd be a little Dave in every Australian comedian currently working. Sadly, homeopathy is a load of crap. Yet I still sense a hint of Daveness tainting the St Kilda air. Or it could be just the waft of a discarded veal parmi from Topolino's.

They say there is nothing worse than being a comedian and dying on stage. Perhaps, but nothing is worse than dying on stage while another act is performing within earshot, and that act is going over rather well. During one of his first forays into the world of stand-up, Flacco was performing to a handful of uninterested human fodder in the downstairs theatre of a popular alternative 'creative space' (as they were dubbed in the 1980s). The only sound, apart from Flacco's meandering monologue, came from the upstairs theatre: riotous laughter, floor thumping and general mayhem, muted only slightly by the wooden boards that were the ceiling of this downstairs arena of death. A troupe of comedians was working a full house of three hundred above my head into a frenzy. Meanwhile, I worked my audience into an irritated stupor, this irritation fuelled all the more by the fun times above. I knew what they were thinking: 'I wish I was having what that audience is having.' I shared a similar sentiment. I wished I were onstage with the performers above.

As the saying goes, be careful what you wish for. It was some time later that I met one of the owners of those heavy boots, a man who would play a major role in thrusting Flacco into the sideways glance of minor celebrity. His name was Steve Abbott aka Johnny Goodman aka The Sandman, performing with the Castanet Club, all eighteen feet of them, including those of Glenn Butcher, Angela Moore, Doug 'Gargoyle' Ormerod, Mikey Robins and Maynard F# Crabbes to name but ten.

Small, silent audiences are a test for any apprentice comedian. Without the laugh track, other tools are required. A simple solution to my youthful predicament would simply have been to acknowledge their thoughts and my own. Stop talking, pause, look upwards, look to the audience and say, 'At least the ceiling is enjoying itself.' Something improvised on the spot to release the awkward valve somewhat. Better still, acknowledge the dilemma then take your dozen patrons out of the room, through the dressing-room and upstairs to watch that show from backstage. I was too green, too caught in the script, too scared to take the leap. As Al Murray confirms, stand-up comedy is a cruel but honest tutor.

> What I loved about comedy rather than theatre is it's direct and you find out if you are any good straight away. You talk to actors and you know, they're in *Hamlet* and they don't know how it's going. 'Is it going well tonight?' 'I dunno.'

Some comedians thrive on the tiny crowd. I was one of fewer than a dozen paying customers attending a performance of The Sandman in the Belvoir Street Theatre in Sydney. Sandy didn't flinch, wallowing in his inability to attract any sort of attention. 'Failure requires no preparation' is one of Sandy's standard quips. In The Sandman, Steve Abbott created a brilliant character who revelled in his own inadequacies. On some nights, with even less of a crowd, he escorted his mini throng into the theatre restroom, where the acoustics were much better.

> There was a period where usually a big house for me was about five or six. During those sparsely attended Belvoir Street Theatre shows there was one night in particular where there were only three, so I took them out of the theatre and we drove around in my car for a couple of hours. I really like it. It allows me to go off script.

On the night I attended, he slid open a fire door to the side of the stage allowing access to an alley where theatre patrons pass as they enter and exit the building.

> At the end of each show I started singing 'Nobody Ever Comes Back From Goodbye' as the audience filed out. So the seven or eight people who were at that show would leave and go to the bar and have a drink, meanwhile I'd open the fire door and I'd keep singing that song to no-one, and often they'd stay at the bar for some time, and a half-hour later I'm still singing that song to an empty theatre. One time my son Max, who was about five years old at the time, came to my show and he felt sorry for me. Here was his dad

performing to no-one. So he came and sat in the audience to fill out the seats.

When his crowd eventually left the bar, they filed out of the building and down the alley, past the fire door where a lonely figure with a guitar continued performing to empty seats. Some would then come back in to see the rest of the show. But there was no rest of the show. This is typical Steve Abbott style: loose, precarious and rarely thought through.

No matter how small the crowd, it pays to always give it your best shot, as Steve Abbott and I discovered while working to a subdued Sunday afternoon crowd in the Belvoir Street Theatre. Thespian luminary Neil Armfield once aptly described the dynamic between our stage personas: Flacco was always ten steps ahead of the audience and Sandman was ten steps behind. It made for an erratic night of comedy, as Steve corroborates.

Sometimes we would test people's patience by leaving the stage with nothing happening for minutes on end. It was merely people looking at a miniature calico tent onstage with a light that went on and off. There was no script. And that night only one person was laughing, but he was absolutely pissing his pants, which in turn started others laughing. And it turns out it was Warren Mitchell.

Warren later wrote a letter to the theatre, saying it was one of the funniest things he had ever seen in the theatre in his life. High praise from Alf Garnett himself. Now that's what I call a fan letter.

Paul McDermott recalls working to a small room in Cork, a town where the All-Stars had worn out their welcome even before setting foot in the county.

We'd had bad press from the Catholic Church after performing in Dublin with the *God & Satan* show. We got to Cork and the word was out not to go and see these fellows. We were doing songs like 'The Virgin Mary Weren't No Virgin When We Knew Her', so perhaps it was understandable. We had booked a fifteen-hundred-seat theatre in Cork and there were about thirty people in the audience, so we took them to the pub next door. Next thing we know, the publican was giving us and the audience free beers, I was dropping my trousers and wrapping myself in the curtains, impersonating a Roman god or emperor, performing *Romeo and Juliet* on the bar. It was wild. We did a two-hour show in the pub, and the publican shook our hands and everyone was embracing at the end of it. Then we walked back into the venue to find the staff all standing there looking at us, and they said, 'We are going to sue you.'

Melbourne comedy heavyweight Anthony Morgan could work to five people in a tent in Edinburgh in the middle of the day and still win them over. Rod Quantock built an entire show around taking a small gaggle of an audience to other people's larger and more successful shows. Al Murray subscribes to a similar ethic.

I've never not gone on because there's no one in. No, I've not done that. Because even if there's just eight of them you've got to make tonight special, haven't you? And they've paid and you don't want to make them feel like saps for turning up. I think that's a mistake comics often make in that situation. They go, 'Fuck me, there's no one here.' And the people who are there think, 'Well I'm here, do I not matter?' I was in a group once that outnumbered the audience, in Edinburgh – there were three people in the room, there were four of us. They can be great fun. Personal.

Television exposure can swiftly increase the size and scope of your audience and performing opportunities. That is, if you can cut the mustard. On the small screen you only get one shot. And you do not want to walk out of that studio with egg on your face and a plate full of untouched mustard.

THROUGH A CATHODE RAY TUBE, DARKLY

Television is a medium because
anything well done is rare.
FRED ALLEN

I died and was resurrected many times on those tiny pub stages in the late eighties. What the experience gave me proved invaluable for the challenges faced on the set of Ted Robinson's *Tuesday Night Live: The Big Gig.* An hour of live television comedy, set across five stages with a dozen cameras and a capacity audience of about two hundred and fifty, but the lack of legal restrictions meant they just packed in as many as possible. It was standing room only as the audience was manhandled from stage to stage and out of range of speeding cameras and cranes between acts. How Ted Robinson managed to get this thing off the ground in 1989 is a tribute to the man's tenacity.

There were often battles, and the battles were generally about stuff you wouldn't think there'd be a battle about, but there was extraordinary pressure for *The Big Gig* not to go live. Everyone was afraid of giving this bunch of lunatics control of the asylum. Because you have to remember that when you are live on air, you *are* the ABC. You are the sharp end of whatever it is. And so there was enormous pressure to stop it going live and I kept saying, 'I've never done a live show like this to air but I think it gives it the element of danger it needs, and think of the oomph it's going to give the performers.'

Oomph is putting it lightly. On the performers' side, the requisite skills were the ability to hold the room while simultaneously working a dozen cameras and remaining hilarious. One take, no room for error, and nail it all in less than five minutes. This was real live-to-air television – not live to air as it is in twenty-first century parlance, where a live performance is shot before a live audience, edited, passed through lawyers' hands, edited again and aired days or weeks later. *The Big Gig* went out each Tuesday night at 9 pm. We were in the studio and the viewing audience at home, with only a cathode ray tube between us. Ted attempted to sell this idea to other networks before it landed in the ABC's lap. He remembers one rejection quite fondly.

It was one of the sweetest little rejections I ever had, because he said, 'Come in, sit down,' and he was a truly commercial TV guy but he loved all things television, and he said, 'I know about you, I've seen your career, I've seen everything you've ever done, I absolutely love it all – but don't think you can get away with that shit on my network.' So then I went to the ABC and there was some resistance to Wendy [Harmer], or particularly to a woman hosting it, and there was quite a lot of pressure, which is very funny given the way the world turned out, but I hung out for Wendy. I might have used one of my favourite ploys by not admitting I'd been to commercial networks and saying, 'Oh well, if you don't want Wendy we'll go to a commercial network. And so it became Wendy.'

The dynamic on set was one of palpable tension. Everyone was on edge: the talent, crew, ABC commissioning editors; we were all in this thing together. Performers paced the corridor surrounding the studio, head down, mumbling lines – Glynn Nicholas, Wendy Harmer and Jean Kittson, swearing and cursing at her mutinous brain as she tried to digest another densely worded script often penned by the genius hand of *Big Gig* head writer, and her future husband, Patrick Cook. Just the occasional nod to one another as we passed, and with it the recognition of sheer terror in our collective eyes. It was specifically the solo acts that roamed the corridors; on every circumnavigation you'd pass the D.A.A.S. dressing-room, where sweet harmonies rang out, or the Empty Pockets, Matts Quartermaine and Parkinson, enjoying the camaraderie that comes from working with at least one other human. The soundtrack to all of this came courtesy of the house band, the Swinging Sidewalks, all horns and revelry.

Every now and then momentary chaos erupted as floor manager Hugh Johnson tore down the corridor, looking remarkably like Salman Rushdie running for his life. Hugh grabbed an arm. 'Got him!' he'd shout into his headset before a jittery comedian was manhandled into the studio like a hog to the slaughterhouse. Once in the studio the first sight the comedian faced was the back of the audience, a writhing horde generally roaring with laughter at the sharp observational wit of Anthony Ackroyd or the twisted waterfall of sinuous jokes from Jean Kittson's creation Candida. A round of applause, then back to Wendy Harmer, who swiftly threw to the next act. 'In three . . .' whispers Hugh, and you silently count down 'Two, one,' before a tiny red light flashes on the camera directly ahead. Now, what was my first line again?

I had honed the material in pubs and clubs for several years yet I felt myself perched behind Flacco's eyes, peeping out. The audience peeped back, some with crooked smiles, all slightly puzzled, a couple downright angry, a yawner, a talker and a fellow pale-faced performer in the rear, preparing for launch immediately following Flacco's five-minute flight of fancy. There was, however, a single loud laugher in the front row. A real snorter. This guy was lapping it up. Or so I thought until I glanced down. It was Hugh, on orders from upstairs to lead the laughter. About two minutes into my set, things turned particularly quiet, until I heard a faint *ha!* from Hugh's headset. 'I may die up here,' I thought. 'I may embarrass my family, but at least I'll get another shot at this thanks to Ted Robinson's singular *ha!*'

Richard Fidler lays the the All-Stars television success squarely on the shoulders of Ted Robinson.

The Big Gig was 'inspired' by *Friday Night Live*, the show we'd done in the UK in '88, and they didn't shoot us very well. It lacked impact, we could never figure out why. No director had known how to shoot us. But with the use of hand-held cameras to cut and slice the way we were shot meant we could do stuff right down the barrel and grab the camera, and Paul of course instinctively and entirely appropriately used it for sexual purposes. Normally one would see a hand-held camera as a phallic thing; Paul saw it as a vagina. He disregarded the lens entirely as a prophylactic, he just saw the hole and went for it. Plugged it. Which, of course, was perfect.

The impact of the All-Stars was instant; their fanbase exploded from their first appearance on *The Big Gig*. Richard puts it down to a form of calculated totalitarianism.

We were unknown to the Australian public by and large; we were far better known in Britain so I thought, 'How do we make ourselves look famous?' So when we were doing the audience warm-up before we went live to air, I said, 'Look, this is our first time, would you mind doing us a favour and giving us a standing ovation, and could we just practise that, please.' So when we were introduced the live audience gave us this huge welcome, and it looked like, well these guys must be incredibly famous, everyone loves them already, you need to know what's going on here. It gave us the opportunity of using the template of the fascistic address, a *1984*-type address to the nation, a parody of that. It worked perfectly within the format of *The Big Gig*. It worked like a charm.

Mandy Jones used to wag school to go to the live recordings of *The Big Gig*. Little did she suspect she would one day grow up to be an official D.A.A.S. fan club coordinator. But for the moment this year eleven student had to hustle for tickets and a spot close to her heroes.

It was the whole lottery of the thing. At the end of each show, whoever was hosting would say, 'Call after 10 am tomorrow to get your tickets for next week.' You just had to ring and ring and ring because there was no voicemail. It was just ring, engaged, ring again. If I didn't get through after forty-five minutes all the tickets were gone.

Mandy and her colleagues put a lot of adolescent woman hours into landing the prize of watching the All-Stars perform for seven minutes.

You could get a maximum of four tickets. So you'd turn up on the night and get ushered into the ABC cafeteria and have the watered-down wine and you'd choose your position well. You wanted to be closest to the exit doors from the cafeteria so that when you were let in to the studio you could get down the front, and we always knew which stage D.A.A.S. were on and you'd stand there. But it also meant you'd be on camera all night. I remember one night Wendy Harmer handed me a banana and pulled me up on stage: 'No, I'm not here for that.' We just wanted to be there to scream. Then we'd go home on a buzz and the next morning try to get in again.

Greg Fleet remembers his time on *The Big Gig* with just the barest hint of seething, blood-boiling resentment.

I was working with the Empty Pockets and Ted Robinson hated me. I don't know how he even knew who I was but he thought I was shit. The three of us had done Edinburgh, so he got the two of them who were a double act to do the television show and they kept hassling him on my behalf to get me involved. After the first series he caved, but he was very open about his hostility towards me and he just didn't like me at all.

Why not just tell it like it was, Greg? Don't let me stop you. All I'll do is put everything you say into a book. Carry on.

The Empty Pockets and I – by this stage we'd developed such a bitter nature – we'd have some sketch, we'd do it in the rehearsal and it'd be, like, four minutes long and it would be what we thought was a great sketch, but we'd all know what was going to happen. Everything would be set and then back in our dressing-room, maybe an hour before the show, one of the assistants would come in and say, 'Listen, we're going to have to knock your sketch back to three minutes.' It was a four-minute sketch. So we had about half an hour to cut it back to three minutes – and why? Because the Dougs were doing this sketch where they were being lowered through the roof on a rope and a helicopter comes in. It was a routine that did not have a single joke in it, but was really complex and, of course, eventually the helicopter lands, they take off the bat costumes and do some awesome Doug Anthony sketch.

Quite finished, Greg?

After a while we'd go, 'Okay, we've got this sketch,' and they'd look at it in rehearsal and go, 'Really funny sketch,' and we'd go, 'Are you going to come to us later on and tell us we have to cut some of this back because the Dougs have to release eleven Dalmatians into the audience and hit three of them with a tiny rubber hammer?' And they'd go, 'No, of course not.' And then they would.

Ted knew what he liked, and more importantly, what he didn't like. And what he didn't like was Greg Fleet. Until, eventually, the ice on the Predator's brow thawed.

It took a number of years, but over time he grew to like me and a genuine affection grew between us. But it was like the southern soldier and the northern soldier who become friends as old men.

Michael Petroni, on the other hand, was welcomed into Ted's exclusive flock. Bob and Flacco were booked to perform at The Pat while we were still on the dole, so we purchased a one-way stand-by ticket each to get to Melbourne and we thought that the door takings from the shows would buy our tickets back. That was the extent of our ambition, as Michael recalls.

> But the more important thing that happened was that Tim Ferguson came to see our show. He already loved Flacco and then he saw Bob . . . almost instantly I was offered a spot on *The Big Gig*.

Michael presented some scripts for Ted to peruse, but Ted insisted on Bob performing a song he'd seen him do at The Pat. Among other dubious lyrics, it included the lines: 'You're a pinko, nigger-lovin' son of a bitch, I'm going to cut you up and put you in my fridge' – a delightful ditty that would later turn up on *D.A.A.S. Kapital*. Michael was, understandably, a little hesitant to include this tune in his first-ever national television appearance.

> So instead I performed the opening monologue to my set that involved me standing in the audience in full Bob costume, and people didn't know who I was or what I was doing there. And then I rose up out of the audience on a hydraulic pedestal. I guess I just waited until I had everyone's attention, and I just started in on the monologue. 'Hi, I'm Bob and I've got a problem . . .' I was certainly not in control of myself enough to say I was 'working the cameras'. It was terrifying and exhilarating all at once to be plucked quite literally out of nowhere and to be put on a national television show that went live to air.

Ted Robinson has no memory of Bob's first spot. When I recently reminded him he said, 'Fuck, that sounds like a good idea. Oh, that's very clever, I'm pleased I did that. If you want a surprise entrance for Bob that's as good as any.' But Ted does remember the night an unlikely performer almost shut down the production by unleashing a taboo expletive live across the nation.

> Everyone was pretty well disciplined about not swearing, and in the middle of something the Dougs were doing, of all people, Richard Fidler said, 'Fuck!' I thought that could be the end of the program, because I knew what a thin line it was dangling on.

Richard recalls dropping that F-bomb during a Five Blind Boys sketch. The Five Blind Boys were Richard, Tim, Paul, me and a character called Silent Neville, who was never seen or heard but the Blind Boys were sure existed.

> I think maybe the problem was we had dark sunglasses on (swimming goggles, in fact) and couldn't see a damned thing. And it was so easy to forget you were live to air . . . as soon as it came out of my mouth, a second later I thought, 'I just said fuck on national TV', when it was not a commonplace thing at all, and no-one said anything, no-one seemed to notice except for Michael Shrimpton, the head of entertainment at the time. He rang up Ted, I think . . .

He did indeed.

The next morning at about 8.30 I was in the office and I got a phone call from our executive producer and he said, 'Robinson? You said "fuck" on my network last night.' And I said, 'Well, I didn't personally,' and he said, 'Well, one of your jesters did.' I said, 'Yeah, sure, it was a bit of an accident, a slip of the tongue, he didn't mean to, but our batting average isn't bad so far,' and he just laughed and that was the last I heard of it. But it was a pretty big deal at that time. In fact, it may have been one of the first two or three times anyone had ever said 'fuck' on air. And it was fucking Richard!

Richard offered another D.A.A.S memorable moment, arguably the first gay kiss on national television.

During one of our *Big Gig* mock dating segments, the three of us went on looking virginal, saying we are looking for a partner, and I was in the middle doing my lines when Tim and Paul just looked at one another, realised they were in love and started to, not just kiss, but really tongue kiss passionately. There is a substratum of teenage girls that finds gay attraction powerfully erotic. There was a whole subset of fan fiction about us as a group that was full of gay sex scenes between the three of us . . . It might have watered it down if I'd have participated in it . . .

Later in the series Bob and Flacco were to perform a poem together. Flacco was dressed as a young child, with Bob in his usual psycho-killer camouflage flak jacket. Our little poem went something like this:

FLACCO: In my youth I had a passion.

BOB: In my ute I had a passenger.

FLACCO: I'd stand for hours at the edge of my bed.

BOB: I stared for hours and beat his head.

FLACCO: Where I would chew spinach and wish upon a star.

BOB: When I was finished I let him out of the car.

FLACCO: Toppling backwards I dozed off.

BOB: I ran over him backwards and drove off.

FLACCO: Within no time I entered the land of nod.

BOB: I waste no time, I finish the job.

FLACCO: I slept for hours.

BOB: I drove for hours.

FLACCO: Wet with fever.

BOB: White-line fever.

BOTH: I dreamed . . .

Then we'd repeat the poem with the characters swapping the lines. It was risky TV but it worked. Even the executive producer called Ted Robinson to congratulate him. It went straight to our heads. We were drunk with praise. Our inevitable downfall began as we rehearsed a second poem in the *Big Gig* studios, flushed from the success of our previous outing. I can't bring myself to recount the tale of our descent into humiliation and ostracism so I'll leave it to Michael.

So I thought I was an artist extraordinaire. We were on the stage and it's a tech rehearsal and it's a live-to-air show so there's lots of things that everyone has to get right besides

Paul and Tim in the classic despotboiler, *The Fascist Gun in the West*.

Richard Fidler and Mark 'Bob Downe' Trevorrow scan the script for any sign of humour.

Flacco as the Fairy Godfish, and Richard Fidler as Richard Fidler.

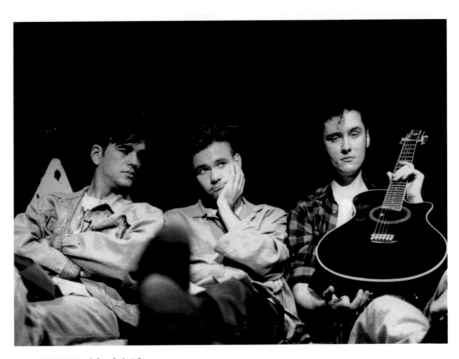

FERGUSON: (*thinks*) I love you mate.

McDERMOTT: (*thinks*) I'd love to mate.

FIDLER: (*thinks*) Sesquipedalian. Mmm, that's a big word . . .

The common-or-garden-variety Flacco – self-fertilising and completely rooted.
Stuart Spence

Flacco and The Sandman. A mismatch made in heaven. *James Penlidis*

David A. Taranto and Janet A. McLeod backstage at the Esplanade Hotel, St Kilda, 1995. *Peter Milne*

Flacco, 1996. Pre-show. Premeditating.

Beria (Paul Livingston), Khrushchev (Dennis Watkins), Malenkov (Steve Abbott) and Stalin (F. Murray Abraham) on the set of *Children of the Revolution*, 1996. *Philip Le Masurier*

Mr Book (Sir Ian Richardson) flanked by Assistant Stranger Number 1 (Paul Livingston) and Assistant Stranger Number 2 (Michael Lake) on the set of *Dark City*, 1998.

Flacco and The Sandman eventually parted ways. No hard feelings – just a few sour grapes.

Paul 'Flacco' Livingston and John 'Gomez' Astin, *GNW Night Lite* dressing-room, 1999. *Steve Abbott*

FLACCO: I distinctly asked for Pink Ladies and all I get is Granny Smith . . .

Stuart Spence

The All-Stars reunite in 2013 to launch the *D.A.A.S. Kapital* DVD. *Tor Goldsmith*

Richard Fidler,
professional
conversationalist,
settles back into
his day job.

Meanwhile Tim and Paul ponder a reunion. 'If we build it, will they come?'
Tony Virgo

'Oh my god, what have I done?' Cameron P. Mellor on accepting the role of
D.A.A.S. tour manager, 2014. *Tor Goldsmith*

With Anne-Sophie Marion and Samantha Kelly recruited to manage the production, the new D.A.A.S. crew were ready to roll. *Paul Livingston*

Tim Ferguson brought his own wheels. *Paul Livingston*

The D.A.A.S. faithful came bearing gifts, among them a selection of custom-baked cookies. *Courtesy of Patty Macintosh*

They built it. They came. They queued around the block. *Tony Virgo*

A pensioner, a cripple and a songwriter awaken the monster. It's alive . . . but does it have legs? *Tony Virgo*

D.A.A.S. backstage with Dane Hiser at The Harold Park Hotel prior to the warming of the corpse in 2014. *Erik Bergan*

It soon became clear – you can't teach an old dog new tricks. Especially when he can't even remember the old ones. *Tor Goldsmith*

LIVINGSTON: (*thinks*) I came out of retirement for this.
McDERMOTT: (*thinks*) He came out of retirement for this. *Anne-Sophie Marion*

'The Guitarist' reliving someone else's youth. *Tor Goldsmith*

Flacco, Version 2.0, gracing the stage before said stage is disgraced by D.A.A.S. *Tor Goldsmith*

me remembering my lines, but I was absolutely ignorant of all that. And we were bitching about how long we had to stand up there for and my radio microphone was uncomfortable and I think we were even complaining about the set and how close or how far apart we were from each other and how were we to hear each other. We were bitching and bitching with our radio mics on. So everything we said was going up into the cans of Ted Robinson (via every headset in the studio), who was trying to get a show together that was going to air that night.

And suddenly it was like there was this draft, a cold draft blowing through the studio, and everyone went silent and all we heard were the footsteps of Ted Robinson coming down the steel spiral staircase and making a beeline for us, grabbing us both by the arm, and saying . . . I can't remember exactly what he said, probably because I have mentally blocked it out, but it was said with that very, very quiet anger. He didn't yell, but it was the intensity with which he said whatever he said . . . I could have shat my pants. It was terrifying. So from that point on whenever we bitched we didn't have our radio mics turned on.

As Michael recalls, our fate was sealed with our second poem. After we'd finished, the audience blinked, turned their backs and wandered silently towards the host, Glynn Nicholas, who scrunched his face in embarrassment and said, 'Well, that was Art . . .' Sadly, I think Glynn was right. But we did receive a single fan letter congratulating us on the finest anti-war statement the viewer had ever seen on television. It was news to us, but we were happy to have fooled at least one viewer into thinking we were smarter than them.

Mr Petroni was having a bad run. When Flacco was invited to perform for two nights at Mietta's, I immediately offered the support spot to Michael. Mietta O'Donnell was the grand-daughter of two of Melbourne's most influential restaurateurs, Mario and Maria Teresa Vigano, and true to family tradition Mietta's restaurant, salon and cocktail bar just off Collins Street became the hub of Melbourne's cultural elite. This elegant, softly spoken woman had a habit of opening her doors to all manner of performers to amuse, delight and confuse her patrons. But there was at least one occasion when she may well have regretted her generous support of up-and-coming clowns.

Flacco was to present his solo monologue *On the Dangers of Literature*. This show was my juvenile attempt to rise above my working-class roots and ingratiate myself with the highbrow crowd by employing obscure references and very long words in a sesquipedalian feast for the mind. Michael was to open the show with Bob, the trigger-happy serial killer. The event that assured the demise of Bob, and the banishment of Michael from Mietta's for all time, came after the conclusion of our second and final show. I sensed Michael's pain as he recalled the episode.

After every show Mietta would treat us to wine and fine food. We'd sit in one of the plush booths to the side of the dining room. It was lovely. And on this particular night Mietta and her partner, Tony Knox, came up to the table and they had this very special book. It contained the signatures of all the famous people who had passed through Mietta's.

Michael and I, having grown up in the same working-class inner-Sydney suburb, had never been exposed to haute cuisine and fancy wines. We were two fish out of water, guppies among tropical exotica. Mietta maintained her composure as we sculled her red wine (no doubt selected from her comprehensive list of grand cru burgundies) like cordial. I suspect I know now why Tony always wore a subtle frown fixed to his brow – it was in fact a grimace. That grimace was about to be tested to its limit when a large leather-bound book with guest signatures dating back decades was presented to us. Tony opened it to a page for Flacco to sign.

It was like a holy relic. And they wanted Paul Livingston as Flacco to sign, and he did, then they looked at me, kind of embarrassed, they were such polite people they thought it would be rude to just withdraw the book without offering it to me. I didn't want to sign the book – I certainly wasn't worthy of signing it – but they very tentatively proffered it to me, and because I was so nervous when I reached for the fountain pen I knocked my glass of very expensive red wine over the very important page with the fresh signature of Paul Livingston as well as the signatures of Frank Sinatra and Liberace. Their faces blanched and Tony grabbed a cloth and began fussing, and they hurried away with the book whispering to each other and I sank into my seat just wanting to die.

The 'incident', as we now refer to it, capped off a trying couple of days for Michael. That final show had not gone smoothly for Bob.

Mietta's had a tiny stage, and there was nowhere to change; you were either behind the curtain or under the piano. Flacco huddled under that piano for half of the show and then he would come out, on my introduction. And I basic-ally got partway through my set and had what I call my *Shine* moment, where everything went quiet. I couldn't even hear my own voice. It was a total out-of-body experience. And I literally just gave up and walked offstage, leaving Flacco, who couldn't see, but could only wonder why I'd stopped speaking. So there was this awkward gap in the show until Flacco realised that I'd either died or run away, so he had to crawl out from under the piano and start his show, except he had to make excuses. It was terrible. He must have frigging hated my guts at that point.

I don't remember any hatred. Panic, yes – and, in retrospect, embarrassment at my lack of manners, culinary knowledge and wine appreciation. Mietta's tragic death in a car accident in Burnie, Tasmania, on 4 January 2001 came as a shock. I have no idea if she ever forgave the guest book incident, but I do know she would be proud of Michael and me these days, being the class traitors, culinary enthusiasts and wine bores that we are.

MOVEMENT II

Larghissimo (from the Latin *ad libitum*, to drag out every note)

THE PLAYERS

PAUL McDERMOTT: Impassioned hedonist, internuncio of oddball haircuts, sex god.

TIM FERGUSON: Suave, beguiling, still pretty.

RICHARD FIDLER: The guitarist.

PAUL 'FLACCO' LIVINGSTON: Spear-carrier, boiled egg on stilts, sexual domino.

CAMERON P. MELLOR: Hanger-on.

MINOR PLAYERS: Shady tour managers, illegal-substance enablers, assorted comedic couldabeens, wouldabeens and nevercouldabeenorwouldabeens.

LOCATION

The entertainment world.

TIME

Late 1980s–early 1990s.

THE PATHOLOGY OF THE ALL-STARS

I actually don't have a bad hairline . . .
DONALD TRUMP

- pathological lying
- glib and superficial charm
- no sense of responsibility
- grandiose self-perception
- a poverty of heartfelt emotions
- lack of remorse
- cruelty to animals
- staying eerily calm in scary or dangerous situations

These are the commonly recognised traits of your prototypical psychopath. That being the case, it makes for a clear diagnosis of the youthful Doug Anthony All-Stars as psycho-comedians. That this list appears to be a recipe for the celebrity persona in general is beside the point. The D.A.A.S. self-esteem engine was a three-piston-headed loco-emotive, benumbed of compassion and fuelled by sweat, deceit and cold-blooded bloodsportsman-ship. They knew no fear; they instilled it. As for animal cruelty? One need look no further than their signature tune, a mindless ditty that successfully channels the spirit of English sculptor Eric Gill, a lousy sculptor but devout Roman Catholic, most famous these days for his fervent erotic horseplay with canines. Not to mention my own treatment at their merciless hands. They petted me lovingly at times, taught me how to beg, one even allowed me to hump his knee, yet they felt no hesitation in feeding me to the lions or, in this case, their minions.

Initial impressions can be deceptive, and Rod Quantock's first sighting of D.A.A.S. in a small town outside Canberra gave little hint of what was to follow.

> We were doing a conference dinner for the Gas Association of Australia or some such thing, and they were these three very neat, clean-cut, tidy, sanitised, disinfected boys from Canberra Uni who were just doing covers basically. They sang well, but apart from that they were just the Kingston Trio. There was nothing to like or hate in terms of what they did.

It wasn't long before a darker side of D.A.A.S. made its presence felt, as Frank Woodley recalls, having supported the All-Stars with the Found Objects.

> I was still a virgin at that time. I didn't lose my virginity until I was nineteen. I wasn't exactly terrified or intimidated

by it, but there was an aggressive kind of sexual energy that I was a bit uncomfortable about. I have a memory of performing at Le Joke at the Last Laugh and we came downstairs and the Doug Anthony All-Stars had been performing and there was a kind of a party after their show and I remember seeing Paul McDermott doing a very sexual dance, sort of as a display. It was a kind of performance for all the staff and those who were hanging out, but it was a very sexually provocative thing. They had their clothes on. There was just some sort of rooting action going on, where genitals were rubbing up against each other. It was all so new.

Greg Fleet offered a definition of Paul that made a lot of sense to me.

He was the devil. I was very impressed with the whole thing; they were doing exactly what I wanted to do. They had that kind of punk vibe, an educated private school punk ... They seemed to have that really great balance of underground and mainstream, whereas the harder we tried to be underground the more underground we became.

Greg doesn't seem to be capable of offering much praise before his own inner demon is released. D.A.A.S seem to bring it out in a person. Psycho-comedy is like that. Charismatic at first, it wants to be your friend, drawing you in with the promise of earthly delights before ravaging and pillaging your soul, leaving you shaken and shucked. Shucked senseless, to be precise. Or was that just me and Greg?

But I kind of hated them too, because to some degree they terrified me – apart from Richard, who never terrified anyone. Paul and Tim intimidated me, and I thought they'd both be horrible people to meet. They'd be playing psychological games with you and trying to break you, but I was astounded by the mixture of comedy and incredible singing and I kind of hated them for that too, but I never hated them for very long because it became quite fashionable among all my friends to hate them and I thought, 'I don't want to be a sheep.' So I started to vocally like them. So I liked them but I hated them, mostly because I was jealous.

The virginal Frank Woodley remained baffled, like a frightened puppy in a pack of hyenas.

Watching them perform . . . Say you're at the Prince Pat and it's packed to the rafters, and the atmosphere is absolutely electric – I don't know that I've ever been in an audience environment that has been more intense, more charged, than watching those guys.

There was this incredible thing going on, a lot of sexual energy and a lot of psychological manipulation of the audience in a way that I found really interesting but quite disconcerting . . . It seems to relate to the beautiful singing. When they are doing the harmonies in these small venues there's actually something really rarefied in the atmosphere that's creating an emotional effect, but in fact they are using that to open everybody up, and then they are playing with us. And then of course, with all the young women in the audience as well, they're just kind of teasing them. I've got lots of kind of weird little memories like that.

Janet McLeod was similarly impressed by this astonishing psychological orchestration.

They got away with far more than many other comedy trios because they had the beautiful music and the looks. The thing that I found fascinating about them in the UK was the fervour, it was a pop star phenomenon. We'd never seen anything like that in Australian comedy, the level of excitement . . . going into a room and finding all these adults in this heightened state. That level of danger is always appealing to both genders, especially when you are young – when the possibility of getting abused is also appealing.

Abuse masquerading as entertainment was an All-Stars specialty. Frank singles out Paul McDermott for special mention in this regard.

I remember seeing Paul McDermott tell a really banal shit joke, a joke that I don't think he wanted to be shit. He wrote the best joke he could, I believe, and it was quite weak, and then, when the audience didn't laugh, he just said, 'Get fucked! Fuck off!' And that was beautiful. It was like, Hang on, how can you be abusing us 'cause you're shit?

But I liked it. You know how there's that thing in comedy where the audience is always laughing either with you or at you? We are kind of laughing at him, because he's the most arrogant, deluded person. He's kind of the butt of that joke in a way, but because he's abusing us so aggressively, is he really the butt?

Former D.A.A.S. fan club coordinator Mandy Jones had a fan's-eye view of the situation.

I think it was the aggressive sexuality of it. It was just so shocking. My generation had grown up in an atmosphere of casual racism, sexism, homophobia – all of that bad behaviour was normalised and made out to be okay. Then you'd go to a Dougs show and it would sort of border on being misogynistic but it wasn't – it was actually done to prove a point. Mob mentality can change people. A percentage of the audience totally got what was going on and others just couldn't understand the manipulation, and one minute they were cheering and the next they were baying for someone's blood. I think it was a golden age when there was still an innocence, our horizons were so limited because there was no internet and we didn't know what was going on around the world comedy-wise unless comedians came here. D.A.A.S. were just the clash of all that coming together into this seamless amazing experience.

The All-Stars peculiar mix of psycho-sexuality and mob manipulation seemed to hold Frank and Greg in its thrall.

GREG: I remember the first time I saw them do that song with the airman and the soldier ['War Song']. A beautiful song and, you know, we're watching it and afterwards a couple of the comics I was hanging out with who were infamously bitter people anyway, they were saying, 'Yeah, there were no jokes in that. No jokes at all.' I said, 'But it's way beyond jokes.'

FRANK: My reaction to that wasn't so much 'no jokes', it was like, 'Hang on, hang on, hang on, you want me to make the step.' And people were taking the step, and I'm amazed . . . You could hear a pin drop. They are doing the beauty bit now. But I was going, 'You expect me to trust you to open my emotions up to feel vulnerable after you've just been shitting into my mouth!'

That's exactly what they expected, Frank. I just hope you weren't standing in the front row with your mouth agape at the time. Greg Fleet described the dilemma as being akin to being in an abusive relationship. One where you go back time and time again. You can almost feel Frank's innocence being swept away as the veils of D.A.A.S. deception are peeled back in his mind.

FRANK: Just the activating of different sorts of emotions you can then exploit for nefarious purposes. I reckon that's a really interesting thing, you know, because the other thing is, like, intellectual posturing. The Doug Anthonys would use lots of lofty pseudo-intellectual concepts.

GREG: Throwing Sartre into a comedy sketch.

FRANK: And the point is, to give them status, to make you feel that they are superior to you and that you're in awe of them in some way, you're aspiring to be as powerful as them, once again it's that abusive relationship thing. It used to fascinate me but it used to shit me.

GREG: I remember Paul told me someone had seen the Dougs and they'd mentioned Sartre or fucking whatever, and they said, I've read *Nausea*. Paul said, 'What?' And they said, 'Since seeing you I've read Sartre's *Nausea* and it's amazing.' And Paul's like, 'I've never read it.' And this poor person had pored over this turgid fucking book. And Paul's like, 'I wouldn't read that. I like comics.'

Ted Robinson enjoyed the intellectual conceit of the All-Stars.

The real truth is I love the essence of what they did and still do. All those spurious literary drops that Richard would do, having read them on the flyleaf of some book, something about Proust or some such thing. Which is why a generation of people like them. I thought, 'You've no idea what you're fucking talking about as you talk about Nietzsche or whatever, but that doesn't matter – the fact that you are mentioning it at all gives it a kind of resonance which I think is quite interesting and important.' And their own little bizarre take on theatricality, you know, how three guys can have got so far on the one step, the one little piece of choreography, that is still being used today by Paul. It's not quite a box step, it's got a little bit of a kick in there as well. A slight adaptation from one song to another but basically the same step. Do you know what a step-ball-change is?

Like swimming, driving, rock climbing and marriage, dancing is one thing I've managed to avoid thus far. So no, Ted, I have no idea what a step-ball-change is.

It's kind of a basic step; it's exactly what it says. You take a step, you do the next one on the ball of your foot, you take another step. Every drag queen uses that step, Peter Garrett uses that step, I think there should be a history of step-ball-change. It just turns up everywhere.

Ted doesn't just talk the talk, he dances it. Ted started out treading the boards by dancing on them – until he made a career out of dancing around the fragile egos of comedy upstarts.

I have never been terribly interested in the All-Stars' foot movements, but I was impressed by their ability to sweep from highbrow to lowbrow and back again. I was happy dwelling in the one brow, the pseudo-upper brow. The All-Stars were monobrow beaters. What all this meant to the fans is another story. Mandy Jones recalls that there were many in the D.A.A.S. audience who failed to grasp the concepts their objects of adoration were singing about. And others who at least pretended to have a clue.

There were some who had no idea. Then there were the ones who hung on every word, and if there was a mention of Camus it was, 'Oh yes! Yes!' And they'd add it to their reading list. And you could just imagine in public libraries every-where the day after, all the Dostoyevsky and Camus books have gone! . . . But I think that a lot of it just went over their heads . . . There was that real mix and I think there was a tension to that as well. The ones who knew the references were always making it very obvious and the others were just like squealing or screaming through the show, 'Tim's pretty!' And the older ones were there to hear the lyrics and appreciate the comedy.

One fan had barely reached puberty when he first began taping and watching *The Big Gig* over and over. His parents had no problem with him watching the show, it was just that young Patrick needed to be in bed by 8 pm.

I was too young to know who the hell half these people were or what the references were, but I could get something from the heft of the language. To me, listening to comedy and watching it over and over again was a big part of how I learned about language. It was a big part of how I learned to manipulate language and use language and deconstruct language.

One reason why Patrick has used the word language five times in two sentences is that little Pat grew up to be Patrick Stokes, senior lecturer and discipline convener in philosophy (as Patrick makes quite clear, that second title does not mean that he takes the bookings at an S&M brothel). The All-Stars' habit of drop-ping the odd obscure name pricked the mind of young Patrick.

That stuff does stick with you and comes back later on. The name Kierkegaard, I heard that name twice in my life before getting to university – once in a Monty Python sketch and once in a Dougs routine somewhere. So when I saw the name in Sartre's footnotes in my first year as a philosophy student, I thought, 'I remember that guy,' and that then sent me down the path to where I'm now one of maybe two or three people in Australia who is a Kierkegaard scholar.

Patrick compares being one of Australia's foremost experts on the works of Kierkegaard to being the president of Antarctica:

. . . or being the tallest building in Adelaide. There's not many of us; that's just what I fell into because Kierkegaard is a weird, miserable, sometimes hilarious, often impenetrable, sometimes exhilarating figure to work on, but he's very odd. He had some good jokes actually – I mean, by nineteenth-century standards. He's good fun. And then he's writing these incredibly dark references alongside.

Patrick was in year eleven by the time the All-Stars split up. But the damage was done.

A lot of people grew up watching the Dougs in their early teens and by their late teens it had become one of those things that was sort of already bedded down into nostalgia, and I guess even though [the Dougs] were well past their teens when they were doing all that stuff, it still spoke to that kind of very particular teenage mindset. It was kind of smartarse and violent and inward looking in a way that teenagers naturally are, so in that sense it very much resonated. The Dougs' version of 'Throw Your Arms Around Me' is the definitive one. For people my age, that and Jeff Buckley's 'Hallelujah' are probably the two sad, late-night, back-of-a-hostel guitar songs. And only one of them gets played at funerals, and it's not the Dougs'; there's that degree of decorum at least. But that moment of absolute beauty and clarity juxtaposed with 'I Fuck Dogs', it has a certain kind of resonance to it.

Patrick has managed to merge the highbrow and the low into his career; he's currently teaching a course that sounds a lot like the name of a D.A.A.S. show: Love, Sex and Death.

Technically, can there be such things as non-substitute masturbators? Comedy was a good sort of training for that.

I have no idea what that means, but it sounds rude. D.A.A.S. should be proud of Patrick. He took the pseudo out of their intellectualism. The sad news is Patrick went on to dabble in comedy. After one gig, his father told him he wasn't funny at all. In summing up, Patrick is philosophical, of course.

People always say to me, 'What's the connection between doing philosophy and doing comedy?', and for years I couldn't put my finger on it. It's only in the last couple of years that it occurred to me what they both do is dissolve obviousness. The structure of a joke is to take something that appears obvious then do something completely incongruous with it. A lot of what you are doing in philosophy is redescribing things in a way that suddenly brings incongruency out so you can then start to unpack what that is or what that means. So in a way they are both kind of driven by the 'Hey, isn't that weird?' reflex. A lot of my education in language comes from comedy, and that is useful for a philosopher because you are trying not to be bewitched by language, you're trying not to be bewitched by the way language sort of drags us into settled understandings of things. So in that sense it did have some sort of formative impact.

Well done, D.A.A.S – a germ was planted in a young man's mind and it bore fruit. Other young men were not so lucky. Frank Woodley's psyche does not seem to have survived the onslaught of early D.A.A.S. exposure, though for a man who was obviously unsettled by the antics of the All-Stars, Frank seems to have attended a lot of their early shows. The D.A.A.S. lair was enticing.

I remember seeing them once at the National Theatre – this was after *The Big Gig* started – and having a really strange, alienated experience where the crowd was going berserk. Lots of screaming, lots of laughter, but very much a rock star sort of thing and me just feeling like, 'Oh, I can't enjoy this now because it's not for me anymore.' There was no focus, it was just unbridled excitement.

My memory of experiencing Flacco for the first time is quite strong. Not exactly the same as the Dougies, but it's like this theatrical thing where you're bringing the audience in, but you're kind of alienating them at the same time. You're playing this little game, it's another abusive-relationship concept in a way, but with Flacco sort of alienating them and creating intimacy in this strange kind of dance. It's not all easy for the audience.

I think Frank may have hit on where Flacco and D.A.A.S. inhabit common ground. We are all guilty of abusing our relationship with the audience. Different approaches. Same result. Greg Fleet noticed my distress at the thought of Flacco being dragged down to the creative depths of an All-Star. He tried his best to soothe my bruised ego, in a Fleety sort of manner.

I've certainly never studied clowning but maybe it's something to do with being a clown. There's a pain or a damage in those characters [Frank's and Flacco's] that you are drawn to. If you're not a sociopath you're drawn to hurt, and you're kind of drawn in there and then it's, 'Oh fuck, I'm caught! But it's a joke.' And then you think, 'But is it?' And then you start thinking about what makes someone make that joke. And you go home – and I think people probably did this with the All-Stars – you're going home thinking, 'Yeah, it's all an act, but who makes up that act? Surely someone who's damaged and in need of loving.' Of course, we are all in need of love.

Some more than others, and when it came to that hairy, elfin satyr Paul McDermott, no inanimate object was safe. Janet McLeod describes the mayhem, the sense of anarchy, as the first thing that attracted her to D.A.A.S. And the fact that most stand-up comedians didn't steal your shoes as you walked into their show. No seat was a safe seat in a D.A.A.S. gig; Paul McDermott would travel the entire alphabet of rows to attack, steal from or humiliate an audience member. Janet still bears the scars.

> I wouldn't call myself a particularly normal person, but Paul McDermott scared the pants off me. I still find him scary to a degree.

It was getting late in the conversation, and Greg's convoluted sad-clown, tortured-soul routine sent Frank adrift on a rambling thought stream.

> You've heard about how they are creating artificial intelligence but they do it through having different programs? For example, there's a maze and these ants have to get from one side of the maze to the other in the smallest number of moves possible. And they have different little algorithms or different programs to do it and they send out a hundred ants, and the two that get across in the least number of moves they keep . . .

It occurs to me that perhaps these were mice, not ants. Ants would simply crawl over the maze, would they not? I chose to ignore this flaw in his logic.

> And then there's a program that creates another hundred ants that are slight variations on these two, and again they

keep the two that work the best, and so slowly these things get more and more efficient in making their way through the maze . . .

Everyone has gone quiet except Frank. Is it interest? Or daydreaming?

And it's a bit like in terms of comedy, like when you are creating comedy – even the performers don't know how they work. They don't actually know what the numbers are, what the formula is, in terms of the ones and zeros, the virtual genetic code. The people that made it don't know how the program works – they just know that it works. The performer themselves doesn't really know why they end up performing in the way they end up performing. They go out there and they try something that they've got . . . Like I was saying before, I was so naive about myself – we still are, of course . . .

Some personal insight at last. Note to self: Frank Woodley – no dinner parties.

It was just exuberance. Like, 'I'm kind of interested in the world . . . I'm going to try out stuff and I want attention and I want laughter.' And you get out and you try something and then it works, and then the things that don't work you go, 'Well, I won't do that anymore because it felt shit when I did that, but they love me when I did this,' and then you go on and find: 'They don't love me if I get too into that and they don't love me anymore . . .'

At this point I consider tiptoeing out of the room and leaving Frank to his bliss. But apparently Greg has been listening intently. He sets off on his own little journey into comedy darkness.

> . . . And it's a complicated sophisticated system for a bunch of people who have never really prided themselves on being complicated or sophisticated, so it's like you learn, you become an expert and you go, 'Well, I guess I'm an expert at this, I actually know a lot about it, I know how to do it – it doesn't mean I'm always going to do it perfectly.'

Obviously Frank is contagious. Was it something I asked? Janet McLeod attempts to steer the conversation towards a semblance of coherence.

> It's interesting when you see people who go, 'Right, I've got it, I know how to do this,' and then they keep that particular thing and they fail to realise certain things, like they're ageing and the way they look is different – it's actually part of the entire presentation.

The males in the room go quiet. Is she talking about us? Frank's puppy ears go up, the head tilts, and he's off.

> Me and Col [Colin Lane aka Lano] have an example of that. We would get an audience participant up and Col would do some obnoxious sort of flirting with that person. And when Col was twenty-one and the person was sixteen, it was still

a bit inappropriate but it was kind of . . . You're doing the same shtick now but he's fifty and she's still sixteen . . .

Janet counters before Frank can get another thought in.

I remember you saying to me once, Frank, that there was a certain point where you'd be able to just chuck in a pop culture reference and you knew it was the right thing to say and you knew what reaction you'd get, but there's that point where suddenly Scott Baio doesn't work anymore. FRANK: And the Red Hot Chili Peppers aren't the hot band.

Boom boom.

SUMMER OF THE SEVENTEENTH SHOW

Life is a lot like jazz . . . it's best
when you improvise.
GEORGE GERSHWIN

It takes a performer capable of 'staying eerily calm in scary
or dangerous situations' to venture off the beaten track in
Australia. Would any sane person open their act in Tamworth
with an original song called 'Do the Dead Elvis'? Between
Big Gigs, D.A.A.S. embarked on a formidable tour schedule,
performing hundreds of shows a year and venturing into
corners of the continent unused to having their norms challenged – isolated outposts where a threatened norm was not
the norm. Norms are the redneck equivalent of the G-spot;
enough poking, prodding and nudging of the N-spot soon
arouses the passions.

Michael 'Bob' Petroni was recruited to support D.A.A.S.
on several regional Australian offensives. These tours were

intense, with gigs in different towns each night for months on end. Their 1991 Hell No We Won't Go tour took in most of the east coast of Australia, from Hobart to Cairns.

> The show never stopped. It just kept moving. That was the beast. By Cairns it was very strange. We were all feeling the strain, that's for sure. It had been a long trip. Byron Bay was the turning point for the whole tour. I remember some very late nights and some mind-altering stuff happening. Quite bizarre. And then the pranks started getting out of control.

Cameron P. Mellor drove the van and sold the T-shirts. Life on the road with the Dougs was not easy for this pair of non-alpha males. Michael was aware of the stiff competition between bottom dog and second-bottom dog.

> It was always Cam or I who would be the last to be considered for something. Always jockeying not to be that person. That was the way it would go.
>
> I do remember one memorable line that Paul McDermott delivered. Cam had driven all the way from Melbourne until about fifty kilometres outside Cairns, the final stop on the tour, and he said, 'Michael, I'm shattered, could you drive the last bit?'
>
> I said, 'Sure.' So I drove the last fifty kilometres into Cairns. And when we got there – obviously Paul McDermott had been sitting on this pearler for those fifty kilometres – I pulled in and said, 'Well, we made it.' And McDermott

turns to Cameron and says, 'You just couldn't finish what you started, could you, Cam?'

After driving nearly three thousand kilometres, this is the thanks given by the Brood Parasite. That counts as somewhat psycho-comic, manipulative and abusive behaviour in my book.

Life beyond the tour van was no picnic for Michael either. This tour was pre-*D.A.A.S. Kapital*, and Michael's character Bob was unknown outside of two tiny inner-city venues.

> Well, they didn't want Bob. They didn't know who the hell I was. They didn't associate me with the Dougs. So that was a challenge, to kind of harness their crazy teenage girl energy and win them over, and also deliver them the Dougs. It was a very challenging thing to open for the Dougs in those days. Just the screaming that went on.

Tim Ferguson recalls throwing this sensitive young Maltese psychology major to the D.A.A.S. fans.

> You look at Bob and you think, 'Well, yes, it's funny, but there's something else going on and I don't understand what it is.' Bob's little story where he just went from one relative to the other and was killing all of them and then that was the end, he'd sing his song . . . for our audience at that time it was completely inappropriate. We had teenage girls turning up to watch our act, they were turning up to see Paul's butt wiggle, and out comes Bob talking about serial killing.

Flacco was offered the support spot on several of these All-Star sorties into the heart of Never Never Land. He declined. Flacco's habitable zone lay within a five-kilometre radius of any capital city centre. Outside of that, he was fair game, an exotic mollusc existing in a shallow rock pool surrounded by an ocean of predators. Flacco wasn't ready for the deep end. Being a mollusc, he couldn't even dip his rasping radula in, bless his little dorsal gonad. His stream was never main.

Even within his habitable zone, touring with D.A.A.S. was problematic. We drew opposing audiences. Flacco was born of art, nurtured by the elite. His audience required a modicum of intelligence. Many of the D.A.A.S. devotees had no idea what modicum meant. Was this some kind of pathological psycho-comedic lark? A case of 'throw the freak on stage, stand by and watch the fake fur fly'? Or did they appreciate Flacco's obscurant excursions into nonsensical solipsism? Something had gone terribly wrong. Obscurity was my chosen destiny. I courted it. Flacco was not assembled for the masses. He lacked superficial charm, hair, teeth and jokes. His selectively mutant creator was horrified in scary or dangerous situations – for instance, when communicating with other humans. An article in *Vogue* magazine described Flacco's creator as 'a man so tense he bites his fingernails to the quick and so paranoid that he won't wear glasses, despite being terribly short-sighted, because he doesn't want to know what's out there'. And he had platonic relationships with puppies. In short, I failed the psychopath test. How was I ever to make it in the world of minor celebrity?

After four years of art school, I abandoned the art scene in the early eighties as the global plague of postmodernism infected the artistic milieu, sucked clean the joy, the humour and the heart and left it a shallow husk. That said, I did share some traits with my postmodern academic peers: I publicly shunned acclaim but secretly coveted it; I approached popular culture with humourless irony; and I made every reasonable effort to insert my proverbial cranium into my anus, thus proving that matching internal models to the real world is inherently coloured by the bias of the observer. Or something to that effect.

I so desired to prove to the world that I did not care for its opinion that I succeeded in becoming a culturally invisible man. I could walk down the street knowing that nobody knew that I was really worth knowing. That really showed them. My downfall was to share a squat in Woolloomooloo with a bevy of other Alf-alpha males and Alice-alpha females who not only worked quite hard at their art, but also had an actual sense of humour, and seemed rather keen on pursuing a phenomenon that had hitherto repulsed my inner artiste: they wanted to 'entertain' their fellow men and women.

Here's what I hate about memoirs. The penchant on the author's part to dwell on the minutiae of every aspect of their being. In order to avoid this turgid sand trap, here is an abridged account of my five years in an inner-city squat.

1980   Abandoned art school.

1981   Moved into squat. Settled into daily routine:

      11 am: Wake.

      1 pm: Wake again.

      1.30 pm: Loiter.

      6 pm: Arrive at the Oxford Hotel in
                    Kings Cross.

      11 pm: On to the East Sydney Hotel in
                    Woolloomooloo for last drinks.

      Midnight: Pizza, kebab or similar.

      3 am: Begin restless night's sleep.

      11 am: Wake.

1982   See above.

1983   See above.

1984   See above.

1985   See above.

That's about the extent of my memory of the time. Yet rumour has it I did in fact make myself sporadically useful. A nest of independent animators calling themselves the Even Orchestra enticed me to apply my graphic skills to their enigmatic but entertaining cartoons. I was soon corralled into voicing characters. We occasionally performed live, adding live soundtracks to the films, complete with rear projection, shadow play, puppetry and song. We had a foot in two camps, the highbrow and the low; we played both the fool and the flummery. Enough to garner us an audience.

It was during a warehouse performance of these underground indie films that the first incarnation of Flacco tentatively stepped out in front of the screen. This drew the attention of a troupe of 'alternative comedians' incubating in another corner of the squats. These men grew up to be the brilliant and influential mid-eighties comedy phenomenon known as Funny Stories, who recruited me for my first taste of live comedy: I was hired to play the role of a head on a plate in a performance of darkly entertaining tales. Not long after this I found myself backstage at Cafe Jax in Canberra, a dead cat strapped to my groin, urinating into a flagon of moselle.

Tim Ferguson remembers his first sighting of Flacco in 1986 at the Adelaide Fringe Festival.

> Paul and Richard were both talking about the Even Orchestra, and they were saying, 'You've got to come and see this guy, you just have to.' I'd seen other arty comedians but Flacco wasn't just right out on the wingtip, he was doing a Lois Lane, letting the fingertips go and then grabbing hold of the wingtip again. There was nowhere in my brain where I could put this thing. It wasn't even a force of nature – it was just *of* nature . . .

I have no idea what Tim means by that but I'll take it as a compliment. The Woolloomooloo squats seeded and gave birth to Flacco, a creature born of art, an antisocial construct, anathema to commercial success, fame and universal admiration. A fine wine, to be savoured by the few. But D.A.A.S. would have none of that. Being true psycho-comedians, world domination was just the beginning. As hand luggage on the D.A.A.S. juggernaut, I had no choice but to embrace a broader audience.

Unfortunately, having prised opened Flacco's arms, some were reluctant to accept his embrace. D.A.A.S. invited me to join them for a New Year's Eve performance in Hobart to bring in 1989. Flacco was three years old and had never appeared on television, but my manager scrounged around for extra gigs and landed a spot for Flacco, sight unseen, at a suburban venue earlier in the evening of 31 December 1988. I can't quite remember the name, but it was something like the Mongrel Bar. (I know it had something to do with angry rabid hounds.) I dragged my oversized suitcase, stuffed with Flacco paraphernalia of the time (dead cats, dead rats, car horns, fake bombs and much, much more) to the outer reaches of Hobart. In Hobart, the distance from the city to 'the sticks' is pretty much within walking. I had an eerie feeling I was on page one of a Stephen King novel as I stepped out of the blinding sun and into a mangy bar complete with a heavy metal band churning out industrial boogie in one corner. The rest of the room was home to a motorcycle clan. I made my way through the hefty crowd and introduced myself to the barkeep, who grunted and led the way out the back to my dressing quarters – a square metre of turf between the kitchen and the toilet – where I changed into my Elizabethan garb, black tights, full make-up and props. My mission was to perform a tight twenty minutes between the band's sets.

I lasted five. I hurried off under a shower of beer cans and abuse, desperate to vacate the premises, when the publican, a larger-than-life hirsute gent, grabbed me by my ruffled collar, pulled me to his chest and said, 'I'm paying you sixty bucks for twenty minutes.' I felt a mutual trembling; mine was terror, his was bristling rage. I tried to explain that Flacco was perhaps not suitable for his clientele. 'You're a comedian, aren't you?' he bellowed. 'Get back out there!' He put me down and left.

I had only one course of action open to me. Making a break for it through the bar would be problematic, so I grabbed Flacco's suitcase and located a back door leading onto a concrete expanse enclosed by a corrugated-iron fence of impressive height, topped with barbed wire. There was a gate, eight feet high, padlocked.

There was no going back. After several attempts, I managed to hurl my suitcase over the gate. After several more attempts I managed to hurl myself over the barbed wire. Once on the outside, I found my suitcase had burst and the contents of my burgeoning career spread all over the pavement. I packed up my alter ego as swiftly as I could and then lugged my suitcase and my bruised ego off into the Hobart twilight. I had no idea where I was. I had no money. Somehow, I made it back to civilisation and a biker-free, Flacco-tolerant, D.A.A.S. crowd crammed into Salamanca Place. The good news is I did eventually get my sixty dollars. From the comfort of his inner-city terrace in Sydney, my manager boldly threatened to have Actors Equity black-ban the venue. The cheque was soon in the mail. Minus tax, minus twenty-five per cent management fee. Show business is mostly show, very little business.

Being a character comedian is one thing, being a gay character comedian can up the antipathy, as Mark Trevorrow informs me.

Brighton, England, in front of a bunch of homophobic rugby lads whom the venue allowed to destroy the shows on a weekly basis. I knew I was in huge trouble when I heard the act before me say pleadingly, 'But I'm not a poof.' Oh dear. I was! I lasted about five minutes and just left the stage. The manager forced me to go back on, where I lasted another five minutes. A nightmare.

Richard Fidler shudders to think about the day the All-Stars came to Telfer, an isolated mining town in the middle of the Great Sandy Desert.

It had no cops. It had one rule. If you threw a punch, the police would arrive in a chopper from Marble Bar the next day and you'd be sacked and kicked out of town. It was a two-stratum society: you had the professionals, the managers, the mining industry engineers, the specialists who lived there with their families, and then there was the miners themselves, who were like, they were crims. These were violent dangerous human beings. And they formed the front row at our gig. One of them had an ice bucket and each one of them had a bottle of Jack Daniels. We went on stage and within thirty seconds it was, 'Pooftah cunt! Pooftah cunt!' Then the bottles started flying. We lasted three minutes. We went backstage and said, 'We can't do this', and the bloke who was putting it on said, 'They luv ya! Ya gotta get back out there!' We said, 'We'll get fucking killed!'

Three pretty boys made it out of Telfer in one piece, although at least six locals got sacked the day after the gig.

Steve 'The Sandman' Abbott always made the most of a situation. Even when that situation was hopeless.

It was a Wednesday night, it was wet. Tahir Bilgiç and Steady Eddy were also on the bill, we'd been touring around a bit, and I was to go on before Steady. There was about three hundred in the audience, everyone pissed out of their minds, and from the moment I walked on in my fluorescent pink suit there was no applause. You know when you hear your own footsteps as you walk to the mic? I opened with a couple of stock Sandman lines and immediately this 'We want Eddy!' chant started up. I felt, 'This is not great,' but I thought, 'Don't panic, something will come along.' And as the chant got louder this bikie guy, who was quite drunk, walked from the back of the hall, stood right in front of me waving a twenty-dollar note and said, 'Here, take this and get a cab home.' I tried a comeback. I said, 'I live in Bondi Beach and it's more than twenty bucks in a cab.' It didn't deter this guy at all. He said, 'Well don't take it then, just fuck off and bring Eddy on.' I looked around and there was no sign of Eddy. Eddy's a great guy and super funny, but it takes a while for him to prepare for a show and I had no choice but to kill some more time out there. They started booing and throwing things, and that's when I began to really enjoy it. I laid down on the stage on my back and started singing some of my children's songs – 'Mr Bumble Bee', 'The Alley Cat', 'Mr E's Flat' – and then I spotted Eddy. I immediately introduced him and he came on to thunderous applause. Meanwhile I didn't even get out of my stage clothes. I picked up my bag, shot straight out of the place, got into my car . . . but of course, twenty minutes into the drive home I'd forgotten all about that gig.

I have always marvelled at Steve's insistent optimism. As Sandy says, 'If you make the world around you bleak, the time spent in your house will be like a paradise.'

Thanks to *The Big Gig*, *D.A.A.S. Kapital* series one and relentless rounds of touring, the All-Stars were a household name in Australia by the end of 1991. With fame came instant exile from the uber-urban-intellectual high ground. Without changing a dance step or a smutty jibe, D.A.A.S. were relegated to the mortal sin bin. The charge? Providing entertainment to the hoi polloi. They transgressed the code by appearing on a nationally televised entertainment program, even though selling out on an ABC wage is near impossible. Flacco too was tarred with a modicum of minor celebrity, but his material remained far too abstruse; he was more Beckett than Benny Hill, he had slipped through the cracks. The All-Stars swiftly found their niche, while Flacco remained stubbornly stuck in his Nietzsche.

The 1990s D.A.A.S. fan base was young, predominantly female, and they were in love. It should have come as no surprise that they would not be overly welcoming to an opening act featuring an elderly bald male wearing tights and a sporran, spruiking existential inanities in a very high voice. As one reviewer noted at the time, 'Flacco must surely be the unsexiest comedian alive.' And therein lay the dilemma: D.A.A.S. oozed sex, they symbolised adolescent desire, bald arrogance, bad attitude, unbridled confidence, mischief, haircuts, risqué groin manoeuvrings . . . and then of course there was Richard, the wallflower, the hard-done-by, the innocent, the one you'd take home to meet your mum. And they were all seriously cute. Al Murray concurs.

> It was ridiculous – they were a boy band. In Edinburgh, it's the Fringe, and it's all a bit serious, even the comedy is serious, it's all a bit dour, and they were like fucking rock stars. Which in alternative comedy wasn't a big thing at all. Well, they were three incredibly handsome, charismatic blokes and I think they were man-crush material, certainly.

Paul McDermott blames television for the sudden onset of adolescent followers.

> Television hit and within a couple of weeks our audience demographic dropped to about fourteen and they would form a blockade coming to shows and there would be six rows of almost impenetrable young flesh . . . with brains that you clearly couldn't reach, and they were seeing

something different from other people. So we just made it an even more vulgar and aggressive act. You could get arrested for that shit. It was really borderline stuff. But funny.

Paul recalls a young Colin Lane approaching him at the time and chastising him.

I remember Colin coming up and having an issue with it. I love Colin, beautiful man, but he did have issues with some of the horse semen lines, as we were playing to fourteen-year-olds, and he thought, well, horse semen and nuns was apparently an issue . . . The moral conundrums were part of the show. Previous to that I was never aware of pushing any boundaries, but when our demographic dropped, I was aware that the people who were coming to see us, especially in those five or six front rows, were younger, more hysterical, more prone to screaming and were not listening to what we were doing, and that gave us licence to be incredibly loose with what we would have once classified as our parameters. The lines we once would not have crossed, we now gleefully leapt across.

Richard Fidler recalls the transition from art-house-friendly japesters to post-pubescent poster boys: 'We thought we were the comedy equivalent of the Sex Pistols but it turned out we were the Bay City Rollers.'

Greg Fleet is a touch resentful when it comes to the subject of adoring groupies.

I only had ones that were passed on by other comedians.

Rod Quantock, being the wiser and the elder, has no regrets.

I would hate people not understanding what I was talking about coming to a show. I know my audience; I take the tickets at the door for every show. I know them by name or face but I've never had throngs of teenage girls hurling themselves about. Josh Thomas and I did a show at a theatre in Canberra about three or four years ago and I did the first half – one show, separate audiences – then he came in and did his show. So I was out in the foyer before my show with all these cripples and elderly people moaning and groaning, and when my show's over and I walk out into the foyer again and there's just this ocean of teenage girls, not a male among them. And I thought, 'How can you go on entertaining teenage girls? They'll grow up with you, that's alright. But to actually talk to three hundred teenage girls for an hour?' But there was that sexuality about the Dougs, that daring and convention-breaking and shock. My overarching memory of the Doug Anthonys is just shock. Not my shock, but the shock that they created.

Rod had prior experience of shocking the general public while commandeering the groundbreaking 1983 ABC Television series, *Australia You're Standing In It*.

The show got a lot of complaints. It's interesting to see how the world's changed. The first episode we did, John Eastway was the director, and he said, 'You've got to put one thing in there in that first show that's truly going to upset a lot of people.'

Like Ted Robinson, John Eastway was an adventurous and visionary director. In those days, television directors and producers were often braver than the performers.

We had a thing where Sue Ingleton did a very good Queen Elizabeth and she hated the Queen so much, it was a really fiery interpretation. It was her standing in front of the Government House gates (which looked like the Buckingham Palace gates) with a bottle and a glass, advertising McWindsor Whisky, 'the whisky that the Queen drinks'. And she's absolutely pissed, she's got the corgi, and there's a red carpet. But the red carpet is laid in a staggered line, and she'd walk drunkenly back up to the gate. And then at the end she just collapsed. Well, that was the thing that we put in the show and that created a furore all over Australia. I was on the radio in Perth the next day and I think I took about twenty calls and nineteen of them were hateful calls because of that thing about the Queen. I can't think that we ever set out to shock. Our show wasn't about shock, it was about critiquing.

Flacco has been described in countless ways. My personal favourite is: 'A mutant anorexic in orthopaedic underwear who sounds like a dolphin blowing the SBS news out of its shorts in a spa bath.' This allegedly from a fellow comedian, who cannot be named, because the reviewer refused to supply their source. So being dubbed the least erotic comic on the planet didn't faze Flacco. The description was perfectly apt. If I had intended to create a character to attract a mate, it would not have been a white-faced clown with a falsetto voice and a name resembling flaccid. Any fan who ever found Flacco in any way attractive (and there was a handful) was not the kind of human I'd ever care to enter into a relationship with.

I presume an exposé of the carnal misadventures of life on the road with a comedy boy band is expected here. I would eagerly oblige, but just bear in mind who your source is: this warm-up act was in his early thirties and acknowledged as the unsexiest comedian alive. So I've nothing to report. Not a thing. As for the other gents? They become tight-lipped when I raise the subject. All three are very tame family men these days, so on the record they insist on spreading the word that they were mere innocents, perfect angels. And if you believe that, you probably also believe they were in the Batman films, or performed in New York, or opened their act in Tamworth with an original song called 'Do the Dead Elvis'. Put simply, you cannot rely on anything that comes out of their horny little private schoolboy throats.

Former D.A.A.S. devotee Mandy Jones recalls how she and her older sister Kym insinuated themselves into the All-Stars collective and set up the official D.A.A.S. fan club. Kym was working for a market research company not far from the Last Laugh in Melbourne. She started faxing the All-Stars manager, Doug Hunter. Mandy recalls:

We were both fans, but we were fairly stable. Kym just sort of pestered them, it wasn't stalking, and then one day Doug rang her and said, 'Actually, the guys need some admin support.'

The D.A.A.S. office consisted of a telephone and fax machine in a corner of Doug Hunter's small apartment in St Kilda. There was no computer.

I think Paul had been writing and needed his notes typed up and they said to Kym, 'Would you be interested?' Yep, of course! But then we didn't have a computer either and she couldn't do it on her work time so she used to come to my uni at night and type it all up in the Apple Mac lab at Deakin Toorak, typing up all this amazing stuff that Paul was working on.

Doug must have been impressed by the typing, because Mandy and Kym were immediately signed up to run the official D.A.A.S. fan club. The fact that these two young women had no previous experience didn't seem to concern Doug. There was no meeting, no resumés were required. They were fans – who better to run the fan club? 'Fan club' is a rather twee title for a trio such as D.A.A.S., so they decided to call the club 'Hate Line'.

We had a little laminator and we had a template of a membership card. It was twenty-five dollars to join Hate Line and they would get a membership kit, pre-signed promo photos, a welcome letter and any old newsletters, and a badge. I'd get all the orders, get on the tram and go down to the office in St Kilda, get the merchandise then go back and post it all out to them. We lived in Mount Waverley, so because of the postal address all these fans were hanging out in Mount Waverley trying to work out the connection, and of course there was no connection it was just that we lived there. So we gave our mum the key to the PO box and she would go up and pick up stuff during the week, and if it was too big to fit in the box she'd have to go into the post office and she was always horrified that these parcels were all decorated with skulls and pornographic images. The fans worked out when [the Dougs'] birthdays were and they'd send boxer shorts, and some of the envelopes would arrive and we'd be scared to open them because you could feel something dodgy inside – someone sent a whole lot of hair once, I think they'd cut off a plait. It was a bit like, 'What's going to be in the envelope today?'

With a staff of two and no internet or social media, running a fan club was a time-consuming occupation.

Obviously we were in it for ourselves because it wasn't like it was a paid thing – we were doing it for the love of it. You'd get the occasional ticket. But we weren't pushy. The guys weren't that involved; they said, 'Do whatever you want.' When they were living in Fitzroy they'd go to Marios a lot so we used to go there as well, and suddenly everyone was hanging out at Marios – that was when it was getting a bit creepy. I think many of the fans probably thought they all lived in a house together like the Young Ones. I don't think they imagined them having their own separate lives.

Flacco was not entirely left out of this equation. On any given day there were half a dozen fans loitering across the road from the St Kilda apartment in Robe Street I shared with Dave Taranto. I have to admit it was something of an ego boost to think there were fans of your work who would go to such lengths. Until a friend pointed out that they were probably waiting there in case Tim, Paul or Richard came to visit. Cue sound of ego deflating.

FAME AND MISFORTUNE

I want people to remember me before
I'm dead, and then more afterwards.
RUSSELL BRAND

Walking onstage to a full house of hormonally charged teenagers chanting 'All-Stars! All-Stars! All-Stars!' is just a tad
daunting. Flacco was a jazz comedian who spun 'densely woven,
allusive surreal threads', as one approving Adelaide reviewer
put it. Yet no matter how densely I wove or surreally I spun,
the D.A.A.S. crowd were not quick to wear it. I held my ground,
and always ended my spot with a line that never failed: 'Please
make welcome the Doug . . . Anthony . . . All . . . Stars!'

After a sell-out show at the National Theatre in St Kilda, the
usual eager army of female fans surrounded the venue. Once
herded into our tour van, we made our way through the throng,
headlights sweeping a sea of eager young faces. Tim, Paul and
Richard, heads tucked down, sat low in the van. I was always

seated conspicuously in the front of the van, obviously deployed as a decoy. At the age of thirty-five, I reluctantly found myself the support act for the comedy equivalent of One Direction.

While the fervour and adoration was Bieberesque, D.A.A.S. were not offering up bubblegum and cheesecake; these boys were delivering sweetmeats from hell. There was a darkness lurking in their tunes and tales, pleasantly wrapped and delivered with boyish charm and unrelenting energy towards young disciples who were subliminally initiated into the shadowy underbelly of D.A.A.S. lore, their deftly delivered depth charges of decadence presented in blissful song and dance. This was compulsory entertainment with no easy escape route. One move from your seat and a fetid All-Star would be off that stage and into your face and personal belongings in no time.

There was no going back. I had made the descent from high art to lowbrow comedy, never more to indulge in the films of Peter Greenaway or a turgidly pretentious stage production of Eugène Ionesco's *Rhinoceros*, not to mention a post-studio art performance in an inner-city warehouse in which five women wrapped in burnt hessian expounded the poems of Sylvia Plath in front of a super 8 film of black paint drying. D.A.A.S., for their part, brought light into the art of darkness, and darkness is much more palatable once you shine a torch into it.

Being Canberra lads, all three were politically astute. Unlike many so-called alternative comedians of the day, they weren't satisfied with merely attacking the extreme right. They had no message or agenda to spruik; their main targets were people who spruiked messages and agendas. Their uniforms and artwork were an unnerving mix of the socialist revolutionary left and the Nazi fascist right. Flacco was neither right wing nor left wing, just a harmless, wingless political quail. The only tools at his disposal were clever wordplay and bad puns whereas the All-Stars' sweet harmonies belied their lyrics, like dark Zen anti-koans, weapons of mass corruption aimed squarely at anyone or anything in their path. They pulled no punchlines. Their fearlessness was rare. Bill Hicks shared their approach, as did Bobcat Goldthwait, Jerry Sadowitz and our own Anthony Morgan and Sandy Gutman. Most comedians attempt to read their audience and serve its needs. Should you swear? Drop this? Tone down that? Comedy psychopaths couldn't care less what the audience thought. They didn't suffer from the desperate need to have people love them, to gain acceptance, to not rock the boat or simply to entertain the guests on the cruise. D.A.A.S. were out to sink your ship. And there were no life rafts.

Being famous in Australia is a little like being a household name on Mars. Australia seems trapped in a cultural black hole, readily sucking in the faddish whims of the global zeitgeist, but it is near impossible for anything to escape the non-event horizon that is Australia's border. D.A.A.S. made their escape, but Richard Fidler recalls finding nowhere to hide.

> I had this experience where I was in Berlin, during the fall
> of the Berlin wall. The wall had just come down, people were

happily chiselling away at chunks, this glorious bloodless revolution had come about and I was just so enthralled, I really thought I was there as a witness to this amazing historic moment and as I was going through the hospital-green corridors of Checkpoint Charlie I heard a voice go, 'Hey! Doug Anthony and his All-Stars! What the fuck are you doing here? Come over here! I reckon you guys are shit. What's the matter? You up yourself?' And then I was dismissed.

The word 'fame' is derived from the name of the Roman goddess of rumour, Fama. A nasty piece of work, also known as the goddess of gossip, she spread slander and scuttlebutt throughout the empire. According to Ovid she lived at the centre of the earth, surrounded by a thousand windows in order to catch the slightest hint of humanity's dirty laundry. If she were around today she'd have a syndicated TV talk show in the US.

The craving for fame is infantile. 'Everyone! Look at me *now*!' Yet the first thing to happen if that wish comes true is an equally potent craving for anonymity. 'Everyone! Avert your eyes *now*!' It is particularly problematic for a comedian, whose job it is to observe the foibles of their fellows. Perving on humanity is impossible when the voyeur becomes the viewed, the observer the observed. Kafka had it down: live in obscurity and go for posthumous fame. That way you can avoid tiresome interviews, photo shoots and the odd stalker. Kafka could do his shopping in peace. He had no need to purchase Ray-Bans and a baseball cap.

Most people are familiar with Andy Warhol's famous quote, 'In the future, everyone will be famous for fifteen minutes.' What they remember less is Andy's quote a decade later, when he declared, 'In fifteen minutes everyone will be famous.' These days, Fama can be attained simply by existing. It's non-skilled labour. Without the labour.

In the twenty-first century, being known just for being known sets you apart from the pack. Fama for Fama's sake. Social media has fulfilled Andy's prophecy. Fama promises eternal life. That's the attraction. Celebrities fade but never quite die. Yet comedians die all the time. Resurrection and death are the norm. One night a hero, the next night a casualty. Comedians are accepted among the famous but at the same time expected to behave merely as light relief for the truly, seriously adored; they are to host award nights rather than receive the awards. Some say a true comedian must burst the bubble of self-inflation wherever he or she sees it. Without wise fools to burst the ego-dirigibles of wannabe somebodies and rain on their vainglorious parades, Fama will continue to have her wretched, bitchy way with humanity. Al Murray has a more down-to-earth attitude to fame.

I'm not quite famous; I'm not like 'famous' famous. I never think I am, anyway. The thing I like about it, I really like about it, is I'm not very good at small talk, I'm not good at that kind of thing. I find it quite awkward. And it kind of like pitches you past that. So people are friendly whom otherwise you'd have to make an effort with, and I really like that. It probably means I'm really shallow, but I like that kind of thing, and again, my favourite thing is eating out, eating good food, and I use what fame I have to get reservations at the best restaurants – it's just brilliant. And I mean these are all really, really, really shallow things, but that's what it offers you. And obviously the other brilliant thing is you get to go to amazing places and meet interesting people and all that, but for me it's the, like, um, the shallow selfish shit.

Well said, Al. You can have your fame and eat out too.

Michael Petroni had a brush with fame in Australia, but he has since been scrubbed with far larger brushes in Hollywood, where he has racked up two decades of laudations as a screen-writer in the deep end of a writers' pool renowned for its ruthless predators (while I obviously stayed home mixing metaphors for a crust, as this paragraph attests).

Fame is a very weird thing in that you never know if or when you are actually famous. Even when someone tells you, it's still quite hard to understand. It takes something obvious to kind of wake you up to your fame. Like a bill-board. The penny drops. It's not something you easily accept or understand.

When you become the observed, you need to watch your every move – and those of your pets, as Steve Abbott found out at the height of The Sandman's fame.

There was a time when I couldn't go anywhere without being recognised. I'll never forget one day when I was walking my miniature schnauzer, Esther, and she had a turd stuck out of her arse like a cigar. She couldn't get rid of it so I had to put on the plastic bag as a glove and as I reached down to pull the turd out of my dog's arsehole a car went by and a bunch of guys yelled out, 'Hey! Sandmannnn!' just as I pulled the cigar out of Esther. That's fame for you. Now I'm just some overweight old guy who looks like a hobo that no-one recognises.

Even being considered one of the coolest and most eloquent comedians of his era is not enough to quell the bitter heart of Greg Fleet, who continues to covet other people's success to this day.

I felt much the same about Flacco as I did about the Dougs. Jealous and inspired. It was like we were all invited to New York City but then you guys got invited to The Factory by Warhol.

The gloss of celebrity soon loses its Charlie Sheen once you rub shoulders with the famous. 'Spear-carrier' is a show business term for those on the periphery of fame. In classic plays they are quite literally those who carry spears in the background of the main action – a background hack one rung above an extra. I've made a solid career out of carrying spears. I've spear-carried with the best of them (Warning: Names Dropping Ahead). I've held my spear aloft beside the likes of

William Hurt, Jeanne Moreau, Kiefer Sutherland, Max von Sydow, Sam Neill and Geoffrey Rush. You could say I've worked with the best. You could say that. Except I wasn't working, I was standing by, clutching my spear and watching others work. As spear-carrier I did not get to 'hang out' with any of these dropped names, and I doubt any of the names dropped would remember mine, let alone drop it.

The trick is to attach yourself to a major player. Most of my feature-film roles have character names like 'Assistant Stranger Number 1'. Not terribly impressive until you consider the role demands that the leading player – in this case the late Sir Ian Richardson – never be seen without assistants one and two at each shoulder. Hence the need to appear in every single scene, standing in silence beside the great man. Apart from having no lines to remember, this was a chance to be regaled by Sir Ian between takes. And Sir Ian loved nothing more than a spot of regaling.

During my days as a bar fly at the East Sydney Hotel in Woolloomooloo, there was one regular who repeated the same anecdote each evening to whomever had ears to listen. His claim to fame was 'sharing the stage' with Frank Sinatra on his 1974 Australian tour. Him and Frankie this, him and Ol' Blues Eyes that. The truth was that he once played in the string section of the orchestra at a Sinatra gig. This guy was nowhere near Assistant Stranger Number 1 status. More names will be dropped liberally later, but for the moment I carried that spear for the Doug Anthony All-Stars.

D.A.A.S. Kapital series two went down with the critics like the *Titanic* it was set in. This was of no consequence, as the real prize was the series being banned in Japan and Germany. Or was it? Someone call the fire brigade, the D.A.A.S. trousers are on fire again. It didn't matter to the reviewers that by series two the program had found its feet, the episodes were cogent and entertaining, and it reached a wider and appreciative audience. Never mind. There was a whole planet to play in and while D.A.A.S. set their sights on Edinburgh 1992, I took a longer route via Montreal. As far as Montreal was concerned, D.A.A.S. had soiled that nest and moved on. D.A.A.S. didn't just burn their bridges, they exploded them.

The Just for Laughs comedy festival vies with Edinburgh for the title of most prestigious comedy attraction in the world. Yet the two experiences are poles apart. Unlike Edinburgh, Montreal is invitation only. Those select few are treated like royalty for the week-long event, driven from venue to venue, fed and housed. All that is required is a seven-minute killer spot to spruik around town at small club venues and, for those deemed worthy, a spot at a gala event. Those to whom you were to spruik were largely agency representatives from LA on the lookout for the new Jerry Seinfeld, or whatever was the particular flavour of that month. They were a collective mind with no leader, a hive with no queen. The Borg of the entertainment industry, abuzz with searching for the latest buzz. And they had absolutely no sense of humour. Flacco was roundly ignored by the Borg. No surprises there.

The festival culminates in a weekend of galas. The venue is the Théâtre Saint-Denis, a step up from the low-ceilinged, brick-wall-backed stages of the comedy caves inhabited by the Borg members. The Saint-Denis is a delightful venue, at festival time overflowing with a comedy-literate, intelligent, French Québécois crowd. The LA contingent rarely attended these events; they were ensconced in the celebrity tent city down the road, where the galas were screened and largely ignored. A spot on a gala was not guaranteed. Somehow – and I suspect this is only due to the loyal support of the festival directors – I scraped in on a wild card for not one but two weekend galas.

Working the smaller rooms sapped my confidence. I was convinced I'd never land a gala spot. Other comedians treading the boards that year – Steven Wright, Drew Carey, Ray Romano, Jon Stewart, Penn and Teller, Rita Rudner and Sinbad – were not names I recognised, because this was 1992 and no-one had recognised them yet. When I received my call sheet for the gala I looked down the list of the night's performers. Being a wildcard entrant, my name was not on any official call sheet, but one name was scratched out and another etched hurriedly beside it in red ink. The red ink spelled 'Flacco', due for sound check at 3 pm. The name scratched out was Jerry Lewis. Jerry didn't do sound checks. Jerry just turned up on the night and did what Jerry did, or what Jerry's people told you Jerry was going to do.

By chance I still have the call sheet, thanks to my dear mother Evelyn. It was only after she passed away that I discovered the extent to which she took an interest in her son's unexpected career choice. As my brother and I riffled through her carefully ordered cardboard boxes, we came upon what could only be described as the 'Museum of Me', a slew of memorabilia, print interviews, posters, advertisements, reviews good and bad. A career in a box. Evelyn, bless her, had even attempted to tape Flacco's one-minute monologues from my years contributing to the Triple J breakfast team in the mid-nineties. I can imagine this slight woman in her seventies, waking each morning, sitting through Mikey Robins and Helen Razer's inglorious rants, waiting for the moment to stab the record button on the cassette player once she heard her boy's voice. She often missed the first ten seconds, but the cassettes were all there, dates and times noted on the covers. And there was the Montreal call sheet, with Jerry Lewis's name scratched out and mine inked in.

Jerry Lewis was the celebrity guest at the 1992 Montreal festival. The gala's guest host was another comedy great, Lily Tomlin. Lily introduced Flacco as 'the love child of Pee-wee Herman and the Mayor of Munchkinland'. I walked onto the stage, and seven minutes later I walked off. I could hear warm applause, but the Borg in the celebrity tent hardly noticed I'd had a win in the big room. The locals appeared to enjoy this white-faced creature in tights who spoke too fast and made little sense. It's not often I have the opportunity to gloat, so it gives me great pleasure to admit that I received a warmer welcome at the Just for Laughs festival than did D.A.A.S., who were run out of town for insulting the pseudo-French. I, on the other hand, had neglected to insult the nation, its accent or its national treasures. I'm funny like that. According to the Québécois.

Post-show, as I milled around in the corridor outside the St-Denis dressing-rooms with a troupe of fellow performers who would soon be stupidly famous, Lily Tomlin appeared and began to walk among us mere comedy mortals. (Jerry, by this time, was back in his hotel suite, having performed a six-minute mime piece playing an imaginary typewriter to the tune of Rimsky-Korsakov's 'Flight of the Bumblebee', complete with Coke-bottle glasses and wooden teeth. I vowed to the comedy gods that there was absolutely no way that I would be seen attempting to cash in on past glories once I'd reached the archaic age of sixty. Sadly, a quarter of a century later, those words would be eaten and swallowed along with my pride.) A hush fell over the gathered throng in the corridor, the seas parting as assorted comedians peeled back to make way for Dame Lily. She stopped inches from my face, smiled, and gently laid praise on my performance. I opened my mouth, various sounds came out, but I doubt any of it was English. I tried a little smile, I felt I should perhaps curtsey, anything to break this heavily pregnant pause. My tongue would have been doubly knotted had I realised that I was the odd comedian out among some who were next in line to become international comedy royalty. I had been starstruck earlier that afternoon while sharing a dressing-room with another celebrity guest, the legendary George Carl, a superstar of vaudeville and an American national treasure. Fortunately George was a mime artist, and the chatter was kept to a minimum.

On the final morning of the festival, as I waited in the hotel lobby with my fellow comedians, nursing our post-gala hangovers, I underwent another visitation by a different kind of royalty. Once again the hush, once again the seas parted, and an unfamiliar but well-presented gentleman approached me. He smiled, praised my work, turned and left. No awkward pause. Behind him was a slight young human, attendant to this kingly figure. She quite literally bowed, handed me a business card, averted her eyes and moved on. It was the look in my peers' bloodshot eyes that suggested something of portent had occurred. The card bore a name and a logo. The name meant nothing to me. The logo was Showtime Networks Pty Ltd. On the reverse was a handwritten phone number. I held in my hand the one card that everyone sought. Any Borg in the lobby were whimpering in confusion. I held the grail. Showtime Networks was a division of CBS Corporation, home of America's premium cable television network. The door to opportunity had been flung open. America was calling. I placed the card in my wallet, and promptly forgot about it, until I uncovered it a decade later while poring through my late mother's Museum of Me. I guessed it was too late to call back. What was I saying about regrets?

My mind was elsewhere. I had a three-week season booked in Edinburgh immediately after the Montreal festival and this time I was going it alone. D.A.A.S. would have to fill their toilet cubicle with another victim, perhaps a young Al Murray. Flacco was a part and parcel of a neat little package, the brainchild of the late John Pinder, a giant of a man, and a giant of the Australian comedy business. John had his weighty fingers in the pies of the Last Laugh in Melbourne, the Flying Trapeze Cafe, Circus Oz and the Melbourne International Comedy Festival. John had also achieved much in the way of selling Australian comedy to the Edinburgh Festival Fringe, having instigated Oznost, unleashing a battalion of fifty top-shelf Aussie comics at the Edinburgh Fringe of 1988. His plan in 1992 was to pitch the talents of myself with those of Sue-Ann Post as a double bill. Sue-Ann is a six-foot-plus former Mormon and current lesbian. She is also hilarious. She can lay claim to being Australia's first out lesbian comedian.

> I've been out since my first gig in 1986. Being out onstage was against all advice, including from my gay friends, who said, 'Look, you are funny, but you are a bit scary, and you'll just confirm the stereotype. Maybe you should wait for a smaller prettier lesbian to come along before you do it.'

They'd be waiting a long time. We were to be billed in Edinburgh as Mr and Mrs Average Australia. The clincher was the 6.30 pm timeslot in the Wildman Room, a prime venue and part of the Assembly Rooms, a central hub of the festival. The Wildman Room was a small but famous venue, and the 6.30 slot is perfect for Edinburgh, particularly if you are relying on material that requires an iota of attention. The festival boasts shows from dawn to dusk. Attention spans are waning by nightfall. The crowds are spent, eager for musical or easily palatable acts – or D.A.A.S., whom no-one could sleep through. With my ego inflated to bursting after my Montreal triumph, I was looking forward to my second crack at the Edinburgh Fringe.

Things began to go downhill immediately upon arrival at Montreal airport. A fierce storm had my manager Dale Langley and I grounded, with the result that we failed to link up with the Toronto flight directly to Edinburgh, a mere six-hour hop. After a seven-hour wait in Montreal, we eventually made it to Manchester airport, where we were stranded for another twelve hours. In all, it took just on twenty-six hours to get from Montreal to Edinburgh. It was late afternoon on 11 August as I made my way to the apartment John had arranged. I opened my suitcase, in desperate need of a change of clothes, to find that everything was soaked from my luggage being left on the tarmac during the storm in Montreal. I lay down for a short nap only to wake in pitch-darkness ten hours later not knowing what time it was, or what city or country I was in. I followed the wall with my hands and located a light switch. The body of a large-proportioned man, John Pinder, lay asleep on the couch in nothing but red budgie-smugglers. A beached whale in a G-string. Toto, I've a feeling we're not in Montreal anymore . . .

The following morning John informed us that due to a last-minute glitch the deal for the Wildman Room had fallen through. Never mind, we were offered the Supper Room, a decent but larger venue, and a revised starting time. Midnight.

This was Sue-Ann's first crack at Edinburgh. She was building a strong following in Australia, working principally at the same two venues as Flacco, the Harold Park Hotel and the Prince Patrick. It was at the Harold Park that Sue-Ann had first taken the leap into stand-up comedy.

> The first time I actually got up on stage in Sydney was at the Harold Park Hotel in the open mic section and I shall never forget it. Mandy Salomon was hosting, and she came up to me and said, 'Open section?' I said, 'Yes, what gave it away?' She said, 'You're nervous. Never mind, I'll introduce you, you'll be fine. What's your name?' Mandy then gets up onstage and says, 'Well, we've only got one bloke in the open mic section tonight, please welcome to the stage . . . Sam Post!' So I get up on stage and go, 'Actually, my name is Sue-Ann and I'm a woman.' And they didn't all look convinced. Mandy had disappeared out the back by the time I came offstage. But I wasn't angry – let's face it, it happened to me once a week. It was no big deal.

There were far worse gigs to follow for Sue-Ann. Such as:

> The Private Bin in Canberra, a nightclub where a lot of the Duntroon boys hung out. A public sector meat market. I walked onstage and they immediately started making ape noises and hurling bottles and ashtrays and yelling out, 'Go to fucking Tilley's, you cunt!' I left the stage after three minutes, and then they had to usher me out through the

kitchen because it looked like they were going to rush me and try to beat me up.

Sue-Ann made it out alive and did in fact take their advice. She went straight to Tilley's Devine Cafe, Canberra's leading lesbian enclave.

The natives were friendlier in Edinburgh; there just weren't quite enough of them. Sue-Ann and I needed to fill twenty shows. By the final night, the bar staff knew all our lines; after all, they were virtually the only people to have witnessed the international debut of Mr and Mrs Average Australia.

Edinburgh 1992 was also the first time Sue-Ann met the All-Stars.

I first saw them on *The Big Gig* and I've got to say they weren't really my cup of tea. And Paul McDermott just annoyed me. But I remember after a show in Edinburgh talking to Paul and Tim, and the next morning not remembering if I really had or if it was a hallucination from the Scottish beer, because Paul was so polite and well behaved, nothing like I had imagined him. Tim's a love though.

When an audience did turn up to see our show, the response was mixed.

I remember being treated superciliously by an English comic who said, 'You know, you're quite funny for a colonial.' And one night we had a small audience and again it was that condescending English element who were quite bemused by us, and you decided to just make me and the sound guy laugh. Fuck the audience. I think we scared the crap out of the Brits.

The critics, however, were kind – kind enough after a long day's reviewing to turn up for our show. *The Scotsman*, 25 August 1992, described the 'strange pairing' of 'a large woman with a wide grin and a wicked gleam in her eye [who] delivers a decent chunk of entertaining material with enthusiasm and aplomb' (and a fair amount of Scottish ale too, if the truth be known). Flacco, meanwhile, was: 'Bald, white-faced, looking like a cross between a hobbit and a deranged mime artist.' I decided to take that as a compliment – but kind reviews were not enough to fill the room. The moral of this story is: unless you can sing, dance or otherwise intimidate an audience, never perform at the Edinburgh Fringe after 10 pm.

While Sue-Ann and I worked to next to no-one, a couple of blocks away D.A.A.S. were ramping up their reputation. Without question these boys were on the verge of greatness, you could smell it, as distinctly as the odour emanating from their stage clothes. As for myself? I had a new ex-Mormon lesbian drinking buddy and the head of Showtime Networks' phone number in my pocket. I also had a return ticket to Australia. My bank account and a growing antipathy towards live performance had me back in Australia soon after our closing night. International opportunity never bothered knocking for me again. I walked through its revolving door and came out exactly where I started.

Professional regret is a sorry state of affairs. I try to cope with it by concentrating on the misfortunes of others. Greg Fleet savours a veritable cavalcade of regret.

> Some of the advice I give is the worst advice. I was the one person who told the Puppetry of the Penis boys, 'Seriously, guys, I loved it, but this will never fly, you will be humiliated, just put a lid on it.' And then Madonna was walking out of their show applauding, and I went, 'Maybe I was wrong . . .'

Greg's regret only brings more of my own to the surface. For example, after the premiere of Jane Campion's debut feature film, *Sweetie*, the one that put Jane on the road to international filmmaking glory (and featured me carrying a spear as young Teddy Schneller), I told Jane the film wasn't commercial enough to succeed. And subsequently I never landed a role in any of Jane's highly regarded Academy Award-winning future efforts. I'm also the guy who told David Wenham it would be best not to accept the role of Diver Dan on ABC Television's highly acclaimed *SeaChange* if he ever wanted to pursue a career in films. But I can always rely on Michael 'Bob' Petroni to trump us all. He was offered the opportunity to write *Fight Club* but turned it down. That's got to hurt.

As I limped home from my second and final Edinburgh Fringe, licking my wounds, I left D.A.A.S. basking in the glow of their sixth straight Edinburgh triumph and considering their next move. Corridors of opportunity lay open to them. What point in returning to Australia? After discovering intelligent life, why return to Mars? The answer was clear: their future lay in the UK. Television offers were coming in, they were touring the country to full houses and mingling with the stars.

The Reading Festival originated in the early sixties, making it the oldest rock music festival on earth. Every major rock act on the planet has performed there. Comedy has become a healthy sideline to the main event and in 1992 Australia's Doug Anthony All-Stars were invited to attend. Cameron P. Mellor, by this stage a permanent dogsbody in the D.A.A.S. touring roadshow, recalls being in Edinburgh when the boys got the call.

> We were driven to Reading to do the show, then it was back to Edinburgh the next day. It was all a bit rock 'n' roll. We didn't know what to expect. D.A.A.S. had a dressing-room and a rider. It was star treatment all around.

While headline acts like Nirvana, Public Enemy and Smashing Pumpkins were hitting the main stage, Al Murray, Harry Hill, Frank Skinner and the Doug Anthony All-Stars prepared to hit the Comedy Tent stage. Cameron P. Mellor rallied his troops.

> All I really needed to do for a gig like that was literally get them side of stage and get them on. There were thousands of people inside this tent and they went completely bonkers for D.A.A.S. McDermott was glancing to me at the side of

the stage with this look of 'Can you believe this? What the fuck is going on?' I've got to say they were good. They could not have done anything wrong that night, they were so on the money. I was standing there thinking, 'This is going to go down as one of the All-Stars' greatest moments.'

I'm standing there, arms folded, loving it, until this very polite man walked up to me and he said, 'Oh, are you with these guys?'

'Yeah,' I said.

'Um, we've got a bit of a problem . . .' he said.

'Really?' I said. 'There's a problem?'

Meanwhile there's the background noise of the Dougs in full flight and the crowd going apeshit for them.

'Yes,' he said. 'That guy in the middle? I don't know how this has happened, but the wireless microphone that he's using is on the same frequency as the main stage. And every time they try to do a line check for Public Enemy, his microphone comes up.'

So I looked at him and instead of panicking and going, 'Oh fuck, we've got to fix this,' I felt this weird sense of power knowing that the main stage holds sixty thousand people, so I looked back at him and I went, 'Well, what do you suggest we do?'

'We've got to get that mic off him, get it out of his hands and turn it off.'

I'm going, 'Well, I dunno . . . I mean, they're doing pretty well out there. I'm going to have to pick a moment of the set where I'm not going to throw him off his game.'

He had every right to turn McDermott's mic off. This was rock 'n' roll. But he just went, 'Okay.' And he stood there, in a cold sweat, and more and more people were coming up to him, eyes bugging out of their heads, and of course I was then very conscious of everything that was coming out of McDermott's mouth, knowing full well there was a mixer out on the main stage pushing faders up for Flavor Flav's microphone, and all he was getting was McDermott singing, 'I fuck dogs in the park after dark.'

It got to the point where the guy couldn't hold off any longer and he hands me a replacement microphone with a lead, and there was one part of the show where Richard took over, and I just bolted out onto the stage, pulled Paul's mic off the stand, whacked the leaded mic onto the stand and muttered to Paul, 'I'll tell you later, it's good.'

I ran back to the guy and he grabbed this fucking microphone and turned it off.

The boys continued and went off in a blaze of glory, it was quite triumphant, and McDermott came over to me and said, 'What the fuck were you doing? What the fuck was all that about?'

I just went, 'You wait. You wait until I tell you.'

That was the night that we were broadcasting to sixty thousand people and held up Public Enemy from going onstage.

CONFESSIONS OF A RELUCTANT FARCEUR

I didn't have a really important life,
but at least it's been funny.

LEMMY KILMISTER

While the glow of success, the flush of fame and infrequent bouts of financial security fade with time, performance anxiety remains. After thirty years the stomach still turns, the bladder must be evacuated, the feeling of impending doom and the urge to flee still haunt me in the moments before the curtain rises. Why didn't I take my father's advice? 'Get yourself a trade, son.' This was no trade: it was human sacrifice. I came into this life kicking and screaming and covered in blood and I expect to go out in the same way. There is no dignity in birth so why expect it in death? Dignity is possible only in the middle bit. But not if you are a comedian. It is said most people fear public speaking more than they fear death. One theory has it that the fear is actually one of ostracism, of banishment from the social group. Our piliferous ancestors would risk literal death if they behaved in any manner that risked rejection. Humans in groups were formidable hunters. A lone human was mere prey. Every comedian knows that feeling.

Immediately before a performance, the signals detected by the primal corporeal self convince the body that it's about to be chased down by a mob of sabre-toothed tigers or the odd woolly mammoth. The limbic system takes comedy very seriously. The mind is torn between fight or flight, yet the only thing on the line is pride. Stand-up comedy is a health hazard. In the eighties, comedy rooms were thick with tobacco smoke, passively absorbed by the weakened immune systems of recalcitrant performers. On a good night, the dangers were compounded by the wide open jaws of the audience as they released their brittle squeals of laughter, thus expelling in the direction of the performer whichever bacteria or other pathogens inhabited their inner quarters. A healthier night for any performer would be a crowd of no more than a dozen patrons with no sense of humour. Yet, paradoxically, this is where a comedian is said to die.

Comedians are the architects of other people's happiness. They are no fun to hang out with, to share a meal with, or be trapped in an elevator with. They are either observing your foibles for future financial gain or not the least interested in playing the fool for free. It may seem counterintuitive, but introversion is common among performers. People who appear at ease on stage and screen become complete wallflowers offstage. How is this feat achieved? It's called acting. We are not talking Stanislavsky here, more your George Burns, who once said the key to performing was 'Sincerity – if you can fake that, you've got it made.' Introversion when off duty is a necessity. How are you to spy on your fellow humans if you are the one holding court? When not wearing the motley, the wise court jester is a very good listener.

Half of humanity are introverts, yet in western society the extrovert is the most highly valued. Lauded for their magnetism and charisma, these lives-of-the-parties are considered role models. Introverts are viewed as social weaklings: the unblessed meek who deserve to inherit nothing. It is this humble recluse's opinion that most, if not all, extroverts are at root pathetic, needy, egocentric tub-thumpers. Yet introverts are passed over for leadership, even though they are proven to be more careful, make fewer mistakes and bring a lot more to the table because they've spent much more time in solitude contemplating what should be brought to that table. Brainstorming requires a brain, not a group-thought. Author Susan Cain enlarges on this in *Quiet: The Power of Introverts in a World That Can't Stop Talking*: 'Any time people come together in a meeting, we're not necessarily getting the best ideas; we're just getting the ideas of the best talkers.'

My alter ego Flacco is a raging extrovert and he is, in short, a complete fool. It takes countless hours of solitude to create such an effective extrovert. Al Murray began his career as a doubting, unconfident student.

I was a really, really self-conscious kid and sort of short. I'd have confidence in bursts, and I got to thinking that if you're really self-conscious you're thinking about performing the whole time. You're thinking about life as a performance.

Al nailed it right there. The sensitive kids have to learn how to put on a show in order to survive. It should therefore come as no surprise that the best actors are anxiety-ridden, unstable, nervous wrecks. But for Al, acting for a living can also provide healing.

And I think that got me into the idea of performing, because when you are performing it is a controlled environment. The thing I find really interesting about being onstage is the ritual of it. There's an understanding in the room, you know, that they're all looking at you, they are all pointed in a certain direction. They expect there to be a beginning, a middle and an end. And because I was really self-conscious, the idea of theatre attracted me because you get to be self-conscious but control it and use it.

I've considered releasing a self-help book for extroverts titled *The Positives of Negative Thinking: Releasing the Power of Shutting the Fuck Up*. Paul McDermott is a case in point. Out of the glare of the public eye, he is a quietly spoken teetotaller. But just add an audience and this meek and mild Clark Kent of the entertainment industry morphs instantly into a rakish raconteur, seducing all before him with an abundance of charisma. The two poles of Paul McDermott: the snail in the shell or the smug slug rolled in glitter. I'm yet to uncover any hint of in-between Paul.

Tim Ferguson is the polar opposite, comprised of just the one pole offstage and on. 'Hi, I'm Tim Ferguson,' or Timmy to his friends, and everyone is invited to be a part of Tim's ever-expanding circle. You just go directly to friend, do not pass acquaintance, do not flatter, or offer frankincense and myrrh (mind you a little myrrh and he readily rolls over on his belly; the more the myrrhier, as Tim might say). Ferguson is a puppy to his people – all you need do is smile and he lets you pat him. But don't be fooled, this little kelpie-cross has not been neutered and he has an intellectual bite that is far worse than his excitable yap.

Al Murray came to a similar conclusion while studying D.A.A.S. at close quarters.

> You'd never know which Paul you were going to get. Sometimes the aggression onstage would be offstage and sometimes it wouldn't and you'd think, 'Well, who am I talking to today?' The thing about Tim is there's no change in what he's like at all.

Richard, on the other hand, has always projected a more bookish temperament, forever nursing a hefty hardback, generally non-fiction and with no pictures. His comrades cruelly mocked the studious guitarist for his cerebral indulgences. As if being well read and a good listener would ever pay the rent!

But who's laughing now? The Boab was busy gathering the fruits that would sustain him decades into the future.

Rod Quantock remembers a standoffish Paul.

> I think the first conversation I ever had with Paul was just before a *Good News Week* taping and he didn't talk, he just got into his little bubble, so even though I did a lot of *Good News Week*s I never really got to know him. But last year during the comedy festival I was doing a walking tour and we went through the Town Hall and he was in the foyer. I had fifty or sixty people with me and he was fantastic with them. I'd thought he was going to get really pissed off, because of the image we have of him; I saw a very different side to him. I find him really interesting because he has that really, really, really dark side to him, and it comes out in his drawings and in the music. But that's the reaction I had to the Dougs from when I first saw them [those clean-cut Canberra boys] and the next time I saw them they're this dark, evil, brooding psychotic group of people. Which seemed like a big leap to make. I don't know the truth of it, but I always felt the transition from the nice neat sanitised boys to what they became was driven by Paul.

I agree that Paul was the driving force in the murkier aspects of D.A.A.S. Some people you can read like a book. With McDermott it's a tome of some heft – not easy to get into, but once inside you find that many of the pages are stuck together.

Greg Fleet remembers a more outlandish Paul.

The first time I saw Paul he reminded me of [the deliciously cabbalistic] Ignatius Jones, who was in a band called Jimmy and the Boys. They were always cutting open sex dolls and raw meat and I was seventeen, just out of boarding school, going, 'Fuck!'

ROD: What a waste of meat.

GREG: I was thinking what a waste of a sex doll . . . But I'm thinking, all that stuff, seeing punk, Jimmy and the Boys, Pinter movies on TV, and although by then I was already down that path, seeing people like the Dougs to me was always, well, often my thing was jealousy to some degree . . .

Frank Woodley spotted a side of Tim that others rarely saw.

I've got this really weird memory that I almost feel like, it's so subtle, it's so simple, it's almost a bit rude to mention it, but I was riding my bike around Carlton and I saw Tim just walking around and there were these posters for their upcoming show. It was called *Sex and Violence*, and I'd noticed all these posters stuck to walls and around lampposts and things, and I just happened to see Tim walk past one of the posters and fix it up, on the pole, and it almost struck me as just like the least cool thing you could do, to be getting around fixing up your own posters.

GREG: *Sex and Violence* posters . . . The *We Don't Give a Fuck* tour – oh, hang on, better straighten that up.

FRANK: He wasn't putting up the poster, he was just walking round Carlton . . .

GREG: Correcting other people's work . . .

FRANK: And he noticed that the thing had come off and he just fixed it up, and I felt like I was witnessing somebody masturbating or something, do you know what I mean? A private little moment. I shouldn't have seen it.

I get the feeling Frank never quite got over the effect the All-Stars had on him. Perhaps the magnificent blend of tragedy and pathos Frank brings to the stage these days is a result of having his innocence wrenched from him by three darkly Delphic Canberrans.

And here is where this little symphony takes an unexpected turn. A syncopation, an unexpected arrhythmic dissonance. News that D.A.A.S. had split up came as a shock. I had not sensed any animosity within the group, although by 1994 Flacco was roaming solo with entire shows of his own to peddle. I was told that Tim decided to call it quits to return to Australia and raise his budding family. There was some truth in this. But it wasn't the whole story. Tim had been monitoring a tiny rebellion taking place within his body. Cameron P. Mellor had by this time returned to Australia, but he does recall being in Ireland when Tim first started experiencing numbness on one side of his body.

At that stage we were doing two full shows a night. We were busking all day and he was trying to get pregnant again . . .

We can safely assume it was Tim's partner who was more likely to become pregnant. They already had a young son and were trying for number two.

> . . . and Tim started getting numbness in his leg and his arm, on one side of his body, and at that point it was put down to exhaustion. But why pull up stumps? Why would you stop? It was a mystery.

It was also a mystery to Tim at this stage. Nothing too serious, he hoped, but enough to make the idea of singing, dancing and staying up all night perhaps not the best path to tread for the moment. Paul and Richard were like two lost kittens. D.A.A.S. were a trio, a single organism with three appendages. Tim's departure was an amputation. A fatal one.

MOVEMENT III

Scherzo: Like the burlesque, the scherzo is often associated with the expression of humour, ranging from the lighthearted to the darkly ominous and grotesque.

FROM *THE GREAT SOVIET ENCYCLOPEDIA* (1926)

THE PLAYERS

PAUL McDERMOTT: Early fifties, smelly, disgruntled, cranky. A bounder and a cad in his youth but things are falling apart, especially the people around him.

TIM FERGUSON: Early fifties, seated but enthusiastic, still pretty.

RICHARD FIDLER: Widely lauded and beloved national radio presenter and responsible husband and father. A living treasure.

PAUL LIVINGSTON: The guitarist.

CAMERON P. MELLOR: Stage manager, producer, art director, nurse, van driver par excellence. The years have not been kind. He now resembles the love child of Marty Feldman and Richard Pryor.

MINOR PLAYERS: Assorted riffraff, ne'er-do-wells, roadside cafe workers, spear-carriers, dogs.

LOCATION

Lower hemisphere – somewhere between Kundabung and
Paraburdoo.

TIME

The twenty-first century.

A PENSIONER, A CRIPPLE
AND A SONGWRITER

Irreverence is the champion of liberty
and its only sure defense.

MARK TWAIN, *NOTEBOOK,* **1888**

I'm going to quote Woody Allen's oft-repeated famous line
on immortality. It's been done to death. But it's not often I
get to use the word 'oft', so here goes: 'I don't want to achieve
immortality through my work. I want to achieve it through
not dying.' An easier way to ensure immortality is to breed.
Nothing like bringing into being a litter of freshly birthed
innocent bio-containers to ensure all your phobias, opinions,
beliefs and fears continue long after you're dust. It has long
been my pledge not to stain this earth with progeny.

Since teetering on the edge of global immortality in 1994,
the All-Stars have been heavy breeders. All three have eked

out a decent living in the past quarter of a century, earning enough of a crust to supply all the rusks required to feed their progeniture.

The goddess Fama has blessed them all, but what does fame mean at the end of the day – or, more to the point, in approaching the twilight of one's career? Does it still matter? Did it ever? Ultimately, in the grand scheme of things, none of we *Homo sapiens* is left with anything to show for ourselves, because there will be no-one to show it to. We are mere momentary membranes of meat perched on a nondescript planet in the outer suburbs of the galaxy, with on average only 550,000,000 breaths to inhale before exhaling into the eternal abyss, leaving behind nothing but a useless corpse grinning at the lid. Welcome to the autumn of life, when an old man's fancy turns to thoughts of utter and inescapable personal annihilation. And prescription medications.

After leaving my peers poised for immortality in Edinburgh, I returned to Australia, broke, tail between my kilt. Yet somehow, over the past twenty-five years, I have continued to scrape a living by employing the technique of the remora fish (to paraphrase Steve 'The Sandman' Abbott), a parasitic organism that attaches itself to larger fish for personal gain. During the course of the nineties I attached myself to Steve, feeding off his external parasites, while he in turn attached himself to even larger fish, Mikey 'The Grouper' Robins and Helen 'The Great White Pointer' Razer, working the morning shift on the Triple J breakfast show. By the end of the last century Steve and I were sucking the life out of

Paul McDermott's perennial breadwinner *Good News Week*, a phenomenally successful soufflé of a production that resisted deflation no matter how many pricks it had to endure.

Monty Python's Flying Circus, *The Aunty Jack Show* and *The Young Ones* were at the forefront of a wave of character comedy television shows of the seventies and eighties. For a selective mute like myself, character comedy was the perfect way to release the inner exhibitionist while maintaining the introvert within. In the nineties, character comedy gave way to the American model: a casually attired comedian, typically male, a stool, a glass of water, an air of confidence and charm, and a string of observational one-liners. The Irish genius Dave Allen had been honing this style for decades, a style in its highest form both potent and subversive; George Carlin saw to that. I was never built for stool-and-water comedy, and by the end of the nineties both The Sandman and Flacco were affectionately referred to as 'old school'. At least we were free of the term 'alternative'.

In spite of being an unfashionable character comedian, Flacco was invited back to the Just for Laughs festival in Montreal in 1999. Although embraced once again by the local crowd, this time there were no business cards from high-end television executives. But Flacco did manage to make it to the list of 'Best Jokes of the Festival' with his closing line: 'And so, to make a long story short . . . Rhett and Scarlett split up in the end.' (I now confess I did not compose the line; it was given to me by Steve Johnson, illustrious member of the *Good News Week* writing team, the night before I left for Montreal. Thanks,

Steve, and no, there was no prize money.) I did, however, have the pleasure of sharing a dressing-room with Johnny Vegas, the British comedian notorious for his no-holds-barred, beer-fuelled delivery. I was more than a little intimidated as I sat near the man, dabbing my face with foundation and mascara. Johnny, a largish lad, sat with legs spread and a pint of beer in hand telling me about his day spent seeking out the best examples of classic Canadian pottery to be found in the city. Many comedians nurture secret hobbies. The Sandman is an avid twitcher, a birdwatcher of some renown. I dabble in campanology, ringing bells in church towers whenever possible. Johnny Vegas is a potter. He has an impressive knowledge of crockery from all eras. To this day Johnny still drinks before going on stage – 'to get into a morose mood' – but in Montreal he was the sweetest of dressing-room companions before he went onstage and Mr Hyde emerged. A brilliantly funny Mr Hyde.

Now that I've outed myself as a campanologist, some explanation is due. I am a post-religious being, an atheist in the belfry. Belfry dwellers, it turns out, are an eclectic mob – among them are twitchers, trainspotters, Buddhists and Christians. In days of yore, bellringing was the pastime of rogues and drunkards, and I presume a good way to avoid attending the service itself. In that sense I simply view this pastime as keeping up those old traditions. To quote our tower captain, 'Bellringing is no beauty contest,' which is why ringers are often heard but never seen. Brian Eno is a self-described evangelical atheist and yet Brian regularly sings in a gospel choir.

When you sing with a group of people, you learn how to subsume yourself into a group consciousness because a cappella singing is all about the immersion of the self into the community. That's one of the great feelings – to stop being me for a little while and to become us. That way lies empathy, the great social virtue.

Campanology is precisely that. Perhaps I'm subconsciously taking a punt on Pascal's wager with this bellringing lark. Blaise Pascal, while busy philosophising in the seventeenth century, reasoned it was probably safer to put your money on God existing. Should God exist, you win. If there is no God, you've got nothing to lose. Perhaps I secretly view myself as a Pearly Gatecrasher . . .

St Peter: Sorry, you can't come in here, mate.

Me: But I'm a campanologist.

St Peter: My mistake. Straight through, son.

And just by the way, Quasimodo had terrible technique. Never hunch, and at no time may both feet leave the ground at once. That way leads to heaven, as your lousy technique has you being whipped upwards at some force into the belltower ceiling.

Campanology has also proved a means of filling time after my performing life appeared to have run its course. Earlier this century, my attempt to allow Flacco's television career to end on a high was thwarted by circumstance.

There are certain events in history after which the question is posed: 'Where were you when . . .?' For example: 'Where were you when President Kennedy was assassinated?' (I was in my bedroom listening to a transistor radio. I was tiny, but I cried anyway.) Or: 'Where were you when Armstrong stepped on the moon?' (Watching a blurred image on a black-and-white television in my grandparents' room. I was underwhelmed. Where were the little green men? The shiny robots?) Or: 'Where were you on September 11, 2001?' The answer: with The Sandman pitching a comedy series to the ABC.

Timing, as they say, is everything. Aware that our Sandman and Flacco television use-by dates were almost up (we were both in our forties and by Australian television industry standards that made us professional pumpkins), Steve Abbott and I put a great deal of work into our pitch. We had enjoyed a successful run on Network Ten's *GNW Night Lite*, contributing all of seven minutes of comedy a week for several years. All we were after was another twenty minutes to shoot a pilot for a half-hour series. The title for this proposed series was *The Nerve*. The show was to be shot with a single locked-off camera, The Sandman and Flacco seated, motionless, in front of a white screen, with most of the action taking place offscreen. *The Nerve* would have been a tough sell in any climate.

On that sunny morning in September we were well prepared, with no time to take in the morning news. We had notes, confidence, a great pitch (in our own opinion) and, as it turned out, no-one to pitch it to. We arrived at the headquarters of the light entertainment department of the Australian Broadcasting Corporation where not a soul was to be found. We sat in the waiting area, watching the television, and saw that half of the

United States of America appeared to be on fire. Curious. There was no sound, but a banner along the lower half of the screen read: 'America under attack!' Everyone was in the newsroom. We were seen, eventually, by a highly agitated employee who was itching to get back to where the drama was unfolding. Needless to say, our pitch did not raise a smile. Goodbye, confidence; goodbye, comedy television series. Thank you, Osama bin Laden. The nerve of that guy.

Flacco had a decent run despoiling the small screen for over a decade, but at the age of forty-five, I was a little too young for the pension. I managed to insinuate myself into another niche a few rungs down from the 'minor celebrity' status to which I had grown accustomed. It was not exactly a reinvention; I'd been writing for decades, and as the century opened I made it my business to write exclusively. Superficial beauty and self-esteem are not compulsory for a writer, but bitterness and self-loathing are encouraged, so I possessed more than my share of credentials.

Writing was an option I embraced with gusto. I had re-earned my anonymity. I could observe again. I floundered in the writers' pool, becoming a bottom feeder with one of the foremost comedy writing teams in Australia, working for *Good News Week*. Obscurity became me once again. I settled into my cave, lit a candle and hunkered down to the business of being a 'real' writer. The daily discipline goes something like this . . . Up at 5 am, I jog to my desk and write, non-stop, until 1 pm. A light lunch. Then back to it. Unable to drag myself from the desk I soldier on, writing late into the night, before falling into my high-thread-count Egyptian cotton sheets, spent and sated from the day's efforts yet eager for the dawn. This goes on month after month until the beast is tamed and the manuscript is produced and delivered ahead of deadline to my doting publisher.

That's one way of looking at it. The other would include accuracy.

Here's what they don't tell you in those creative writing courses: writing is painful. The rewards, both financial and personal, are minimal. The terrible truth is that each morning I wake and chant the same mantra: 'Please, no, not again.' Welcome to Groundhog Day. The mission? Achieve your daily word count. That's all there is too it. So why can't I think of a single opening word? Writer's block is a term authors use when procrastination eventually wins out. The great procrastinators are easy to spot; these writers have magnificently organised desks, very shiny kitchenware, unnervingly clean toilet bowls, and their book and CD collections are all in alphabetical order – and, for the most part, not one of the books in their collection has their own name on the cover.

This species perpetually finds more important things to do. Busy, busy, busy. You can spot one of these scribes at any cafe on any given day, talking about writing, complaining of writer's block. The truth is, the entire process is one continual block. Every writer is blocked. Every step of the way. Blocked. You never know what that next word is going to be. And if you decide on one word, you agonise over whether there might be a better one. Or a preferable one. Or a superior one. Or a worthier one. Or an exceptional one. Or a surpassing one. Or an unrivalled one. Surely there's something better than better? Or at least a thesaurus with better words for better? There is no way out. You simply write straight through it, like I'm doing right now. That feels better. Or worthier? Or . . . no, sometimes better is just better.

Every writer has his or her formula. Many find the only way to lure themselves to the desk is the promise of copious amounts of alcohol on completion of the word quota. This is a fair enough option when the default social position of the writer is isolated, single and drunk. The novelty of sharing one's life with an 'artist' wears thin very swiftly. Especially if you are the artist. My daily motivation these days is to achieve one thousand words per day (for your information that was my six hundred and thirty-fourth for the day, so I've broken the back of it and I can already feel my mood lifting).

For the best part of a decade I remained creatively fecund as a writer and no one gave a damn. I could not have been happier. But my fecund coming came to an abrupt end as the new century entered its teenage years.

To say I didn't see it coming is an understatement. Perhaps I was too busy observing to notice, but before I knew it I was back, and carrying a very familiar spear. *D.A.A.S. Kapital*, the series that failed to stop a nation, or the careers of its major players, was to be released on DVD. Grandmaster Ted Robinson organised a cast reunion to be held during the 2013 Melbourne

International Comedy Festival. Tim, Paul and Richard were on board. Sniffing the possibility of a royalty cheque and the chance to both eat and pay rent in the same week, I leapt at the opportunity. Or, rather, I ambled at the opportunity. I was past the age of leaping, past the age of fifty, and I had run out of reasons to leap.

At full capacity the Melbourne Town Hall holds just on two thousand. From comedy galas to *Good News Week* specials and debates, I had known the guttural rumble of four thousand restless legs echoing through the narrow but cosy backstage area. For those who've never ventured behind a stage curtain, it might come as something of a shock to be confronted with the size and scale of these sacred sites. As the audience waits in anticipation in their vast air-conditioned arena, behind that stage curtain lie the cramped quarters of their heroes, flickering fluorescent-lit corridors leading to dressing-rooms that resemble a kind of bed-less asylum ward, the scene of so many thespian tantrums and triumphs.

Bare light bulbs surrounding rows of mirrors do nothing to calm the nerves of the bullet-sweating performers who pace like trapped vermin amid architecture akin to the underground nests of the naked mole rat. Or, in my case, a naked mole rat about to be flushed from its bunker. Like the naked mole rat, I'm well adapted to this lifestyle. My visual acuity is poor. I have little hair and wrinkled pink skin. I lack insulating layers. I'm thigmotactic and I prefer to inhabit small dark places. And I can move backwards as fast as I can move forwards, both physically and metaphorically, i.e. in person and career.

During the heyday of *Good News Week*, the backstage area of the Melbourne Town Hall was abuzz with crew and cast bustling through the narrow corridors, a vast family of mole rats babbling into headsets, running lines, urinating far too frequently and occasionally vomiting violently into their shoes, or someone else's. Personally, I've never been much of a stomach hurler, but I am a pre-show bladder evacuator par excellence.

Before the *D.A.A.S. Kapital* DVD launch and reunion, I arrived at the Town Hall expecting much the same as on previous visits, but here was not the usual hive of activity. There was no outside broadcast van parked outside with multifarious crew members rifling through road cases. The big room was empty – save for Tim, Paul and Richard, sitting quietly and separately in the auditorium. Khym Lam, who played the newsreader and the odd mermaid in the series, was nestled next to Richard. The pair had met on the set of *D.A.A.S. Kapital*, married, gone forth, multiplied and lived happily ever after.

Ted Robinson stood alone onstage, hand held to predator chin, index finger resting on nose, removing said hand only to hurl an order at his crew. Ted's skeleton crew was made up primarily of his offspring. All the while his ever-loyal sidekick, co-producer, legendary show business person and Ted's chief petty officer Pam Swain stood by, ever alert to Ted's next move. Unfortunately Ted never quite knew what his next move was. Television production is somewhat aleatory. This show was not going to air, nor being recorded for posterity. All that was required were four microphones and a projection screen. Nothing one's immediate family can't take care of.

As I wandered backstage there was no wardrobe or make-up personnel, no one at all. My old haunt seemed haunted. I was the only naked mole rat in the burrow. I felt a creeping sense of loss. It was 2013 and it had been some years since I abandoned the performer's life. I grieved for it a little. And thanked it. With distance I had forgotten the pain. This afternoon was a chance to pay my respects to the people who'd made it happen. Soon enough I would be back at my writing desk tapping out oddities for a new audience. I had moved on.

The Melbourne Town Hall filled to overflowing. I could hear their chatter as I paced alone, not really knowing why I was pacing. I had no lines to learn. No costume to adopt. Flacco was not required. Paul Livingston was merely a special guest; I'd just answer a few questions and be off. I waited side stage. No stage manager to give me my cue, no last-minute powdering from make-up. I felt a sense of calm, knowing that those anxiety-ridden days were gone; I would never again be forced to stand here in mortal terror waiting for my intro. A huge weight lifted.

Ted Robinson walked onstage to polite applause and introduced the All-Stars. A gut-tearing roar went up as the three original cast members wandered out. Tim drew the bulk of the applause, carrying a big stick and walking painfully slowly to his stool. Tim knew how to milk this moment. Multiple sclerosis had been nuzzling up to Ferguson for decades. It was now about to take centre stage with him.

After some chat and *D.A.A.S. Kapital* clips, Khym Lam was revealed, further feeding the audience's fervour. I was to enter next, to regale all with tales of the olden days. I have never been much of a regaler, not without the aid of make-up and props. In an instant I felt that familiar pang in the pit of my stomach, my tongue moved to drought mode and I felt like I was choking on a sandpaper slug. My old friend Anxiety was back to say farewell and share in the glory. While Tim rode his MS like a cowpoke on a mule, my latent SM (selective mutism) was kicking in my stall.

The lads introduced me, and as I walked out the audience rose to their feet. 'Great,' I thought, 'my final appearance onstage and it's a mass walkout.' But they stood their ground and they applauded. I have never totally warmed to audiences. I have perpetually visualised them as a jury, passing sentence on my every sentence. But I quickly warmed to this lot. There was no pressure to amuse. Let the Flacco clips do the work, be gracious, and make sure your fly is done up.

The All-Stars' reluctance to sing despite the urging of the audience was a complete fabrication. They were teasing as usual. They had a song they'd prepared earlier. I caught the rehearsal and was moved by the performance. Among the D.A.A.S. faithful there wasn't a dry eye in the house as all three stood and sang along to a projected version of one of their more poignant tunes, 'War Song'. Dwarfed by the image of their former, much younger, less broken selves performing the song, they belted out the tune in six-part harmonies. Here it was at last: the final public appearance of the Doug Anthony All-Stars and of Mr Livingston and his professional albatross Flacco. A fitting farewell. Ted Robinson has only one regret:

None of us quite knew how great the show would be and one of the great sadnesses of my life is we didn't shoot it.

The post-show DVD signing was a delightful finale to the reunion, and a tribute to the dedication and bladder capacity of those who waited in line for hours to be warmly welcomed by Tim, abused by Paul, enlightened by Richard, unnerved by me and charmed by Khym Lam. It was both touching and humbling to meet the people who had terrified me for so many years. I was again soaking up the peripheral glory – and, it must be said, we 'shifted a lot of units' (mind you, no royalty cheques were immediately forthcoming). Paul McDermott was reduced to an uncharacteristic civility by the response.

It was a crazy disorganised shemozzle. But I think we were all incredibly surprised by the outpouring of love more than anything else. I think we acquitted ourselves well onstage, but the thing that I was overtaken by was the emotion at the end of the gig, when people were coming up and we were signing for two and a half, three hours. And people telling us stories about how we'd affected their lives or how they'd first encountered us and what we led them to in regards to either their own artistic endeavours or literary or cultural aspirations. I found it really significant. I'd never had that sort of validation from the group – also because when we split up it was a dark shadow. We didn't really know for years what the fuck was going on. It was just a really deep well of emotion and I'm not normally affected by those things and I found it a little bit profound.

That evening, as I dined with Richard and Khym, it was laughingly proposed that D.A.A.S might consider re-forming. Rich was quite adamant: this event was the perfect final curtain, a priceless farewell.

> It was a lovely feeling. I felt we had honoured that part of our lives.

I wholeheartedly agreed. What was done was done. And not done to death, unlike so many performers, musicians and celebrity reality TV participants. Rich and I knew when the game was up. Quit while you're ahead. Leave them wanting more. That's what I like about Richard: common sense and maturity. One had to draw the line somewhere, and as far as Richard and I were concerned, we had found that somewhere right then and right there. Forgive me for including yet another well-worn Woody Allen quote (well-worn because it is timeless and true): 'If you want to make God laugh, tell him about your plans.' Granted I'm an atheist, but I still had plans. The plan was simple enough – let go of the past, eat, sleep, write. Then repeat until death did I part. Bliss.

When a call came from Paul McDermott regarding a repeat performance of the Melbourne *D.A.A.S. Kapital* DVD launch in D.A.A.S.'s hometown of Canberra in early 2014, I agreed, if only to get away from this desk. I presumed it would be much the same event as in Melbourne – same cast, same minimal crew, with only one difference: Richard was unable to attend.

Understandable, as he was engaged in bona fide employment, having built a solid career in national broadcasting. I was to have a chat and play guitar on a couple of tunes. No problem.

Apart from the absence of Richard, I noticed on arrival in Canberra that there was no sign of the *D.A.A.S. Kapital* DVD I was under the impression we were there to promote. Odd. There was also no sign of Ted Robinson or his immediate family. Odder. And it appeared D.A.A.S. were part of a comedy festival. Odder still. It didn't take long for me to realise I had been lured into what would become the first of many shows in a D.A.A.S. reunion tour. McDermott and Ferguson were right not to inform me. I would have refused. We have all witnessed the sad scenario play out: rock band re-forms after a successful reunion gig only to find out the fans just wanted to say hello and, more importantly, goodbye and thanks for the memories. It can be a sorry end to a once-great career, a destroyer of cherished memories and friendships. Why shit on your own legacy? What also puzzled me was the presence of one Cameron P. Mellor in the role of stage manager. What was his story?

My story went like this. I'd been approached to get the Dougs back together for the Canberra Comedy Festival. Livingston had been roped into coming on as the guitarist and would I like to get on a plane and stage-manage the show? I said, 'Absolutely, yes, I will be there.' Those Canberra shows were pretty amazing, even with 'the new guy' in place of Richard. So it was after that we called a meeting. Now, I had zero emotional attachment to the role of manager because I knew that at some point, if it were to go on, you would have to be managed, and I said, 'Look, you go one of two ways: you either go with a known promoter who probably knows where to place you and how to handle you, and you are probably going to get ripped off, or you go with me and I'm probably going to fuck it up, but I won't rip you off.' And there was a unanimous vote of: 'You do it.' And I think it was 'You do it' because I was in the room. It was just that I was the nearest guy. All I can say is that I was lucky I was dealing with an act that had an extraordinary fan base, because I had no idea what I was getting myself into . . . There were times when I would lie awake at night thinking to myself, 'Oh my god, what have I done?'

Leaving well enough alone was not on the minds of Tim and Paul. It didn't matter that one was now confined to a wheelchair and the other had mounted middle age like a gibbon in rut, refusing to take the passing of his misspent youth lying down. Make no mistake: I had been railroaded, thrown into the caboose of the D.A.A.S. gravy train. With me reluctantly in the mix, three worse-for-wear gentlemen set to work reheating old soup. The question was, would anyone take a sip?

JUST ANOTHER DAY AT THE OFFICE

Why do you have to be a nonconformist
like everybody else?

JAMES THURBER

For a while there, in the years before being ambushed and
forced out on the road again with D.A.A.S. version 2.0, the
delusion that I could survive as a writer seemed to hold true
(Warning: Tub-thumping, Self-aggrandisement and Dropped
Names Ahead). I began my writing career on the cusp of the
millennium with a stage play, *Emma's Nose*, directed by Neil
Armfield and a cast of fine actors. I received many letters
congratulating me on the play, particularly my decimation
of the practice of psychiatry. The play was satirical, based
around the early life of Sigmund Freud, and not only did a
fair slice of the audience miss the point of the play, the irony
was that I was seeing a psychiatrist during its run. I remain
in therapy to this day. I see it as a sort of ongoing surveillance

of myself. I've hired someone to spy on me. I report back to myself after consulting with my spy and then we take it from there. So far, I'm yet to suspect myself of anything.

I followed this effort with a barrage of nine radio plays for ABC Radio National, plus my stint writing for *Good News Week*. George Miller had been a supporter of Flacco for years, and it was an honour to be offered the task of authoring the krill characters, Will and Bill, for *Happy Feet Two*. I saw the pair of tiny invertebrates as a comedy duo, a comic sideline to the main game. I had been thinking along the lines of two comedy actors to voice the krill, perhaps Stephen Fry and Hugh Laurie. Or Steve Carell and Will Ferrell. When the good doctor George Miller informed me of his choices I was puzzled. I thought it was a joke and I laughed – inappropriately, as it turned out. Brad Pitt and Matt Damon were the last krill pairing I expected. George was looking at the bigger picture, of course. It was only after viewing the end result that I realised there is a very good reason why George Miller is the beluga of international filmmaking while I remain a lowly sprat awash in a sea of Hollywood glitterati.

Happy Feet Two premiered at the venue formerly known as Grauman's Chinese Theatre on Hollywood Boulevard, the place with handprints of the stars set in concrete on the forecourt; Groucho Marx, Elizabeth Taylor, Cary Grant and other lesser-known dead people were all willing to shove their paws into the pavement to attain immortality. Most of the finest films of last century opened here. As far as piles go, it's hard to top this one. Being the meek selective mute that I am, I eschewed the red carpet and found my seat among the wealthy and famous for the premier screening.

A review in the *New York Times* singled out for special mention 'two brilliantly orange krill, Will (Brad Pitt) and Bill (Matt Damon), whose dumb and dumber routine approaches Vladimir and Estragon levels of existential dark humour'. Another New York reviewer was not so impressed, taking umbrage at the pair's unsavoury behaviour. This somewhat unhinged scribe accused Will and Bill of engaging in the pursuit of a same-sex relationship and decried the creators of these repugnant invertebrates as members of an alleged conspiracy of liberal animators, engaged in the 'subliminal same gender reinforcement' of America's youth.

This observation came as something of a shock to me. What consenting adult krill get up to in the privacy of their own swarm is not my business but, for the record, the crustaceans in question were not, in the mind of this writer, in any way embroiled in what might be interpreted as a gay bromance, and I cannot recall one production meeting where I or my fellow writers were coerced into implanting subconscious homoerotic mannerisms or pro-Bette Midlerian inclinations into krill – or penguins or bull elephant seals, for that matter – and neither have I as yet heard any rumblings for any proposed production of *Happy Feet Three: Brokeback Iceberg*. Not that there would be anything wrong with that, mind you. One might just as easily imagine *Toy Story*'s Sheriff Woody to be the seventh Village Person – and what of Buzz Lightyear's overly affectionate affectations when in 'Spanish mode'? Dare I mention

SpongeBob SquarePants, who lives in a two-storey pineapple in Bikini Bottom? Perhaps this homophobic reviewer just wants us to get back to the good old days of Archie and Jughead, Tom and Jerry, Popeye and Bluto.

After the release of *Happy Feet Two*, I returned to Australia to wait for the offers to stream in. I sat back and let the krill do the work. No-one took the bait. Not a nibble. After a few months, what I laughingly called my nest egg was looking more nest than egg. Soon I was eggless and on the verge of selling my nest. In accordance with tradition, I descended into self-pity, and spent my days drinking and complaining to anyone with ears about the injustices of show business. Two ears in particular would have none of my self-righteous ranting. A dear friend and a fine actor, herself working a day job to fund her art, proposed that I quit complaining and get a job. Me? A job? A fifty-seven-year-old washed-up writer and burnt-out comedian, sans teeth, sans hair, sans everything?

There was an opening at the Australian Broadcasting Corporation for a rights management, cataloguing and inventory officer. 'Why not apply?' urged my well-meaning but terminally impetuous friend. I had auditioned for dozens of roles, but this was not one of them. I declined the offer. My brassy colleague was not one to be easily dissuaded. She had made up my mind. Such is the power of this woman (combined with my chronic milquetoast manner) that a week later I sat waiting in the foyer of the ABC, a familiar enough arena for me, but this was no script meeting, no interview, no five-minute spot on a comedy show. To my mind, the chances of landing the position were nil, but it would at least keep my delightfully persistent chum off my back. I was confident that once those in positions of authority took a glance at my resumé, I would be laughed out of the legal department.

I started work the following week.

I had somehow secured what in common parlance is known as 'a proper job'. I finally earned my first honest day's pay at an age when most are considering retirement. As my Auntie Dot reminded me on hearing the news of my gainful employment, 'Your mother would have been so proud.' Acceptance into the fold at last. I entered a world I had only ever imagined on the page. The extraordinary thing is it was just as I imagined it. The set was perfect: low ceilings, rows of harsh fluorescent lights, and open plan, of course – what better way to maintain concentration than by putting people who work on the phone all day in a room full of others who work on the phone all day? Is it just me, or does anyone else find it odd that the project managers who implement these open plans invariably have private offices?

I was given a 'workstation' which looked decidedly like a 'desk' to me. I soon slipped into the part. By the end of week one I was the office equivalent of Olivier in *Hamlet*, in my own mind at least. In retrospect, perhaps I was simply astounded that I had lasted the week. I soon began to understand the attraction of this lifestyle. It had perks. And I was a perk virgin. I could sacrifice my salary, I could roll it over, I could be paid for being sick. It was like all my Christmases had come at once – especially when Christmas came and I was paid *not* to go to work. It dawned on me that regular paid work is a big bouncy castle for adults. I didn't need my machete to hack a narrow path through an uncertain future. Here was a clear road to blissful and cashed-up retirement. Why hadn't anyone told me about this?

I was witness to how the other ninety-nine per cent lived. I enjoyed those perks. Would the freelance life ever be the same? Would I ever need it again? The D.A.A.S. reunion tour began not too long after I assumed the position of rights, cataloguing and inventory officer. I would take time off for the odd gig then be back at my desk on Monday morning, happily enjoying the anonymity that regular paid work brings. Walter Mitty never had it so good. My position was still tangentially involved in the entertainment business but from an angle unfamiliar to me. While the title sounds impressive, my task was merely to sort, copy, archive and occasionally shred contracts, agreements and the associated legal minutiae of ABC productions.

A job that should have been mind-numbingly tedious was enlivened by the temptation to research my own history within this fine institution. Thanks to my day job, I ascertained the precise date of my first appearance on the small screen. At the click of a mouse I learned the recording date was 11 November 1988. The program was *Blah Blah Blah*, hosted by Andrew Denton, an early champion and nurturer of Flacco. The program went to air on 7 December 1988, and I received an appearance fee of $131, less tax, less twenty-five per cent management commission. I have little memory of that first crack at small-screen fame. Perhaps I was given the benefit of the doubt, and the jittery nervousness and scatterbomb babble of that slight bald creature caught in the studio lights was mistaken for comedy.

Two of my comedy heroes, H.G. Nelson and Roy Slaven, were also on the bill that night. John 'Roy Slaven' Doyle dropped in to the dressing-room after my spot and congratulated me. I don't believe I said a word to John; I was overwhelmed to receive praise from one of the greats. I am always star-struck when I meet those I most admire. During the filming of *D.A.A.S. Kapital* I lived in a share house in Fitzroy. One morning I wandered out, hungover, to get some milk when I heard someone call my name – not my stage name, my real name. I turned to see a gentleman standing on his front lawn, plastic shopping bags in each hand, and I thought, 'This guy looks a lot like Fred Dagg.' John Clarke then called me over and heaped a generous spoonful of praise on my work. Best hangover cure ever.

The ABC has a long history of nurturing budding Australian talent. I felt I was giving something back by stamping, scanning and archiving contracts for the latest litter of worthy performers, writers and musicians. Either that or I was in a state of denial. Grieving for my former artistic status. Secretly seething with passive rage at these young upstarts, what with their talent, their teeth and their two-year contracts.

My mother may well have been proud of her gainfully employed boy, but thankfully she wasn't there to see me given my marching orders, courtesy of a 'top-down round-table efficiency drive' by those in control of the government purse strings. It seemed only fitting to come full circle on my final day in the office when one of my tasks was scanning and archiving my own agreement for the extension of sales rights for *D.A.A.S. Kapital* (and organising my own royalty payments for the DVD).

I was efficiently driven from my post after almost two years of constant employment. I had worked with fine teams at the ABC in the past, and it was good to know equally fine teams still lurked in hidden corners of that institution. While there was no gold watch or lump-sum redundancy payment, there were handshakes, hugs and homemade cakes and brownies on offer on my last day. I declared I would never abuse or use my work colleagues or their workplace by mocking and demeaning them in the name of comedy. And I aim to stick to that promise. Just as soon as I finish this book.

By the time my regular working life was over, my irregular working life was in full swing. The resurrected corpse of the Doug Anthony All-Stars shuddered into life, but not as the fans knew it. The Larkspur and the Brood Parasite were now joined by the Naked Mole Rat. The Boab was nowhere to be seen, but everywhere to be heard. *Conversations with Richard Fidler* had become one of the nation's most popular radio broadcasts. While Richard had found his feet, I had to fill his shoes.

Rebooting D.A.A.S. after a twenty-year hiatus was never going to be easy. Legends inflate like multiverses as the years pass. In the minds of the fans, the D.A.A.S. legend had distended to the proportions of a bloated blimp driven by high-octane laughing gas. Bathing in past praise is easy. Earning it again is another matter.

The new line-up was in place: Tim Ferguson, Paul McDermott and 'the guitarist'. At first glance, this cast did not readily prompt memories of the vibrant, youthful, sexually deviant, take-no-prisoners brat pack of old. Tim Ferguson, the once-slender Larkspur now confined to a wheelchair; Paul McDermott, twice the man he was in his youth yet no taller; and the guitarist, a senior citizen with all the charisma of a walnut whose best years were behind him even before he began his career. The signs were not good.

I envied Richard Fidler. While the Boab was in full bloom, this naked mole rat of a guitarist needed not only to hold a tune but also to play the fall guy to a relentless barrage of insult and abuse from McDermott, the demonic ringmaster in this little circus. I would be required to kowtow, to slink, to be the patsy, to be the canary in the D.A.A.S. comedy coalmine, while fingering the three major and two minor chords required for the bulk of the D.A.A.S. songbook. A canary in a cage is a perfect metaphor for a performer. The stage is the cage, you do your tricks and are thrown some seeds and then you go shit on a newspaper. Or, if it's a bad review, the newspaper shits on you.

The venue in which we were to reanimate the corpse of D.A.A.S. was the Harold Park Hotel. The pub had been renovated since the glory days of the eighties and nineties, when its Monday night comedy room buzzed with punters and petrified open mic acts. True to its roots, the venue continued in the spirit of its past. Politics in the Pub had returned to the revitalised hotel, and a comedy room, the Laugh Stand, was up and running thanks to comedian, promoter and supporter of all things comedical Dane Hiser, who welcomed this tragic assembly of broken old quipsters with open arms.

In early 2014, tickets for a couple of secret warm-up D.A.A.S. shows at the Laugh Stand sold out in a matter of hours. The Laugh Stand is a compact room and, contrary to what one might perceive, playing to a thousand is far easier than playing to a hundred. In the larger rooms the audience is contained at a safe distance from the performer. They are close enough to see the whites of your eyes, but not quite close enough to see the terror in them. In a smaller venue the performer is inches from the paying public, toe to toe, and well within spitting distance should they turn sour. A bar occupying a third of the space is no mere distraction but a sure sign that many in the audience will have lost a fair few inhibitions before you hit the stage, the stage being no more than a twenty-five-centimetre-high wooden pallet. An attacking breed like D.A.A.S. relishes venues such as this. For a non-performance-fit senior citizen, out of form and lacking confidence, it is a house of horrors.

What passes for a dressing room at the Laugh Stand is a tiny corner of the room fenced off by a black curtain. On 11 June 2014, a larkspur in a wheelchair, a cocky silver fox and a petrified naked mole rat huddled behind that curtain amid stacked chairs and tables. Dane was the least nervous; he appeared to delight in rubbing shoulders and other assorted body parts with the sorry remains of the All-Stars. The audience was pumped, fuelled by memories of their youth and, more disturbingly, memories of *our* youth, something sadly lacking from our act. The premise of the new show was to simply own up. Admit our best days were long behind us. To expose ourselves as the sad, broken wretches we had become. This was not at all beyond our scope; in fact, it was our only scope. But would these hardcore fans swallow it?

Dane walked the few steps onto the stage and held them in his palm until making way for Flacco. I felt like a newborn calf, my legs barely holding beneath me, my topcoat covering shivering knees. Why put myself through this? I could be home in my dressing gown and socks, sucking on a mint and watching re-runs of *F Troop*.

Flacco faced the fray, a close encounter of the umpteenth time, instantly transported to the old days, the birth of my career, small rooms, small crowds, the smell of sweat and alcohol. I could hear the sound they were making . . . was it a cry for blood? Time had warped. It had certainly warped me. I left the stage feeling much the same as when I entered, unprepared and unrequired, thus setting a pattern for the entire tour.

I'd like to say that after Flacco made his exit D.A.A.S. bounded onto the stage. Sadly, the remains of D.A.A.S. were beyond bounding, yet when Paul McDermott wheeled Tim Ferguson onto the stage the audience reaction almost lifted the ceiling of the old pub. Two hours later they rose to their feet as Paul wheeled Tim off the tiny stage. The energy of the audience boosted both men to new heights (and fortunately that same energy took their minds off the hapless guitarist, failing miserably to hold or remember a tune. Richard Fidler I most certainly was not). It would appear the new D.A.A.S. outfit might have legs – or, in the case of Tim Ferguson, flailing arms and a rapier wit. Something was in the air, and it wasn't the scent of the D.A.A.S. wardrobe of old. McDermott was made painfully aware of his new role in this line-up.

I wasn't nervous. I just knew I had to hold it together because I don't think anyone else could. I remember thinking I was on the bow of the ship and I was the only one there, and I just had to keep going. If I didn't get it done it wasn't going to happen. It was like doing a solo show with a couple of tenpins.

Cameron P. Mellor, or 'our George Martin' as McDermott dubbed him, has fond memories of those nights.

We did two nights, absolutely jam-packed to the gills, and a standing ovation on both nights. I thought, 'Yeah, we've actually got something here.'

Janet McLeod was one of the first to witness this new D.A.A.S. line-up.

> The dynamic has shifted: it's not Richard getting picked on – it's Tim. It is not the same act. But it is still wonderful. Paul has had to shift his character. It's actually given him a deeper dimension. He can't just be the angry guy. He's got to take care of Tim while simultaneously picking on him, all the while being confused by the guitarist.

After warming our comedy cockles at the Harold Park Hotel, the first port of call for the Reunion, Rebirth D.A.A.S. tour was the Theatre Royal in Hobart. Built among brothels in the 1830s, it has been trod by some of the world's finest. Noël Coward called it 'a dream of a theatre'; Sir Laurence Olivier advised the locals to never let it go. They have taken Larry's advice and, as Australia's oldest theatre, it was the perfect launch point for some of the oldest gags and gag-tellers in the nation. Even Fred the in-house ghost didn't bother us; I figure old Fred thought he'd be seeing us soon enough anyway.

The Royal is far too classy for the likes of D.A.A.S., who gleefully went about spilling their filthy seed upon its hallowed boards. Enough of an insult to send Fred back to his own grave, just to roll over in it. The audience, however, was rolling in the proverbial isles. The dedication of the D.A.A.S. fans continues to astound me. They adore these men, yet appear to delight in having all that love mocked, disowned and hurled right back in their faces. The D.A.A.S. fans take it all on the chin, or any other part of their anatomy. Tim, Paul and Richard penetrated their psyches at a tender age, and there is a deep sense of thanksgiving underscoring these performances. Perhaps this tour was akin to a D.A.A.S. wake, while the corpse was still warm. Or, in my case, lukewarm.

Post-show, a line of adoring fans waited patiently to meet their heroes, many clearly awed to be in the presence of the Larkspur and the hairy elfin satyr of their dreams. The devotion of their fans is all-encompassing. They come bearing gifts, ancient D.A.A.S. books and merchandise – one couple even presented their three-day-old baby to be signed by the boys. It was little Rex's first-ever theatre experience. The boys declined to anoint the child in Sharpie marker but adored it all the same. On another occasion the boys were requested to sign an urn containing the ashes of a fan who had passed away some months earlier.

I have experienced the awe that overcomes a soul when face to face with an idol. In the nineties, during the taping of Network Ten's *GNW Night Lite*, a stream of top-shelf performers passed through the studio. For me, the most impressive of these was John Astin, a childhood hero and a sublime comic actor who will always be remembered as Gomez Addams from the original *Addams Family* cast. Here he was, amiably chatting to the crew, almost like a 'real' person.

The Sandman and I shared a small cupboard of a dressing-room at Ten's Global Studios; we were the underlings of the *GNW* hierarchy; the two-minute try-hards, the insert guys, minor celebrity in all its unmemorable glory. We could generally be found sitting in the dressing-room facing the mirror, rehearsing our weekly sketch, 'The Gap in the Show', in which we attempted to break the record for how long a performer could remain straight-faced on commercial television without uttering a single word, all the while staring blankly into the camera. Steve Abbott confirms my memory of the day our shared childhood hero dropped by.

> We had hours to wait before we went on, because Paul stuffed up at every taping or Mikey was being indulgent, so we'd often have two or three hours before we were called on. And we were sitting in our little glovebox of a dressing-room when suddenly Johnny Astin came in, pulled up a chair and talked to us for possibly an hour and a half. It was very surreal because as kids we would have run home from school to catch *The Addams Family* on TV and here he was, Gomez Addams.

We sat, starstruck, as John regaled us with anecdotes from his remarkable career, though never in a boastful tone – it was as if this gentleman had mistaken us for equals.

Sandy and I experienced something similar when the Academy Award-winning actor F. Murray Abraham led us into his caravan on the set of Peter Duncan's feature *Children of the Revolution*. Everything was going fine until we were called to set and F. Murray witnessed our sorry attempts at acting in a scene with him. We never saw the interior of that caravan again.

I still have no idea what that F. stands for. Perhaps that's why he spurned us? We kept calling him F. It may not have helped that in a scene which ended up on the cutting room floor, such was the level of my overacting I inadvertently spat in F's face. Sam Neill and Judy Davis were in the same scene. For some reason they stood well clear of me in the remaining scenes we shared. Perhaps they were simply keeping beyond spitting distance of the little bald guy.

John Astin was more welcoming, and all the while he sat in that dressing-room I could not get the thought out of my mind, 'Gomez Addams is talking to *me*.' I presumed it was best not to bring up the Gomez thing; that bizarre creation had probably been a millstone for the man. After all, John was in Australia with his one-man play *Edgar Allan Poe: Once Upon a Midnight*, a serious acting venture, so we steered clear of the 'G' word. Yet without prompting he began offering up tales from *The Addams Family*, of working with Uncle Fester, Thing, Cousin Itt and Lurch. This was, without a doubt, the greatest day of our lives. I later learned from *GNW* producer Ted Robinson that as John had watched The Sandman and Flacco rehearse from the side of the studio earlier in the day, he turned to Ted and whispered, 'These are my kind of people.' Seems we had a fan too.

Following Hobart, D.A.A.S. ransacked Melbourne, Wollongong, Adelaide, Perth, Brisbane and parts in between. In Australia the road is long, the tour vans are adequate, and the tension between the performers is eventually stretched to breaking point. The exception to this rule is Tim Ferguson. Tim was immune to my unnecessary demands, portents of doom and niggling paranoia. They did however raise the bile of Paul McDermott, who struggled to keep his raw anger in check, internalising it until showtime, when this pent-up acerbity was unleashed on fellow performers and fans alike – anything with a face. In light of this, I came to see that my calling was to stoke the fuel for Paul's performance. Where would he be without my constant prima donna petulance? Without my endless jibes, McDermott would have to appear to the fans as his civilian self, a mere middle-aged man nursing a cup of tea, gently thanking the audience for all their care and support over the years, assuring them he could never have made it without them, a tear welling in his left eye (that's the one he uses to emote; the other is perpetually enclosed in a frown). I have made it my mission to be the on-tour bewailer of woe. It's an occupation I take seriously. And it really, really annoys Paul McDermott.

In the space of a dozen performances the D.A.A.S. reunion transformed from 'an evening with' style of presentation into something that almost resembled a comedy show. The D.A.A.S. fans came out of the woodwork, the fibro, the gyprock, the asbestos-ridden insulation, to once again worship at the footlights of the heroes of their youth. There were songs and anecdotes, but the bulk of the show consisted of puerile, scato-logical and repugnant asides and antics. Business as usual for the All-Stars, in other words. After spending the best part of a decade advancing the concept of myself as the gracefully ageing respected elder, a writer of worthy tomes, a mature and cultured gentleman of the arts, it was straight back to piss, fart, wee-wee, poo-poo, laff-a-minute humourland. Perhaps this was fitting for three men groping their way into the murky shallows of their twilight years – some faster than others. Being the most ancient, I should have led the way, and I did my best with kidney stones, slipped discs, a herniated bowel and a memorable but brief bout of leukaemia to my credit. But it was Tim Ferguson out front carrying the baton, wheelchair-bound and trumping his fellow performers on matters of medications and the discomforts of post-manopausal touring.

Paul McDermott was holding up rather well. Although hardly the spider monkey of his youth, this old silverback still had some moves, and unlike some onstage, he could actually remember his lines. Tim had very few moves to choose from, apart from a hyperactive mouth and a brain that wouldn't be stilled. From the confines of a wheelchair, Tim was firing off some of the most piercing and confronting diatribes of comic brimstone ever delivered on any stage, anywhere, anytime. Tim and Paul, the dregs of D.A.A.S., had bitten the bullet (or at least gnawed on it) and embraced those sad shadows of their former selves to wallow and rejoice in deterioration and decline. Fittingly, the remains of Flacco were exhumed and reanimated as the warm-up act for a fire that needed no stoking.

The fourth party in this questionable venture was Cameron P. Mellor. The years had thawed the ice that accompanied our first meeting some twenty-five years earlier in the back seat of a car in London. Our relationship soon slipped into the acquaintance stage as Cameron P. Mellor took on the role of entrepreneur, road manager, stage manager, nurse and van driver for D.A.A.S. 2014.

I think the reason I've been involved is that, magically, what's happened with the reformed group is . . . it's not a victory lap. It has elements of the old Dougs and elements of the old attitudes and approaches, but because of age and disease it's a completely different beast. That to me is the essence of why the new show is so fantastic, because it hardly even rests on laurels anymore. It actually takes what the All-Stars were, uses it as a vehicle and pretty much deconstructs it by the end. Tim's disease is an amazing comic vehicle. It drives this show in an incredibly strange way. The whole show revolves around the fact that Tim has this disease and he's in a wheelchair and he is most probably going to be the first to go. The most rewarding feedback I get from people of like mind who have seen the show is that it's incredibly funny, but it's incredibly moving, and they don't know which way to look. Comedy's got to hurt a little bit, you know; it's just got to hurt. It's a fantastic platform for a comedy show, having a pensioner on one side and a cripple on the other. It's pretty brutal.

Multiple sclerosis is a slow predator, and it proved no match for the Larkspur's new set of wheels during that first year breaking in the new D.A.A.S. incarnation. Ferguson's energy was relentless. Whether he was procuring it via the pharmacist or in the purer form of adrenaline I can't be sure, but night after night that winsome amalgam of protoplasm in a wheelchair seduced, amused, deceived and unnerved every other seated body in the house. The act (if it was one) didn't stop once he'd left the stage. After a marathon two-and-a-half-hour performance, Tim held court in the theatre foyer, taking the time to meet, greet and engage each member of the audience who'd waited patiently in line to shake that quivering hand. Airport staff, taxi drivers, tourist groups in hotel lobbies were all targets for Tim's unrelenting charm.

Tim's humour is often at the expense of his slightly more able-bodied band mates. He flings screwed-up notes to the audience: *Help! They won't feed me! They use me as a sex toy! I don't want to go in the harness!* While being wheeled through airport thoroughfares, Tim yells to startled onlookers, 'But I don't want to get on the plane! I don't want to go back to the institute! Don't let them touch me like that again! I am not an animal! Correction. Technically I am an animal, but that's no reason to neuter me!'

I would keep my distance, walking a few steps behind, but McDermott would often play along. 'Keep it down, freak! You're nothing but a lead weight. If you don't be quiet there'll be no Tim Tams for Tim tonight!' One of the many perks of touring with a guy in a wheelchair, especially a guy in a wheelchair who exudes charm like a newborn koala, is the off-chance of an airline upgrade. The procedure is simple enough: you wheel your anatomically challenged companion to the gate lounge and allow him to plead (and perhaps dribble, just a bit, for effect). Tim has several game plans at the ready should he confront any resistance from airport staff. The Larkspur knows that guilt has the power to thwart any oppressor with her hand on the seating arrangements. If the staff member has legs, and knows how to use them, half the battle is won. It is another story for Tim's patient and loving 'carers' and co-workers. Seething in economy is a common side effect of a Tim Ferguson upgrade. While Tim sips spumante and holds court at the pointy end, Messrs Livingston and McDermott endure the second-best seethe in the house.

Paul McDermott birthed a sure-fire catchphrase early on in the tour. At any hint of an awkward moment he points to Tim and declares, 'He's in a fucking wheelchair, people!' Moment diffused, audience chastised, momentum regained, ice broken, show goes on. Catchphrases are the all-purpose ratchets in the comedian's toolbox. If the mood in the room slips, simply crank it up with a handy catchphrase and they are back. 'I'll rip your bloody arms off!' 'You tell 'em, luv!' 'It's a joke, Joyce!' 'Coupla days, bewwwdiful!' 'More cowbell!' 'Loadsamoney!' 'You stupid man!' All Get Out of Jail cards for the gigging comedian. Tim's new catchphrase is far more menacing. After softening them up with a few sugar-coated left-field jibes, he stares down the audience and then states clearly and quietly a warning to all mortals gathered before him: 'Tick-fucking-tock.'

Paul McDermott is in awe of Tim's fearless positivity.

If I was in a wheelchair I'd just be a little black cornflake of hate. I'd be a nasty piece of work. And I don't think any amount of happy pills would help. But Tim has always had that element of positivity. It was effortless with him. He would have everyone just eating out of his hand, as wonderful and as flimsy and as transparent as a piece of gauze. He was always on, he was always the performer, and to this day I don't know if I know the real Tim at all. He still has that beautiful ability to just find the best in people and situations. Although I rail against it at times, he always sees two sides of every argument and always finds himself in the middle of them, whereas I have very set opinions. Pretty well stuck in concrete. Have an opinion. Stay with it.

Tim derives a special glee from confronting others with his and their own mortality. It's a hard but necessary medicine to swallow in a world of deathly denial. Tim savours those moments.

In terms of what we are doing, the whole MS thing is a gift. Flacco's been bald for a long time. It's nothing new. But this wheelchair is an unsettling sight to keep looking at, and once I've made them laugh a couple of times, it has that emotion under the laughter of being unsettled. Is this fair? Is this even allowable? [In newsreader voice] 'The emotional journey under the laughs . . . It's the surge of the tide under the white froth of the giggle.'

When we were young men [the All-Stars] played on the fear, and it was the fear of us getting physical. But now it's a different kind of fear that we are playing with, it's visceral. It's right on the bone. No-one's going to have to hit anybody. Paul doesn't have to put anybody into his armpit. I don't have to kiss their girlfriend right in front of them and say, 'Oh, sorry, mate, I thought you were a chick,' to the girl.

That fear is the underbelly of this present show. Fear of death, fear of decay, fear of the Little Black Cornflake of Hate. Some friends of a friend of Tim's friend who witnessed a show didn't get the joke. They didn't approve of what McDermott was doing onstage. Tim couldn't quite fathom their gullibility.

> You know the bit where Paul's telling the story about me shitting in the spa? And I'm leaning off mic, feeling awkward? They fell for it. They believed this was a surprise to me. I was talking about it with Dermo this morning and he said, 'That's where we want this to be!' And I thought, 'Fuck, yeah! There's been fun and games and now Tim is acting a little bit like: "I didn't want this to happen, it's too much. This is embarrassing! I shat in a spa!"' With the jets on? I mean, come on! But they swallowed it.

Offstage, Mr Ferguson gets on with life. He tours, he teaches, he talks . . . he talks a lot – but rarely of his 'predicament'. Yet onstage predicaments become playthings. Multiple sclerosis is mocked, ridiculed, held to account and flaunted before the public. A casting-out of demons, but this is no pointless exorcise; D.A.A.S. have been raging at the dying of the light since they were performing pupae. Tim's alter ego Wayne Kerr declaimed on *D.A.A.S. Kapital*: 'Sex is my adventure.' These days the D.A.A.S. cry is: 'Death is my adventure.' These guys are pillorying the dying of the light.

For the best part of a decade Tim hid his condition. Now he was exposing MS in all its gory, much to the discomfort and occasional delight of the audience. MS was no laughing matter. That's what was so funny about it. Drugs had fuelled more than the occasional D.A.A.S. show in the early years, but no one would have imagined the amount of prescription drugs needed to keep this present incarnation of D.A.A.S. inhaling and exhaling. Tim had the most comprehensive stash, I had a decent crop, while McDermott survived on nothing more than a Berocca drip. These medications were not in any way performance-enhancing; they were a performance necessity. Tales of ailments minor and major were comedy grist for the new D.A.A.S. show's mill. We were all falling apart, but none was prepared to go quietly.

EVERYTHING OLD IS NEW AGAIN . . . SORT OF

The most painful state of being is
remembering the future, particularly
the one you'll never have.

SØREN KIERKEGAARD

My mid-life brush with leukaemia ten years ealier was far
more enjoyable in retrospect than it was at the time. It can be
difficult to raise a smile while staring into the Grim Reaper's
sockets. It was fairly obvious by my blood test results that
something was up as my blood count was so low. I'd also been
fascinated by tiny bruises erupting on my arms and legs. I recall
staring at my knee one day, as you do, when a tiny burst of
purple spread across my kneecap without prompting. I pressed
it and there was no pain. I remained merely fascinated. I even
joked about it to my GP. She was not amused.

A short time later, at the tender age of forty-seven, I received a verbal diagnosis from one of Australia's leading haematology specialists.

MOLE RAT: What's the prognosis, Doc?
DOCTOR: *(undecipherable terminology delivered with a straight face)*
MOLE RAT: *(quizzical look)*
DOCTOR: A form of leukaemia.
MOLE RAT: *(long silence)*
DOCTOR: *(long silence)*
MOLE RAT: So what do . . .? What happens? Who? When? Why? How?
DOCTOR: In this case, most treatments are ineffective.
MOLE RAT: So . . . any idea of . . .? What's the usual . . .?
DOCTOR: Six to eighteen months.

A biopsy would be required to confirm the diagnosis and stamp my near-death certificate. A 'needle' the size of a bicycle pump that might appear more at home in a Warner Brothers cartoon was procured to draw a sample of bone marrow from the small of my back. Not being a large gent, my small was somewhat smaller than most. I was handed a gas mask and told to 'suck when necessary'. After some degree of effort, marrow and blood were prised from my small. I let the mask fall, sweating and spent. My medical assailant studied the marrow under a microscope, frowned, and then informed me that he would have to go in again. Same hole. I grabbed that gas mask and no doubt would have sucked the chrome off a tow bar given the chance. He was not at liberty to inform me of what he'd uncovered, but he did ask if I might sign a form giving him permission to show the results to his students. Obviously the spoils of my small were a big deal in medical circles.

For reasons unknown to me, it took a full week before the results were made available, a week in which I attempted to come to terms with the fact that my months were no doubt numbered. I had lost my mother to cancer only weeks before my diagnosis. Over two years I watched the demon do its worst. I knew the territory. I felt oddly calm. As if I were swimming in an aquarium full of molasses. It was later revealed that I was suffering from clinical depression – in this instance something of a friend rather than foe. It muted the terror. I was going to die. Nothing unusual there. This is what happens to people you love. And one thing was certain: I loved none more than myself.

My biopsy result was delivered via telephone. It was good news and bad news. The bad news? I had leukaemia. The good news? It wasn't about to destroy me anytime soon. My particular strand affected less than two per cent of sufferers worldwide. I had contracted one of the rarest forms, and these days hairy cell leukaemia is known to be particularly responsive to treatment. A week-long intensive course of chemotherapy was all that was required. The specialist had treated only two other cases in his long career. One of his patients was still alive and well after fifteen years. He didn't mention the other patient. I didn't push it.

I immediately did what most people do in such a situation. I went home and consulted Dr Google. I typed 'hairy cell leukaemia' into the search engine, and the initial result was a site called Hairy Women Naked. It didn't exactly cure me but it took my mind off the situation for a short while. As far as I could ascertain, those select two per cent lucky enough to be diagnosed with HCL appeared to be doing okay. There were horror stories – hairy cell left unchecked can wreak havoc – but my cancerous horse was yet to bolt. I'd been diagnosed sufficiently early that a swift shot of chemo should be enough to keep the hairy beast at bay for five years, whereupon the process is repeated. The only catch is the repeat treatments diminish in results each time. At the time of writing, a dozen years have passed since that initial invasion of my small. There has been no return.

On 2 June 2003, I began my introductory course of chemo-therapy at St Vincent's Hospital in Sydney. As I walked towards St Vincent's that morning, my hairy cells stood on end when I noticed paparazzi hovering around the entrance. I didn't expect this. Obviously word was out that a certain minor celebrity who'd been off the small screen for years was about to face his Battle with Cancer. I moved through the throng of reporters and news teams without attracting a second glance. I later gleaned that the rumour mill was alive with reports that Delta Goodrem was undergoing tests for what would later be diagnosed as Hodgkin's lymphoma.

I had no idea what to expect of the chemo ward. Visions of Frankenstein's laboratory haunted me as I sat waiting among a gaggle of disturbingly silent humans. I had the feeling I was sitting in a departure lounge, but no-one was too keen on the destination. My trepidation was quelled once I'd checked in. The atmosphere was warm and relaxed, my fellow chemo club members lounged around in what appeared to be business-class barber's chairs, drips and tubes hanging from various limbs as they perused magazines or chatted calmly to each other. These people all appeared strangely familiar to me. It had something to do with the hairstyle. Hairlessness is a great leveller. In this exclusive club, it was polite to acknowledge one another no matter what your status on the outside; high-flyers and the homeless mingled amiably. An uncommon courtesy was the norm.

While I didn't cross wards with Delta, I did become aware of another whom the paparazzi were poised to harass that morning. As I settled into my cosy chemo recliner I noticed Belinda Emmett seated across from me. Belinda was no chemo-club neophyte, having been diagnosed with breast cancer in 1998. I had never met Belinda, but I had worked with her partner, Rove McManus. Yet I kept my distance; I felt it was polite to leave ill celebrities be. It is enough to have the vultures of the press hovering outside without a pale, bald, sickly gent saying, 'Hi there, I know your boyfriend.' It just didn't seem appropriate. In retrospect it would have been perfectly appropriate.

On day four the effects of the treatment began to seep in and a thin cloud of fatigue and ennui descended on my psyche as I passively received my next five-hour fix of Cladribine via a cannula inserted into a vein on my right hand. Words appeared to swirl before me on the page of a book I had been reading,

Life Everywhere by David Darling, a study of the possibility of life in other corners of the universe. I had begun reading it as I sat by my dying mother's side just across the road at the Sacred Heart Palliative Care Centre only weeks before. The irony of the title did not strike me until a palliative nurse asked me what I was reading. '*Life Everywhere*,' I said, simultaneously realising I was surrounded by the nearly departed.

Joining in the conversation and camaraderie in the chemo ward came surprisingly easy to me. I met many in only a few days. The common complaint was the way friends and family had come to perceive them since their diagnosis. Cancer strikes fear into the well. It is as if one had suddenly morphed into another species, doomed in the eyes of those unmutated-celled creatures. Their fear of death seemed greater than ours. For the uninitiated, the whole chemotherapy process is forebidding. For those in the chemo club, there is the promise of hope. That's why we were there. It is a place where the possibility of healing can prevail. I exist to this day purely because of the marvels of medical science. I fucking love chemo. Bring it on.

I say that now, but after reading my diary notes from the days following my final dose I'm not so eager for any return bouts.

SATURDAY, 7 JUNE 2003: First day out of chemo – Body aches – Bloating - Muscle pain - Diarrhoea.

SUNDAY, 8 JUNE 2003: Much the same. I read point eight on the Cladribine factsheet. 'This drug may cause infertility.

The desire for sex may decrease during treatment.' Chemo is definitely not a turn-on.

MONDAY, 9 JUNE 2003: Absolute shocker – Never felt worse – Pressure on chest – Pain in everything – Fatigue – Sore eyes – Breathing, sinus no good.

TUESDAY, 10 JUNE 2003: Dehydration - Reluctance to piss - Headache - Dry mouth on waking.

WEDNESDAY, 11 JUNE 2003: More of the same. Groggy.

THURSDAY, 12 JUNE 2003: Severe sternum pain - Painkillers not working – Shivering with pain.

FRIDAY, 13 JUNE 2003: Possibly the worst day of my life? Called hospital at 1.30 am. Fever and unbearable chest pain. Advised to come in immediately (caught taxi) – After tests, blood, urine, X-rays, levels were dangerously low. 4 am. Antibiotic drip. Morphine for the chest pain. 4 pm. Problem solved. I'd been instructed to inject myself in stomach daily to promote cell growth. Overdid it apparently. Checked out on my own insistence.

SATURDAY, 14 JUNE 2003: Pain gone. Depression appears.

Then over the next five weeks.

Fever, sweat, delirious, stomach gurgling, body rebelling, pains in lower back, lower stomach, rashes everywhere, gums swollen, styes in eyes – Went to dentist. My tooth was in fine shape.

I have no memory of any of this.

Thanks to hairy cell leukaemia I'd had a very small taste of what it is like on that other side; I had earned my cancer patient L-plates, and been given a brush with mortality that would come in handy a decade later treading the boards with the resurrected corpse of D.A.A.S. The plague had left me. I passed my short course of chemo with my colours flying. This would be the first and only course of any kind I had ever successfully completed. My mum would have been so proud.

The lovely Belinda Emmett held on for a few more years. For the moment, Delta and I are still standing. I had 'survived' my 'battle' to live not only another day but another four thousand, seven hundred and forty-five and counting.

Within a few months my body bounced back, but my psyche had taken a dive. I was diagnosed with clinical depression. The effect of antidepressant medications on my mood was striking and immediate, as those closest to me at that time would attest. Almost instantly my selective mute button switched to off. I felt uncommonly confident. I could not stop talking. Loved a chat. High on myself, I determined to rebuild my career, this time on my own terms. I made my own phone calls, I pitched ideas, I even agreed to a spot on a panel show, *The Glasshouse*, where I managed to get a laugh with no props, no make-up and no script. This was a first (and, it would turn out, a last). I had metamorphosed into a short, bald, toothless Tony Robbins. As Tony says, 'There's always a way – if you're committed.' I found out later that some of my friends were keen to have me committed. In the space of a few months I had gone from pitied cancer patient to loud-mouthed, drug-fuelled pain in the arse.

I remember holding court in the back seat of a rental car when our driver, Steve Abbott, my closest friend and co-worker for over a decade, addressed me curtly, employing a command that had never been aimed at my person in living history. Steve turned, glared at me and said, 'Shut up.' I'm told the command had no effect.

> You started making decisions that were totally out of character. Things that you would never do normally. We were up in the Hunter Valley on holiday. And for that whole trip you were in the back seat and you just wouldn't shut up. And normally you'd say nothing. I remember turning around and saying, 'You've just got to get off those pills because we can't be friends anymore.' I'm thinking, 'It's a different guy. I don't know this guy. And he's irritating.' You just kept babbling. Not only were you talking, other people were talking and you were still going. Who was this guy? Normally it's like if you actually have a verb in a sentence it's something to celebrate.

Due to the sudden appearance of outstanding wellbeing, I was weaned off the antidepressants and my anxiety instantly returned; I selected the mute button again and regressed to my former self. But thanks to the manic efforts of 'Hyper-Paul', I was stuck with a full calendar of events: public-speaking commitments, anti-cancer rallies in public malls, weddings, parties, almost everything. Yet while I'd revelled in the organisational aspects of my career, I had ceased any form of solitary, creative activity. My detour into extroversion proved that the condition is akin to what The Sandman calls the Hummingbird Effect: a lot of arm-flapping but absolutely no forward movement. Steve Abbott eventually forgave me for being overly conversant in his automobile, and before long The Sandman and Flacco were a professional item again.

The goodwill of the audiences and their warm welcome was uplifting, but age was wearying me, and the thrill was going. Steve had the same idea, and The Sandman delivered his official retirement season, Exit Sandman, at the 2011 Melbourne Comedy Festival. For his final efforts he received a one-star review. Perhaps a fitting end for The Sandman, who semi-famously said, 'I have a fear of success, failure and rejection, so no matter what people think of me I'm never happy.' The idea of being on the road with only myself for company was not an option. Hotel rooms become post-show penitentiaries. It's not loneliness, it's the disparity that fazes. You may have been the hero of the night, yet the reward is a minibar, free shampoo and conditioner, and tepid toasted sandwiches at 2 am.

I was made aware of a post by a Perth blogger, YeLPar, an ex-taxi driver recalling his days picking up the odd minor celebrity. Including The Sandman and Flacco.

They were two pretty funny comics back in the day . . . They were doing a gig at the Regal Theatre in Subiaco when they jumped in my cab post-show one night. Gotta admit I got pumped at the thought of belly laughs all the way home . . . er, not. They didn't sound anything like The Sandman or Flacco – what the? What's with the normal voices and why are you discussing missing your timings in the second act and what do you mean you're getting room service and hitting the sack as soon as I drop you off at the hotel? You're stars and Perth is your oyster!!! Everyone's just the same in reality, aren't they? Just two schmucks doin' a job, like you and me.

Loneliness on the road is the last thing I need worry about touring with the revamped D.A.A.S. This time around it's a full van and straight back to the hotel after the performance, with Mr McDermott complaining that there are not enough English Breakfast sachets and too many Earl Grey in his complimentary minibar selection. Further to this, the offending sachets are not the paper ones to which he is accustomed but some kind of vinyl affair. A tour can begin with no ill feelings and perhaps even a touch of enthusiasm. This usually wanes somewhat about four hours into the drive to some godforsaken town in the backwaters of this wide brown land.

What was once a charming quirk in a comrade becomes cause for a crime of passion. A simple example: a brief stop at a roadhouse. After ordering his beloved English Breakfast tea, the All-Star in question insists on requesting further pots of boiling water on the side in order to extend the life of the single teabag supplied. Mr McDermott does not respond kindly to lukewarm; the water must be boiling, and in a separate pot.

One of these days that pot of boiling water will be upended on McDermott, either by my own hand or the hand of a hapless young backpacker on ten dollars an hour, driven to boiling point by a Little Black Cornflake of Hate who shows no respect for the serving classes. Small wonder Cameron P. Mellor dubbed him The Diplomat. But then, of course, what happens on tour makes its way into books like this . . . eventually.

Books like this were not the kind I had in mind when I decided to dedicate myself full time to writing. Courting respect after a life playing the fool was never going to be easy, and now I feel fatally compromised after being thrust back into the life of the low comic, serving up generous portions of poo, pus and perversion courtesy of my association with two-thirds of the Doug Anthony All-Stars.

At first I vowed to be on my best behaviour, not to rock the boat, to hide my pent-up resentment at ending my career precisely where I'd started it. To assist in this endeavour, I signed up for six weeks of blissfully silent mindful meditation. The ancient art of mindfulness has become the *dernier cri* of the average upper-middle-class westerner. Mindfulness is particularly attractive to those types who employ terms like '*dernier cri*' to impress others, even though they themselves have little idea what the term means.

My mission was to become a beacon of self-centred equanimity. Mindfulness works a treat in the midst of sprawling mountain retreats. It is a breeze to be at one with nature and the universe when nature and the visible universe have been pruned and tamed in order to attract wealthy clients who wish to loosen their minds and find eternal peace while not being dead. The problems begin once your mind full of mindfulness returns to the everyday task of actually making a living in this none-of-your-busy-ness culture. Maintaining one's hard-earned imperturbable air while in the confines of a tour van is no easy feat. Counting each breath while inwardly fuming is problematic. Fume wasn't dealt with on the retreat. No amount of diluted eastern spiritual practice can cut it on the road. Yet Tim Ferguson somehow maintains a curious air of bliss, twenty-four hours a day. It could well be the drugs coursing through the insulating covers of his nerve cells, or it could be the inherent nature of a man who learned the rewards of outward charm and a hail-fellow-well-met demeanour at an early age. As any D.A.A.S. fan will attest, Tim is, quite simply, still gorgeous.

But for this hairless, sleep-deprived, ageing recluse, charm has never been the *dernier cri*. These days I'm merely a domesticated senior citizen, invisible to most, a background blur of a human ensconced in well-earned obscurity and infused with inner fume issues. Generally the saw-toothed graph of my mood swings is hidden beneath a silent exterior. Enigmatic, as Tim has tactfully dubbed me. I launched into adulthood under a cloak of uncertain shyness. I eventually overcame my lack of self-esteem and overthrew this bashful, reticent self only to reveal an innately quiet being, yet passively very aggressive and burdened by a hunger for isolation in a world of mindless chatter and social bling. No-one noticed the switch. You do have to watch the quiet ones. What else are you going to do?

You can't listen to them. Needless to say I don't enjoy being in the thick of it. I crave the thin of it.

Cameron P. Mellor was not backwards in coming forwards regarding his observations of the qualities of the new D.A.A.S. line-up.

Personality-wise you are effectively dealing with old and sick men, who really genuinely – well, two-thirds of them – would rather be doing something else. I hear that, and I see it on a daily basis. I mean, in McDermott's life there's a lot to do. He's got to walk the dog. The dog has to be walked. Livingston's got his apartment, and he's got to shut the blinds and barricade the door. I mean, going outside for him is very challenging. Of course, the only one in the group who ever shows any semblance of enthusiasm about performing is the guy in the wheelchair, but of course he's the guy who has also directed a feature film and is writing another one and teaches comedy; Tim, as we know, is a machine.

And the complaining . . . Once I get the two Pauls out of their flats and to a venue, either by plane or by van, then it's this waterfall of whingeing. Basically nothing is right. It's either something to do with the sound or the fact that there aren't enough water bottles on stage or there are no pots of tea available. All this leads up to this sort of zone where the pain of this process ends and the enjoyment starts, and it's around about ten minutes before we go up. Flacco goes into a kind of stealth mode, and McDermott's had about nine shits, he's done the set list and of course the guy in the wheelchair's just sitting there happily drawing pictures.

As far as Paul McDermott is concerned, Cameron P. Mellor is the perfect fit.

Cameron is just this effortless, wondrous glue between all of us. I don't think there's been anyone who's done the road managing and the touring of any group in the world who has ever suffered as much as this man. I mean, we serve up a pretty merciless onslaught of barbs. He's a bit of Teflon. He doesn't seem to notice . . . I've sat on jokes for days, full knowing that when I unleash them for optimum cruelty, waiting for the moment, it's viperish – it's like the cobra. And he wears that well. I know some people who might fall apart under that onslaught. And these are blows that graze bones. They go pretty deep. Tears are good. I love tears. I haven't seen any yet but I'm sure he cries alone. But we would not be doing it if not for Cameron; he's become that essential fourth leg of the table.

To his credit, C.P. Mellor endures the idiosyncrasies of the D.A.A.S. ensemble with all the fortitude of a Trappist monk, albeit a somewhat peeved little mendicant. As far as the performers' inner peace is concerned, mindful compassion is unrequired for onstage D.A.A.S. duties. Unleashing unwholesomeness at full throttle is de rigueur in a *dernier cri* kind of way. Live performance is the ultimate in-the-moment experience, no need for saffron robes and incense. For the solo stand-up comedian, there is nothing else but the moment. There are very few other moments in life that demand such singular attention.

Although, there is always masturbation. Why is there no mention of this on mindfulness retreats? There is plenty of talk of quieting the monkey mind, but when it comes to spanking that monkey, the lips are zipped. Surely it's the perfect Zen practice? It's not often your mind wanders during the five-knuckle shuffle. It's rare to nod off when you're auditioning the hand puppet. Yet if performing stand-up is truly all in the moment, then whence comes the promised enlightenment? The awakening? The attainment of nirvana? At the very least, when you are in the throes of Garfunkeling your Simon there's usually a happy ending. But let's just keep our hands on the wheel and our minds on the road for now, shall we?

Like hotel rooms, all dressing-rooms look pretty much the same. The term 'dressing-room humour' does not apply in my case. I take all my fears, loathings and inadequacies into that room. McDermott and Ferguson eschew dressing-rooms in favour of the green room, where the pair feast on snacks and dare to engage in dressing-room humour outside the dressing-room (I've even heard them whistling, and quoting *Macbeth*). I am a card-carrying sceptic, yet I cannot shake my theatrical superstitions. I must always paste a small image of the legendary Danish comedian Victor Borge on my dressing-room mirror. I can't imagine performing without my pre-show ritual thanksgiving to Victor, my comedy demigod. I saw the Master perform live not long before his death. He was in his late eighties and I expected little; I was ready to forgive him for being feeble, forgetting lines or wetting himself mid-quip. But there was no need to practise pity – Victor held an audience of thousands in the concert hall of the Sydney Opera House for over two hours. The laughter wasn't patronising, nor was it mere tittering; there were full-blown guffaws out there, even the odd chortle. It was the audience who were in danger of pissing themselves.

Victor's ability to seduce with words and a very fine Italian suit impressed me. This Danish gentleman oozed class, style and flair, and he was utterly hilarious. I wanted to be Victor. I immediately had a Savile Row frockcoat made for Flacco. Incidentally, being comedy royalty did not protect Victor from criticism. One local reviewer accused the octogenarian of resorting to old material, and noted a joke that this reviewer had heard before somewhere. It didn't seem to matter that it was Victor who actually wrote the joke some thirty years before the reviewer was born. It's like complaining that the Rolling Stones performed 'Jumpin' Jack Flash'. (The joke, by the way, went something like this: What did the Mexican fireman name his twin sons? Answer – José and Hose B.)

Victor Borge's gentle coaxing is in complete contrast to the D.A.A.S. approach. The D.A.A.S. audience don't part with their money for a mere witty massage. They want to be comedically abused, harassed and violated, over and over and over again.

Ferguson softens them up, tapping their brains with feathery verse before nailing them to their seats with no-holds-barred reminders of their mortality. McDermott wastes no time; the jesting gloves are off. He is a comedy cage fighter. Before you know it, you are pinned to the ground under a barrage of bilious bile – and for some perverted reason, it feels good. Post-millennial D.A.A.S. are not out to impress; finely honed insights into the human condition have never been their forte. Raining insults, accusations and political incorrectness onto their audience remains their first line of attack. These men don't need dressing-rooms. They don't dress up. They are in the dressing-down business.

The ubiquitous tiny speaker in a top corner of the dressing-room feeds thin live sound from the auditorium, the chatter of that most feared and unpredictable of species, the audience, as they settle in above the bunker. Tim Ferguson and Paul McDermott appear free of the harrowing anxiety that besets most performers. Backstage the pair lounge about, ingratiating themselves by showing the utmost courtesy to the staff and crew, soaking up both compliments and the complimentary alcohol. Victor and I don't need to witness this spectacle; my dressing-room door remains closed, or slammed self-righteously shut. Let me make one thing clear: this is not self-serving on my behalf – I'm only thinking of my fellow players. Why should they endure the habits of a professional thespian? The stretching, the vocal warm-ups, the meditation and the endless running of lines in order not to let the audience or my fellow performers down. It's not about me. It's never about me. And that's what really gives me the shits.

Inevitably the call comes: 'Five minutes, Mr Livingston.' Then it's dead man walking. The only sound until you hit the stage are your own footfalls on the boards. It's even worse if that's the only sound you hear when you walk off.

Apart from the odd bout of selective mutism, I'm also over-sensitive to noise. There are two sounds in particular that I cannot bear: birdsong, with all its treble scrapings, and human laughter, a high-registered squawk that is like fingernails to the blackboard of my psyche. The late Scottish comedic icon Ivor Cutler shared this disgust, and if an audience dared laugh – or, worse, clap their hands – Ivor would gently place his fingers in his ears until the sound abated, then he'd thank the audience before moving on to yet another hilarious ode that would have those fingers stopping his ears once more. The Sandman used to pre-empt my fear of praise by instructing the audience not to clap or Flacco might take flight and hide in the ceiling of the venue.

Stand-up comedy is a slippery eel of a beast. You never know if the comedy gods will make an appearance or if your demons will win out and you find yourself laughing on the other side of your faith. For the comedian, it's constantly a case of death and resurrection. The only change these days is the speed of the cycle of rebirth and death. In this twenty-first century, the public eye and the private eye have merged into a bizarre cross-eyed organ. What happens on tour happens on Facebook. This phenomenon has seen many comedians playing it safe, domesticating their material, stepping on no toes, rocking no boats and generally vetoing their voices.

This new world order has rendered professional reviewers obsolete. Thanks to the mobile phone, reviews positive or negative silently leave the venue even before the end of the performance. It is possible to come offstage after giving your all (or in my case giving my somewhat) to discover your best material has already made it from crowd to cloud. Or a tentative tryout sketch that died a terrible death has been jettisoned into the webisphere for all eternity. In the nineteenth century vaudevillian performers were able to eke out a living with a single routine for their entire career. Now a performance that may have taken months of painstaking preparation is often uploaded, with unsteady vision, lousy sound and audience commentary upstaging the performer. It's like one huge virtual heckle. Audiences seem more intent on capturing the moment than experiencing the moment.

I prefer to keep the house lights down so that the audience is completely wiped from my field of vision. When I walk on stage all I see is a void. If in fact a void could be defined as see-able. I can hear the void when it is pleased, and I try my best to please the void, but the idea of making eye contact does not generally put me at ease. On a good night their collective mouths hang agape, teeth showing and screeching with glee. The cheerful hairless primate is not a pretty sight en masse. These days a sea of faces illuminated by iPhones, iPads and iDon'tgiveashits documenting the whole sorry enterprise penetrates my beloved void. It's like Carols by Candlelight except

these candles can be lethal. It only takes one slip of the tongue
and one audience member's deft opposable thumb to make or
break a career. Small wonder performers are treading the boards
more carefully. Stand-up comedy is not for the squeamish, but
then again, in the safety of the motel room after a lousy gig,
no-one can hear you squeam.

MOVEMENT IV

Presto (in quick tempo)

THE PLAYERS

PAUL McDERMOTT: Silver fox.

TIM FERGUSON: On a roll.

RICHARD FIDLER: Last seen in Iceland.

PAUL LIVINGSTON: Still the guitarist.

CAMERON P. MELLOR: Crestfallen.

SAMANTHA KELLY: Engaged.

MINOR PLAYERS: Fans, friends of fans, sons and daughters of fans.

LOCATION

The road.

TIME

Is running out.

ALL IN THE FULLNESS OF TIM

[We are] medicine men putting a smile
on the face of the public, helping
them to forget about their woes and
helping them see from the heart.

JIMMY LITTLE, *VOGUE*, FEBRUARY 2000

Who would have thought that the medicine men comprising
the latest incarnation of the All-Stars would require so much
medication to keep delivering their snake oil? Come 2015,
the rebirthed D.A.A.S. were primed for an event they hoped
would cap off another triumphant year. Edinburgh was calling.
Rumour had reached Scotland that the boys were back and
performances were soon locked in. The stages were set,
posters were released, accommodation secured. Until tragedy
struck. Through some miracle of funding, Tim Ferguson was
given the green light to direct a feature film, a film that had
been a decade in the writing and the pitching. The date of

principal photography was set. It was the day we were to open in Edinburgh.

What were we to do? Especially when Timmy looks up at you with those doe eyes. And of course, he's in a fucking wheelchair. As Gore Vidal once said, 'Whenever a friend succeeds, a little something in me dies.' What are friends for? Through gritted teeth (or in my case gritted tooth) and fake smiles we almost convincingly wished our comrade well. Edinburgh would have to wait. Professionally, life was getting better and better for Tim, but for the two ugly sisters it just got bitter and bitter.

I have witnessed the physical and mental ruination that feature-film directing can inflict on a once robust hominoid, men and women crushed by this daunting enterprise, hopes dashed, sickly and spent, awash in a sea of self-loathing and alcohol. With spirits broken they disappear into the long dark corridor of post-production. Tim Ferguson is, to say the least, the exception to this rule. Tim returned to D.A.A.S. base camp after summiting this personal Everest with all the deportment of a man who had just spent two months in a rural health spa resort. As Mr Ferguson advises his audience, 'MS, get on it!' I have little idea what the inside of Tim Ferguson feels like. We don't talk about it, yet there is no MS elephant in the room. Tim deals with it, we deal with it, it's no big deal to deal with it.

The one annoying aspect for me is the inability to indulge in any of my infamous on-the-road gripes about my own meagre, yet significant-in-my-own-eyes, human frailties. 'Look sick for personal gain' was one of The Sandman's signature lines. While on tour, Sandy once dubbed me the Master of Minor Ailments.

You had a few bad years there where you were the canary of the comedy world. Basically if there was any virus, any illness or influenza going around the dressing-rooms, you'd drop off the perch and the rest of us would run because we knew there was a virus coming.

I was proud of that title. But touring with D.A.A.S., no matter how hard I try, no matter how many viruses I play host to, I can never win. Ferguson beats me hands down. And the fact that he refuses point blank to complain or make demands is frankly frustrating. Nothing seems to halt the man's progress, snail's pace though it might be. If directing a feature film won't stop him, I may never be able to complain of my complaints again.

To garner a hint of what might be going on in Timothy's inner recesses I have studied what others have said about living with multiple sclerosis. Here's a short sample from one anonymous sufferer:

Take an ice pick and jam it into your ear or cheek whenever the wind blows on it, or a stray hair touches it. If you want something easier to do, get someone to punch you in the jaw, preferably daily. Glue or sew small steel wool pads to the inside of your shirt, pants and undergarments and wear them for an entire day. Hook bungee cords to your rear belt loops and rear pant leg cuffs, then for your arms hook bungee cords to your shirt collar and cuffs on shirt sleeves, then go dancing.

Or this:

> Look at MS as a bonk-buddy who gets emotional. Just
> when you think they've gone, they're back, messing up the
> kitchen, smashing the crockery. Then they are gone again.
> But just when you relax and think all is well, they return
> with a vengeance, making all sorts of wild declarations
> about who bought that CD and whether sharing a bubble
> bath was a clear sign this was a real relationship and who
> owns those underpants . . .

Who writes this stuff? People like Tim. Or, in the case of the
second example, Tim Ferguson himself.

I did my best to keep my crown: I tried influenza, fibromy-
algia, sigmoid diverticular disease, chronic sinusitis . . . I even
slipped a disc in my neck, the C6/C7. No sympathy. I have
suffered glaucoma, a malady an eye specialist once assured me,
just quietly, could best be controlled by smoking marijuana.
I also drop various pills for high cholesterol, and a doctor assured
me, just quietly, that a good treatment for high cholesterol is a
few glasses of red wine a day. I came down with all the symptoms of prostate cancer, a camera was inserted into my penis
and the hospital staff surrounding me laughingly threatened to
release the video to the world. I was not amused. The wash-up
here was that a proctologist diagnosed a case of LOI – lack of
intercourse – and he assured me, just quietly, that I needed to
go out and mate with something. To sum up, in the space of
a month I was advised, just quietly, that to attain full health
all I needed was a healthy dose of sex, drugs and alcohol. I did
my best. I suppose two out of three isn't bad. I'll let you guess.

Injury has haunted my career. I was once knocked sense-less in a stunt mishap. I was playing the role of a hot-headed chef in *Babe: Pig in the City*. In the slapstick finale I had elected, unwisely as it turned out, to do my own stunts. The ill-fated scene required the hot-headed chef to stand quite still with the star of the film – a delightfully appealing piglet – cradled in my arms, as a stunt person on a hydraulic cable flew past my face, lifted the chef hat neatly off my head, and flew off out of shot. Perhaps I had chosen the wrong-sized hat, as all I can remember is the call of 'action', then suddenly time stood still, or at least moved very slowly. The stunt person collected not only my hat but also the top portion of my hot head. I felt a strange but comforting warmth running down my face. Some distance away the director, Dr George Miller, called 'Cut!'. And quite a cut it was. Worthy of eight stitches above my right eye. I don't remember much about the incident apart from tales of being wheeled into emergency wearing a chef's outfit covered in blood. Needless to say, I was not required for any more stunts on the shoot.

In the award-winning New Zealand film *The Navigator* I caught fire twice, was dropped from a helicopter only to disappear under four feet of snow, dangled from a rope over a forty-metre cliff and trampled by a Clydesdale horse – not to mention having pig shit rubbed over my face and body by a kindly make-up artist who had some powdered swine poo left over from *Mad Max*. Film acting is a sure way to be relieved of any self-esteem.

Another life-threatening role was that of a humble postman in Yahoo Serious's second film, *Reckless Kelly*. I accepted the role imagining that I'd be spending two days on the north coast of New South Wales in moderately well-paid luxury. It was late afternoon when I arrived at the production office. I was introduced to a stunt coordinator who had been given forty-five minutes to teach me to ride a motorcycle. This was news to me.

'Have you ridden one of these before, mate?'

'Not as such, no.'

'Never mind, it's as easy as riding a pushbike.'

'I can't ride a pushbike.'

'Well, just pretend you're driving your car with all the doors open, ha ha.'

'I can't drive a car.'

He stopped laughing. Any activity requiring steering with a force faster than walking pace was beyond me, yet less than an hour later I was tracing a passable arc around a football oval on my postal scooter. The shot would require no more than that.

Shooting began at sunrise on Friday, 13 December 1991, at Tomaree Head near Shoal Bay. The set was not a football oval. The first assistant director walked me to my vehicle. It was also unrecognisable. The scooter had spent the night in the art department and gained six feet in height and just as much in width in assorted postage and parcels. No need to panic; I was advised they were all empty boxes. I climbed aboard. Yahoo decided to shoot the rehearsal. I couldn't see the director from where I was parked. I couldn't see the set I was supposed to drive into. I was on a dirt track, a cliff to one side and a sheer drop to the ocean on the other. Another reason I couldn't see was due to a pair of thick goggles the character was to wear. And to top it off, someone then sprayed layers of red dust over the entire ensemble.

I heard the director call 'Action!' through the assistant director's two-way radio. 'Roll film. Sound. Action Postman.' I revved the engine. The last words I heard as I sped off were Yahoo's instructions crackling through the two-way. 'Release the animals . . .' At the end of the dirt track I kept my eyes on the horizon and began my right turn up a sandy rise into shot. Six large kangaroos bounded towards me. I struggled to control the bike on the loose sand and make it onto flat land, all the while negotiating two emus, a wombat, assorted ducks and minor mammals before stopping the bike, dismounting and delivering my line, 'Letter for Mr Kelly?' Cut.

Yahoo was happy with the take. Except he'd like my final mark to be a few inches forward of where I had come to a halt. I was proud of myself for surviving, and I headed back to my number-one position feeling a tad cocky. I waited for the call of 'Action!'. I sped forward, knocking the odd roo into the briny. I accelerated into the turn and was faced with an indignant emu running determinedly towards me. This bird was not going to back down. I froze in panic. Unfortunately, when you freeze in panic on loose sand on a motorcycle, you tend to heave back on the handle – the handle in this case being the accelerator. I rode straight out of shot, took out the lighting rig, ran over the animal wrangler and came to rest among several cages of exotic birdlife. Once the dust settled, I looked up from the rubble to see the producer with her head in her hands and the co-star of the film, Anthony Ackroyd, barely able to contain his laughter.

I was duly banned from bike-riding duties, and for the close-up two large men silently pushed the bike and me into shot. 'Letter for Mr Kelly?' My humiliation was comprehensive and complete. The whole debacle was caught on film. I saw it in rushes. It looked hilarious: I flew out of shot and a puff of red dust flew back in. Sadly, it ended up on the cutting-room floor, where much of my finest feature-film work seems to lie.

Of course I'm not the only comedian to almost lose life and limb on set, as Richard Fidler was only too happy to remind me.

> Do you remember the day I got shot in the eye? We decided to be assassinated on live TV. Aaron [Aaron Beaucaire, the late and much loved special effects and pyrotechnics expert on *The Big Gig* and *D.A.A.S. Kapital*] had created a little condom full of fake blood, a small explosive, strapped under our shirts. So at the moment we were to be shot the explosive would go off, break through the shirt, and blood would explode out of it.

This segment was shot earlier in the day before the show went to air at 9.30, so the footage could be rolled in live.

> The one thing that no one had thought through were our bolo ties. I had a particularly heavy bolo tie with a

metal tip and so the explosive went off on my chest and the metal tip flew up and jabbed me in the eye. I hit the ground and I remember Hugh Johnson (our beloved floor manager) shouting, probably under instructions from Ted Robinson, 'Don't get up! Don't ruin the take!' I was writhing in pain. I couldn't see out of that eye. I was carried by two of the tech crew past the reception desk at the ABC in agony, clutching my eye with my chest covered in fake blood. The woman at reception was horrified and I remember saying to her, 'It's not as bad as it looks.'

Perhaps it wasn't, as Richard was rushed to the nearest ophthamologist rather than the hospital emergency.

He said, 'Young man, you have suffered a terrible accident. Sit down. I will put cocaine drops in your eyes. You hate me now, but in a moment you will love me!' And sure enough, he put cocaine drops in my eyeball and the pain went away instantly.

Obviously Richard was in no condition to perform that night, being off his eye on cocaine, so Glynn Nicholas stepped in to take his place.

So they wrapped his head like a mummy and pushed him around the stage. The following week I was back, after having 'intense plastic surgery', they said. As they slowly unwrapped the bandages everyone screamed, and of course, it was my normal face. He's hideous! He's hideous!

These days I can relate to this aspect of Richard's role: the butt of Tim and Paul's jokes, our genuine suffering becoming a plaything. But occasionally we underdogs do get the last laugh.

> Years later, I was sitting next to Paul McDermott as he told that story of me being carried out, except in Paul's version he and Tim had carried me out on their shoulders and it was Paul who said, 'It's not as bad as it looks.' So I let him finish and I said, 'You were not there at all, you were in the studio, buddy.' And it really freaked him out when I reminded him of his absence. A little case of false memory syndrome. Ha!

And so the Brood Parasite lives on to tell tall tales! (I have not checked this story with Paul for confirmation because I love Richard's version so much.)

I often feel I'm a human guinea pig, the perfect host to eager microscopic aliens. While playing a game of 'Who Would You Be If You Lived in the Middle Ages?' Mikey Robins instantly dubbed me the very first plague victim. I had a reputation to uphold, but despite my best efforts, as I enter my fourth decade of a painful career, I have been usurped by an upstart in a wheelchair. Tim is the undisputed master of major ailments these days, and not a peep out of him. Unwilling to go down without a fight, in an effort to regain my crown as the group's most sickly, I saw my chance during a run of nights in early

2015 at the Yarraville Club in Victoria, a D.A.A.S.-friendly venue hosted by the inimitable Matthew Hardy. On the morning of the final show I awoke with strangulating abdominal pain. My rule of never taking any notice of the rule that the show must go on was broken by the fact that when compared to Tim, even the most intense pain was not enough to get me off the performance hook. I gave an impressive performance of a man pretending not to be in abject agony before being rushed to the nearest hospital by Cameron P. Mellor, our trusted van driver and tour manager, jack-of-all-trades and master of absolutely none of them. Not even apprentice of them.

The nearest hospital to the Yarraville Club was in Williamstown. I may have been doubled over in agonising pain, but after only moments in the waiting room I believed my life was in more danger from the atmosphere than my ailment. The room was overfilled with super-sized citizens and their overfed offspring, all eyes on a small television blasting out the latest episode of *I'm a Celebrity . . . Get Me Out of Here!*, barely audible over the screeching of infectious porcine suburban progeny.

Another call to Nurse Mellor had me transported to the Alfred Hospital, where attentive staff ushered me into a ward in no time. As is my wont, I self-diagnosed the worst possible scenario. A peptic ulcer? Major organ haemorrhage? A tumour the size of a Williamstown kiddie? After much prodding and poking about my person by a parade of unnervingly youthful staff, my diagnosis was delivered. A generally benign case of sigmoid diverticular disease had been working tirelessly over time to build a Great Wall of China of poo in my intestines.

In short, constipation. The young medicos decided to blast the damage out from below. Al Murray once suffered quite the opposite fate.

> An attack of the shits. I was doing a thing at the West End, and at half-time I said to the stage manager, 'Look, I'm really hungry. Can you pop out and get me something from Burger King?' So he bought me this chicken burger and ten minutes into the second half there was this great gurgle in my guts and I thought, 'Oh no, I'm done for.' That second half [of the show] normally took fifty minutes and I did it in twenty-five. I just raced through the stuff and ran off, buttocks clenched, going, 'Turn the fucking radio mic off!' And I got to the toilet as it happened. Wrenching, it was. Wrenching. Radio mics are dangerous things.

With my condition deemed non-life threatening I was left alone with a jug of liquid and a box of pills on hand to induce the journey south. Presently a young intern approached my bunk and enquired, 'Is this your first enema, Mr Livingston?' I had never had the pleasure. Come morning, after a night spent expelling a tsunami of faeces through the convenient slit in the rear of my hospital gown, I told my sorry story to my colleagues. Alas, there was no sympathy forthcoming from my fellow performers. Sadly, this is one of the pitfalls of touring in late middle age. My grazed anatomy simply can't take it anymore, but does anyone hear me complain? You bet your sorry arse they do.

FINELY HONED MAYHEM

Comedy is simply a funny way of being serious.
PETER USTINOV

In March 2015 it was Sydney's turn to be used and abused by
D.A.A.S. I stood alone behind the curtain at the Seymour Centre,
trying my best not to listen to the audience. A shimmering pool
of anticipation, primed for laughter, their rumblings aggravated
the butterflies in my stomach. Flacco, fortunately, cares only
about himself. As soon as Flacco walks onto the stage I am left
in the wings. I envy him. He stands defiant, silent before the
throng, like Superman, heckles bouncing off him. He enjoys
his work. He revels in it. How does he do that?

As Flacco works the crowd, McDermott paces backstage,
a pitbull in a cage, while Ferguson chats amiably with the stage
crew. When Flacco introduces D.A.A.S. the audience shifts up
a gear. McDermott springs onto the stage and is instantly on
the attack. It is never wise to sit in the first three rows of a

D.A.A.S. concert. Paul seems to have forgotten something. He leaves the stage and wheels Tim Ferguson out and fear turns to love; after all, he's in a wheelchair, he can't attack them, can he? They are lulled into a false sense of security. Some lethal bile lies hunched and prone behind Tim's mild-mannered exterior. The audience needs to remain alert; to nod off might mean one of the players, the one who can effectively still use his legs, might clamber over the audience and resuscitate the hapless snoozer. This show is unpredictable, it pivots on disaster, it risks its life. It is a near-death experience. Cameron P. Mellor observes this potential train wreck night after night.

> The minute the boys go on, from my vantage point side of stage, the pleasure I get is just basically seeing the looks on the guys' faces as, pretty much every night, the show kind of disintegrates and then it gets pulled back up and held, and then it disintegrates again. I've seen thirty-five shows and there hasn't been a dull one yet.

Samantha Kelly, our trusted production manager, is side stage with Cameron most nights. She keeps one eye on the show and the other on the audience.

> You get a lot of your repeat offenders who come to every show. Three nights in Adelaide, three nights in Perth, every show front row, and they would laugh and react every night like it was the first time they'd heard it, and it's fascinated me and scared me until I finally had this realisation that, standing backstage watching the show,

I was doing the same thing! I know what's coming up and I just laugh again! Maybe I'm no different to the girls in the front row.

Cameron corrals the fans post-show, keeping watch over the steady stream of D.A.A.S. aficionados who wait in line to meet and be greeted by the team.

The fans are still just as rabid. Some have let themselves go a bit, they are a lot older, but the fanaticism is still there. There's a lot of people who are quite genuinely moved by a) the show, and b) having the guys back. When we do the signings and you're having one-on-one interactions with people who have basically had their lives changed by the All-Stars . . . The true fanatics, the ones who you would find in your cupboard holding up a dead rabbit . . . there's something about Paul that appeals to them. And he treats them with contempt. He's horrible. He's just horrible.

I have the best seat in the house. In truth I have the best stool in the house (sigmoid diverticular disease notwithstanding). Onstage I stand most of the time, in perfect silence, sometimes in judgement, sometimes in utter confusion, sometimes despair, but always deeply impressed by the puissance of these men. I also play guitar – no sweat there; no-one is listening to the music, and the exquisite two-part harmonies drown out my sour notes. The D.A.A.S. fans are quick to get to their feet at the end of the performance. Scanning the crowd from my privileged vantage point I can clearly see that every one of those eyes is focused on Tim Ferguson. It would be incorrect to assume this was a patronising act, a good-on-you-wheelchair-guy-for-having-a-bit-of-a-go kind of obligation. In any case, McDermott soon knocks that one on the head by hurling abuse as they rise to their feet: 'That's right, stand up. Have you any idea how that makes *him* feel? What a pack of insensitive [expletives].' The ovations are well deserved. Wheelchair or no wheelchair, night after night, it is clear to me that this revised version of Tim Ferguson has found his feet. So to speak.

On seeing D.A.A.S. perform again after more than two decades, Al Murray remains deeply impressed with the men who inspired him to keep going.

> The thing I took away from seeing them was that you should put on a show and you should try to be spectacular. And try to make tonight the night every single time . . .

Tim and Paul wrestle the show into a slightly different beast every night. To say the show is unpredictable is an understatement. Neither cast nor crew really know what is going to happen at any given point or when proceedings will actually end. Samantha Kelly enjoys this disintegration of form.

> You never know what's going to come out of Ferg's mouth. Cameron and I would always laugh at those moments where we think, 'Okay, we are nearly at the end of the show, yep,' and then Ferg opens his mouth. Tim has no respect for cues anymore. McDermott's waiting for the cue or he's just

thrown one to Tim and Tim is oblivious. It drives Paul mad but people think it's part of the show.

Fellow comedians can make for a tough crowd. They often revel in your failures. Steve Abbott was among a small coterie of comedians attending the Seymour Centre show.

I would have to say I really loved that show. The Dougs were always good at what they did. But this had a level of warmth. It was both touching and disgusting. Very funny, and very moving. I remember watching D.A.A.S. from side stage back in the day and I realised they were really great at what they do. And when I finally got to perform with Paul I thought that he was top shelf. But seeing the new D.A.A.S. show from the audience, where it got a standing ovation that was thoroughly deserved – even though it went about eight hours too long; normally I get to the hour ten mark and I'm looking to kill someone – this was a long show, but one of the best I've seen in years . . . I think I just said something positive.

After the two-hour-plus performance there is the compulsory meet, greet and merch-signing routine. Later, we settle into a Seymour Centre dressing-room, sipping the complimentary wine, post-morteming the show. Partying like it's 1954.

Paul McDermott reminded me that there had been in days of old 'acts of madness, drunkenness and debauchery, you know . . .' In all honesty I wasn't aware. So I pressed Paul for more.

There was the time when I hid all the ecstasy – which was popular in the days of my youth – I hid the ecstasy, cocaine, marijuana and various pills behind a framed picture in a hotel room, in a town that cannot be named, thinking to myself, 'That's a good plan.' The following morning we set off for the next town – and because it's Australia, it was about four hours away. About two hours out of town I went, 'Oh shit, I've got to go back, I've left the drugs in the room.' And so we had to go all the way back, and Richard, not being a partaker, was not happy with me – justifiably, I must say. So we got back to the hotel, and this is where Tim's charm comes into play. I said, 'Tim, can you distract them with your beauty while I grab the stuff?' And I went up to the reception desk and said, 'Excuse me, I believe I may have left something in the room,' and the woman at the desk said, 'Oh no, we've had the cleaners go through and they found nothing.' So I had to plead: 'Just take us around there, it will only take a moment.' So she acquiesced and as she was unlocking the door, Tim went, 'Flippant, flippant, flippant, flippant! Lah de da de da de dah!' And I was in like a ferret, got the picture off the wall, grabbed this huge bag of drugs, put it straight into my pocket. Thank you, Tim. But there was at least one person in the van who was absolutely disgusted.

Some of the more revealing tour tales come from outsiders. Never underestimate the cool veneer of indifference shown by hotel staff. These people are seriously bored. Particularly on the nightshift. This breed are gossip-seeking missiles. My

Paul McDermott caught 'spanking the plank' before show time. *Tony Virgo*

Tim Ferguson swamped by a fan mid-busk during the 2016 Melbourne International Comedy Festival. *C.P. Mellor*

Timothy Ferguson hypes himself down pre-show. *Tony Virgo*

Flacco and Samantha Kelly share a moment backstage. One best described as 'awkward'. *Tony Virgo*

Paul and Paul, or Cocky and Pompous to their friends. If they had any friends . . . *Melissa Lyne*

The Doug Anthony All-Stars present *Near Death Experience – The Musical*, 2016. *Shane Rozario*

Q. Who is the odd man out?
A. All of the above.
McDermott, Ferguson, Robinson and Flacco. *Tony Virgo*

'War Song' – 'And the general sighed, "This is our last stand," . . .'
Anne-Sophie Marion

Tim Ferguson – on a roll. *Tony Virgo*

Tim Ferguson, last man sitting. Next port of call, Scotland, UK. *C.P. Mellor*

The author could barely contain his elation on returning to Edinburgh after twenty-five years. *C.P. Mellor*

The signs were everywhere: D.A.A.S. had returned to the Fringe. But would it turn out to be a case of 'GO BACK. YOU ARE GOING THE WRONG WAY'? *Tor Goldsmith*

A genuine Edinburgh Tattoo.
Courtesy of Bridie Mayfield

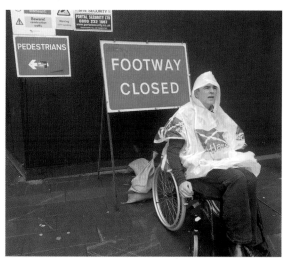

Edinburgh was no place for a wheelchair. The streets were cobbled, just like the D.A.A.S. show running order. *Samantha Kelly*

The Scottish summer weather failed to rain on the All-Stars' parade. *Di Star*

An Audience with Al Murray, featuring three Australians, one Al Murray, a crowd of hundreds and the ears of four million BBC listeners. *C.P. Mellor*

Al 'the Pub Landlord' Murray had been the warm-up act for the All-Stars in the early nineties.
Tor Goldsmith

Two decades on and D.A.A.S. get to return the favour.
Tor Goldsmith

Comic luminary Stephen K. Amos unleashes the All-Stars on his *Talk Show*, downstairs at the Gilded Balloon. *Tor Goldsmith*

Backstage. Gilded Balloon. 1.30 am. The calm before the All-Stars storm the *Late'n'Live* stage. *Janet McLeod*

Tim Ferguson's personal stage hands . . . and legs. Why take the elevator when these guys can give you a lift? *Samantha Kelly*

Onstage. Gilded Balloon. 1.37 am. The storm after the calm. *Janet McLeod*

The legendary Mervyn Stutter interrupts the All-Stars' final show at The Pleasance to present a parting accolade. *Tor Goldsmith*

Edinburgh, 2016. They came. They sore. But not sorry. Next stop, London.

Livingston – Indignant. McDermott – Intoxicated. Ferguson – Indefatigable.
C.P. Mellor

D.A.A.S. waiting for their emotional baggage handlers. *Samantha Kelly*

Backstage, Soho Theatre, London. No time for reflection. *C.P. Mellor*

The Mahatma of Malodorous Mirth, Jerry Sadowitz, enveloped by devotees.
Soho Bar, 2016. *C.P. Mellor*

Soho Theatre, Saturday, 20 August 2016. A final standing ovation. Brexit
– stage left. *C.P. Mellor*

London, August, 2016
TIM: These streets aren't exactly paved with gold . . .
CAMERON: Stop complaining. At least they *are* paved.

TIM FERGUSON: You know, the one thing I really hate is sight gags.
PAUL McDERMOTT: Does my finger smell funny to you?
PAUL LIVINGSTON: (*thinks*) This is going straight into my book . . .
Samantha Kelly

advice is to keep everything close to your chest, except the staff themselves. That road leads to despair, and unwelcome tweets.

In mid 2015, in a motel somewhere along the New South Wales coastline, the cast and crew of D.A.A.S. were following their regular regimen: show over, meet, greet, then back to Tim's room to sip minibar wine and order dubious food from room service. After the compulsory forty-five-minute wait, our room service waiter – let's call him Kelvin, a very young, very green staffer, perhaps on his first shift – makes his entrance with our late-night twenty-three-dollar toasted sandwiches.

Most of the D.A.A.S. road train were present – Tim, Paul, Cameron P. Mellor, Samantha Kelly and me. We could sense Kelvin's innocent young neurons churning over the possibilities of what he·had stumbled upon. His face tilted a little, like a confused puppy. 'Why are you still up?' he said. We were performers, actors, thespians; 2 am is 'our' time. I don't think Kelvin had seen 2 am before. He wasn't judging us, he was genuinely confused; he had entered a world that made no sense. A pensioner, a cripple, two seedy middle-aged males and one attractive female, post-midnight and still awake!

What might Kelvin suspect? Even a demeanour as virginal as Kelvin's would be aware of internet porn and that industry's location of choice, the out-of-town motel room. The fact that I was still in full face make-up may have tipped the scales somewhat. Kelvin appeared more than a little apprehensive. Tim attempted to cut the air with his Stanley blade of wit. 'Haven't you ever heard of Hillsong?' Young Kelvin's shoulders relaxed. Of course he'd heard of Hillsong. Now it all made sense: the guitar, the one in the wheelchair in need of healing, the joyous sense of camaraderie. Kelvin's respite was only momentary, however: as he approached the table to set down the sandwiches, his eyes fixed upon the back of Tim's wheelchair. Samantha, ever alert, leapt across the room to stand between Kelvin and Tim's rear view. But it was too late; the poison had entered the boy's system.

In order to stem the tide of boredom, one of the many ruses employed on this tour was to pin a sign on the back of Tim's wheelchair in order to amuse each other. The joke had worn so thin we hardly noticed it anymore. In this instance the sign, in bold felt-tipped pen read 'Fuck me up the arse – I still love it'. Young Kelvin nearly dropped the complimentary mustard. He placed the tray down, left the room swiftly, and perhaps handed in his badge and left the building. One for the grandkids, Kelvin.

Around this time the new D.A.A.S. collective was considering seeking corporate comedy work for the trio, a lucrative means of earning an actual living out of comedy. By embracing the corporate sector, a comedian can make more in twenty minutes than a month of one-nighters. Flacco has never been a corporate animal; he is a work of art, finely honed and delicate, an acquired taste, not to be easily consumed by the masses, and therefore a money-making black hole. Corporate gigs are an exchange of capital. And it infuriates me, primarily because I can't for the life of me devise a way to make it work. The venues are rarely performer-friendly, being for the most part capacious well-lit conference centres, a hundred or so large tables peopled by beings more interested in who is at their table than who is standing on what passes for a stage. This is court-jestership in the true sense. Playing to the privileged, the well-paid, well-fed, alcohol-lubed, cocaine-snortified powerbrokers. Your mission? Make them laugh. Mission virtually impossible. I've been advised, as I sit in my ivory tower (that I'm still trying to pay off), by wealthier comedians than myself not to worry about selling your soul for the corporate dollar, because the last thing you should do is put your soul into it. Leave your soul, your ego and your best material at home. Take the money and saunter.

On the odd occasion I have agreed to lower my standards – perhaps for a worthy cause, or when a fellow comedian needs support, or when I'm so absolutely broke that even my soul is telling me to swallow the last of my pride and take the gig. Some time last century, The Sandman and Flacco were flown to Queensland to grab some capitalist coin. The venue was a cavernous nightclub. The stage was an absurdly ostentatious creation, a mix of fake palm trees, an artificial waterfall for a backdrop, all set around a Perspex stage perched above a bubbling pond. This mob had spared no expense.

After the short limousine journey from the hotel to the gig, we were given our call times. Sandman to go on at midnight followed by Flacco. This was news to us; we were under the impression we would be on at 8 pm sharp, then a quick slink back to the hotel where we had left our souls. Gig accomplished and swallowed like a bitter pill. It was to be a long four hours until midnight. I didn't mingle. I don't do mingle very well. I do 'stick out like a sore silent thumb' really well, but I leave the professional mingling to The Sandman. Come midnight the crowd was well fuelled with alcohol and associated illegal substances. I stood side stage, or perhaps poolside is a better description, as The Sandman, unannounced, walked on to no applause. The Sandman's low, slow laconic suburban gems sailed effortlessly over the heads of a crowd who were fed up, with fine food and too many speeches. They were ready to party. As usual, Sandy did not give up, and managed to extract a few laughs – or was it pity? – from a single table of guests.

Flacco hit the stage at 12.20 am, precisely the moment thunderous dance music started on the upper floor. I was in no mood to dance but half the audience were. The other half remained seated, completely unaware of my presence. What to do? Think of the money, do your stuff and get off. Two of those options worked fine. The other? Not so good. I thought of the money, I did my lines, the problem came when I left the stage. One had to negotiate a gap of about half a metre between the Perspex sheet of the stage and the club floor. It was a tricky negotiation. By the time I'd finished my set, I was so eager to get the hell out of there I stepped off the Perspex and straight into the pond. The water was chest height. I stood holding both hands above my head, half drowning, not waving. My predicament went unobserved, as crowd, crew and The Sandman were by this point mingling elsewhere.

My pathetic attempts to climb out of the pond were funnier than my set. I was like a drowning gazelle; I'd get one foot up onto the floor then fall back into the drink. Eventually I emerged, dripping wet from the chest down. I had no other clothes; I'd arrived wearing Flacco's very expensive Savile Row topcoat and suit trousers. It was time to meet and greet. The Sandman called me over. For the next half-hour I chatted with various patrons; none noticed that I was wringing wet. The venue was dark, my suit was dark. Only I was aware of my trail, a soggy track tracing my journey as I wandered, cocktail in hand, chatting to the corporate masses.

Eventually The Sandman and I were bundled into our limousine. Upon leaving the vehicle I glanced at my seat. A generous puddle of water had pooled there. Let the limo driver make of it what he would. At least it wasn't pungent. And this was Queensland – no doubt he'd had worse than this deposited on that velveteen upholstery.

We flew home, souls intact, a little wealthier for wear. But I swore that would be the last corporate gig I ever agreed to.

Until. The weekend of 15 June 2015. Paul and Tim have no qualms when it comes to snatching the corporate dollar. When an interstate offer too sweet to refuse came their way I was expected to toe the line. After Cameron P. Mellor assured me there was no aquatic theme on the agenda, I agreed. A twenty-five-minute spot. I was to say nothing, just play guitar, an invisible well-paid extra. It wasn't D.A.A.S.'s greatest moment, but it was over in no time, it was before midnight, and we had a guy in a wheelchair on stage with us. The priceless part of that weekend for Cameron P. Mellor and me was the trip from the airport to the hotel, wherein C.P. Mellor and I learned we weren't quite the men of the world we assumed ourselves to be. There remained at least one human behaviour that had slipped through out collective guard.

While waiting to retrieve our luggage, our designated limo driver's opening shot was how he always picks up his rifles at the oversized baggage desk. Righto, Alvin, we get the picture. During the drive to the hotel, Alvin, unprompted, offered his advice on a top night out for a pair of worldly gentlemen such as we. The main enterprise Alvin recommended to us was the popular local practice of 'dogging', a term with which Cameron P. Mellor and I were not familiar. But we did like puppies – who doesn't? Our great regret is asking Alvin to please explain.

According to Alvin, certain parklands in Perth offer the best spots for after-dark dogging. Instantly I presumed my worst fears were about to be realised. I pictured Alvin, rifle to his shoulder, blasting the odd dog as its owner took it for evening walkies. My worst fears didn't come anywhere near the truth. Alvin had this advice to offer to those new to a night of dogging. 'First of all, bring your own mask. Fox is good, or a rabbit. Then some basic guidelines apply. Windows up, interior light on? Look but don't touch. Windows down, interior light on? Look and touch but only through the window. Doors open? You are invited to join in. In a public open space? Ask permission first.' I don't really want to give you any more hints other than that. Google it if you're still confused.

It was pretty clear Alvin was fishing for a couple of doggin' buddies. C.P. Mellor and I thanked him, but maybe some other time, eh? We just wanted to get out of the car and take a shower.

When we arrived at the hotel, wide-eyed and a little pale, Paul McDermott casually informed us that he was well versed in the art of dogging. No surprises there. After all, this is the man who penned the lyric, 'We all fuck dogs in the park'. Paul was delighted to enlighten us as to the ins and outs of 'goin' a-doggin'. Then he asked for Alvin's mobile number.

NEAR DEATH EXPERIENCE

There are nights when the wolves are
silent and only the moon howls.

GEORGE CARLIN

Some people thrive on the road. The late Jimmy Little was
one of them. I first met Jimmy while carrying a spear on the
set of Wim Wenders' epic road film, *Until the End of the World*
(or *Until the End of the Film* as we dubbed it). Jimmy revelled in
performing. In 2009 The Sandman and Flacco were performing
at the Apollo Bay Music Festival in Victoria. We were staying
in a classic beachside motel, self-enclosed like some kind of
suburban piazza. The rooms were perfectly square with blonde
brick inside and out, all facing a common interior courtyard.
I had a top corner. Jimmy was across from me in a ground-
floor room. You see these motels in Hollywood films. Without
exception, something horrible happens in them.

The staff departed at 5 pm and returned at 9 am. The keepers had left the zoo. The room next to Jimmy's was home to a few dozen local teenagers who partied hard and loud throughout the night. We both had daytime gigs at the festival the next day, and after trying to sleep in the bathroom, which only echoed the revelry outside, I took to the wardrobe, stuffing it with as many blankets and pillows as I could scrounge before adopting the foetal position and attempting to get some sleep. Come morning, I crawled out of the cupboard, overtired and furious.

On my way to breakfast I ran into Jimmy downstairs. I could only imagine how horrendous it must have been for him down there among the rabble that spilled out of the room next to his and into the courtyard, music blasting into the early hours. Jimmy was a seasoned performer, with a lifetime of touring behind him, but at the age of seventy-two, a respected elder renowned for his equanimity and gentleness, surely this would have pushed the great man to his limit?

Jimmy looked refreshed. He gave me a big smile when I mentioned the noisy neighbours. 'Yeah! Some of those songs were great!' he said. 'Those young people were having such a wonderful time. It was fantastic!'

I envied this man's unflappable attitude. The last time I saw Gentleman Jimmy was in the green room of an ABC radio studio. He flashed that familiar delighted smile and said, 'Hey, Paul! Guess what? I'm having dialysis!' I've never seen a man so excited about his own major organ failure.

Jimmy passed away in 2012. A life well lived.

D.A.A.S. were booked to perform in Cairns on Friday, 24 July 2015. While the young D.A.A.S. left no deep northern township unravaged, Flacco parted ways with them at the border. For an obscurant creation like Flacco, certain isolated patches of this Oceanian continent were off limits. Cairns is a three-hour flight from Sydney. That gave me more than enough time to work myself into a paralysis of foreboding. 'Are you going to visit the reef?' friends asked. Reefs tend to be associated with oceans, and I can't swim, let alone snorkel (what can I say? I'm a Pisces, living proof that astrology is bunkum). I was horrified. I hadn't worn shorts in fifty years, and I wasn't about to start. Apart from nurturing a panic attack, I also spent my travel time editing Flacco's introduction to around thirteen seconds. I figured I could be offstage before the first meat-seeking missile hit my fragile eggshell mind.

The Tanks Art Centre in Cairns is an impressive complex, and my confidence is always bolstered by a venue with 'art' in its title. Nestled in a rainforest, three massive concrete fuel tanks constructed during World War II dominate the site. The tanks were decommissioned in the late eighties. Abandoned lumps of exotic architecture attract arts funding bodies like subtropical intestinal worms to human excrement. Both the tanks and the natives were friendly. I needn't have worried. But it filled in the hours. Dread is an excellent time-killer.

Buoyed by the architectonics of the Tanks, I let Flacco off the leash to have his way with the locals. After introducing the All-Stars I exited the stage with a spring in my step and promptly careened onto a concrete floor, unseen by anyone, but heard by the many as I unleashed a range of colourful expletives into my still very much live lapel microphone. There was no pond to save me this time. Embarrassment gave way to pain, but apart from the odd bruise I managed to steer clear of reefs, oceans and tropical ulcers, and my trousers remained long.

A month later the D.A.A.S. Facebook page boasted of a brand-new show, and a new tour. This was the first I'd heard of it. A year on the road is generally enough time for one show to morph into its next incarnation. To ensure this process plays out you need to be working most nights. D.A.A.S. were currently touring at a gentleman's pace. In fact, we were touring at a dawdle, as befitting a pensioner, a cripple and a songwriter. Any new show would be undercooked, unrehearsed and understandably bad news for my nervous system.

My stress levels were back to peak functioning by the time we debuted this alleged new show at our home ground, the Harold Park Hotel. The following morning D.A.A.S. were booked on a flight to Perth, where two shows at the Regal Theatre sold out in no time. In my opinion the new show was nowhere near ready, and the decision to call this shambles of a show *Near Death Experience* might prove prescient. I was so full of passive aggression over the timing of these gigs it spilled over into hyperactive aggression. Unfortunately, Cameron P. Mellor was in the right place at the wrong time. The hulk broke loose and it wasn't pretty. C.P. Mellor bore the brunt of my brief but brutal tirade with all the aplomb of a soft-shelled turtle, fresh from the egg and caught in the hungry gaze of a frenzied raptor.

After my little outburst, McDermott told me I was acting like a pre-pubescent menstruating schoolgirl. Living and working in quarters as close as these, it is easy to nurture paranoia. I for one was convinced the Cairns booking may have been a ploy to rid the band of the ageing guitarist. I have the suspicion I'm seen as excess baggage, a highly paid session muso. I'm well aware that I'm expendable, that there are other elder gents out there who can manage three basic chords and not open their mouths for two hours at a stretch. My use-by date was passed in a former century. They know I fear any venue that has a bar in the actual room, yet our 2016 bookings were peppered with just this style of gig. Small rooms – tryouts, they were calling them.

McDermott can appear friendly, in a calculating deceitful way. Ferguson, however, is a tougher nut to crack. He has the appearance of joviality and rambunctious camaraderie. 'Hang me by my scrotum over a shark tank? Sure thing! Great idea, boys. Rig me up!' You can read Tim like a book, but it's a sketch-book, and all the pages are blank. Most irritating of all was the van driver, Cameron P. Mellor, who had taken to inserting his creative twenty cents into our collective ring. The man doesn't know his place. After starting out so apologetically – 'It's my first time at this, boys, be gentle' – by this juncture the angry turkey was dangerously close to displaying something approaching confidence. But it takes a lot more than merely looking like Marty Feldman to be a comedian. So ended 2015. On a note so sour it would make a jazz musician wince.

Come 2016, D.A.A.S. were off to a bold start. Tim Ferguson, actor, comedian, author, filmmaker, artist and jaunty raconteur was soaking up the adoration, the wheelchair only adding to his charm. The canine version of the present line-up of D.A.A.S. would probably be the eager Doberman pup with shonky legs, a complete mongrel and a half-blind, half-deaf miniature Mexican Hairless Xoloitzcuintli. The D.A.A.S. central planning organisation (i.e. everyone except me) decided to venture into smaller venues. To hone material and somehow rein in the unwieldy two-and-a-half-hour-plus *Near Death Experience* show. Sydney's Comedy Store was one chosen venue – a venue I have avoided for decades. Mainstream was never my stream; paddling in the safe shallow waters of art's eternal billabong was more my style. Fear of being eaten alive has kept me from such main streams. These fears were not quelled by a wardrobe-sized dressing-room infused with the odour of vomit – the ghostly remnant, no doubt, of a fellow comedian's pre-show preparations.

Yet I needn't have feared. First, I was merely the guitarist, and the crowd was not there for any fancy plank spanking. Second, venues like the Store were McDermott and Ferguson's stomping ground. Third, the Comedy Store was not the bear pit I had imagined; objects in my imagination are often vastly larger than they appear in real life. The audience, the staff and the fellow comedians were welcoming, generous and enthusiastic. The Larkspur and the Little Black Cornflake of Hate revelled in the cosy quarters of the Comedy Store. Had the Comedy Store changed? Had I changed? Was the reaction mere pity for the old and decrepit? Was it the guy in the wheelchair? Whatever it was, it worked.

The idea was to develop a tight set for two major shows at the 30th Melbourne International Comedy Festival. Flacco first performed at the MICF in 1987, a small fringe event with a large vision. At that time I played to a couple of hundred punters at the Prince Patrick Hotel. This time we were booked to play two nights, and two separate shows, at the Melbourne Town Hall, the venue where the *D.A.A.S. Kapital* DVD launch was held in 2013. This time we needed twice as many bums on seats to sell out the venue. With hundreds of other performers vying for audiences, we had some work to do.

On arrival in Melbourne five days before opening night, we were met at the airport by a television crew. I couldn't remember the last time a television crew had met me at the airport. That's because it had never happened before. Our beloved peer Libbi Gorr was commandeering a segment to be aired on the ABC's *7.30 Report*. Libbi and entourage followed close on our heels the entire day. First stop was a busking session outside the Melbourne Town Hall. Tim and Paul made it clear they wanted to return to their roots, and the way to sell tickets was to hit the streets and attack the general public in their natural habitat.

It had been thirty years since my first sighting of those three smelly, arrogant lads busking in an Adelaide mall. I pooh-poohed them then. And I pooh-poohed the idea of joining them this time around. In short, I was full of pooh-pooh. I was beyond busking. Had been for quite some time. Most of my life in fact. It was only the presence of the ABC camera crew and my not wanting to look like the taciturn malcontent that I really am that saw me subject myself to this humiliation. Busking in 2016 is incomparable to the eighties. These days council approval and a licence are required – that is, if you pass the audition. Contemporary buskers utilise sophisticated sound systems, making it more like a less-than-perfect concert than a spirited acoustic plea for spare change. Tim and Paul decided to ditch the microphones and instead wander the streets playing tunes to hapless citizens on park benches. About twenty minutes into the stroll, with no television cameras in sight, I packed up my guitar and returned to my hotel room. I don't think the boys even noticed I was gone.

A couple of warm-up performances at Janet McLeod's Local Laughs and the Famous Spiegeltent gave me some hope that D.A.A.S. still had what it took. Final rehearsals took place in Tim's hotel room. Rehearsal is perhaps not the best description of the D.A.A.S. preparation method. A map of the show is agreed to, but this is a map with no compass, and I for one can never tell which way is up. The frown I wear in my role as the guitarist is not just disgust at the puerile antics of my fellow performers, it is also an effort to ascertain where exactly we are on this meandering path to the end of the show.

On night one of our Melbourne Town Hall performance there were more citizens than seats in the audience. Here I was again, pacing the corridor I had three years before presumed I would never pace again. The audience was large and vocal. I felt tiny, bald and sixty. Flacco, as usual, could not have cared less; after all, he was only thirty years old, younger than most of those in the audience. He relished his thirteen minutes of fame before bringing on the All-Stars. An hour twenty turned into an hour forty, but no one was complaining at the end of the show. The second night was much the same. Somehow, D.A.A.S. 2016 still had some lead left in the old pencil. After witnessing D.A.A.S's sold-out performance at Sydney's Enmore Theatre on a Sunday in May 2016, Ted Robinson had this to say:

> I actually doubted – and I know I shouldn't have – that the audience would forgive the fact that Richard wasn't there, and I think the device of just referring to you as 'the guitarist', it's not even noticed. It's Tim and Paul. I think it really is a situation where they are both celebrating Tim and the memory of D.A.A.S., but without dwelling on it or being morbid they are kind of both confronted by their own mortality. It is really a very interesting thing. I think it is an act of overlong genius. But I was delighted with every moment of it.

'Every moment of it' was the problem – the show seemed to be expanding rather than contracting. At just on two hours it was running way too long. Currently, it was a ramshackle meandering beast, resistant to tightening; it was a show about falling apart, very slowly. A show without ambition, it was not trying to get anywhere. The show needed no ending, it was not racing to a conclusion, it was meandering towards the inevitable. Tim Ferguson is not one given to pause and reflect, so I was delighted when he paused momentarily to reflect on our current *Near Death Experience* over a coffee in Cafe Madame Frou Frou.

> This is the best thing we've ever done. *Near Death Experience* has really surprised people. Paul's new song [titled 'Us'], about the pensioner, the cripple and the songwriter, points to the problems we all share, and by the time we've sung it, there is no problem. It's towards the end of the show, so we are kind of saying, 'This is a self-indulgent wank,' when it hasn't been at all . . . we are talking about stuff no other comedians are thinking about.

We are briefly interrupted by a passing stranger who thanks Tim for years of laughter. Tim, as usual, is gracious, funny and light-hearted. Once the stranger is out of earshot, Tim continues:

> We are not actually pointing at ourselves. We are not saying, 'Look at Tim, he's in a wheelchair.' We are saying, 'Look at us as young men; you were young then. We are all in this boat together.' I think that is the thing that is the most shocking for them. As opposed to holding up a kitten and saying, 'We are going to drown the kitten now.' And you might cry if the kitten was a cute kitten. But we are not

saying that, we are saying, 'You are the kitten, and now we drown you.' It's a multi-layered attack on their emotions, which I like. Because a comedy show at the end of the day is an emotional journey. And if you keep the emotions moving underneath the laughter it keeps the surprise element alive. Because it is possible to feel many things and laugh at the same time. Doing a comedy show just to bring joy is not something I could even contemplate. I don't understand what that is. Just to make you feel happy? Here's a funny thing: porcupines!

Time for Timmy's meds. Cheque, please!

Meanwhile, Paul McDermott muses on the alchemy of this particular *Near Death Experience*.

I don't think you can dismiss the idea of camaraderie. There is a history between us all; we were more or less kids. There's a sense of shared stupidity – we've never done anything that vaguely resembles responsibility in our lives. We haven't had to engage in society in the same sort of ways as other people do and part of that is temerity. There is a vast amount of shyness in a couple of members of the group who would prefer to be anywhere else sometimes, but you get onstage and do what you do and adopt whatever persona or strength you need to get through that.

The All-Stars have come a long way in thirty-odd years. But deep down, there is still that worm at the core of D.A.A.S. slowly eating its way to the surface. Paul recognises this creature.

It's a different beast now but it's still the same sort of monster. It's a self-serving demon. In the old days it was always a juggle of emotions, but we are not young-sters anymore and there's not as many brawls. If the All-Stars had a manifesto in those early days then this is the culmination of it. This is the peak of it. This is the proof that the satire, that parody, that cruelty we once turned towards other people we can now turn towards ourselves, and we can still find something valid to say. In some ways I think it's the best work we've ever done. And the reason for that is, of course, we are in closer proximity to ultimate tragedy, and comedy and tragedy are so closely linked. It's not just old men – it's old broken men who are aware of their predicament, and Tim, who is incredibly gallant, performing with MS and being an Adonis when he was younger must be . . . that's an extraordinary journey for that man to take. So many dilemmas to overcome but he seems to do it with such effortless grace.

High praise from McDermott, but when I mention that Tim is performing better than ever before Paul becomes once more the Little Black Cornflake we all know and love.

Well, to be honest, he didn't put in a lot in the old days. I mean, what do you need when you are that tall and that handsome?

Next stop? Northern Queensland and parts thereabouts before the most daunting destination of all: a return to the Edinburgh Fringe in August. Mark Trevorrow describes Edinburgh today as:

> . . . so unfeasibly huge that it's lost its sense of centre and community. We were lucky to establish ourselves there when we did. God knows how anybody cuts through now. But of course they still do. I'm just being an old fart.

Old and fart make up the bulk of the new D.A.A.S experience. What fresh hell were we entering into? Eddie Izzard could offer no advice for the All-Stars on returning to the Fringe after an absence of over two decades.

> I'm not sure, because the last Edinburgh I did was 1993 and I thought that because a lot of London goes up there I'm not going to do it anymore. I'll play Edinburgh when the Scottish people are there. There will definitely be some people who will remember [D.A.A.S]. I don't know whether they'll have to go and re-find them all over again, but if they have the same vibe going on . . . I mean someone like Tim in a wheelchair saying, 'Fuck it, I'm going to do it.' . . . That, I think, will be amazing.

Show business impresario Jon Thoday is a founder of Avalon Entertainment Ltd, one of the world's leading entertainment management companies. Jon first sighted D.A.A.S. upstairs at the Gilded Balloon in Edinburgh in 1988, the year the All-Stars were nominated for the Perrier Award. When I spoke to Jon before the group's impending return to the Fringe in 2016, he recalled his first impression of D.A.A.S.

> I can't think of anything like them, before or since. They were loved by the comedy community back then . . . I'm really excited about seeing them. There's a great community of people here in the UK who remember them. The truth is that they were one of the best live acts I've ever seen and I don't think people forget that. I never saw them do a bad show.

Jon had no doubt they would have gone on to huge success had they stayed in the UK, and he was very much looking forward to seeing them, albeit in their dotage.

> The festival is transformed. I think there may have been fifty or sixty comedy shows back then. There are hundreds now. It's a massive thing. I think they'll go down amazingly. I'm fully confident.

The one daunting comment Jon made (apart from the fact he was feeling 'fully confident') was to assure me the fans were excited about seeing all of D.A.A.S.'s greatest hits. The current plan was to hit the Edinburgh audience with a brand-new experience. A *Near Death* one. The only thing that hadn't changed was the All-Stars' determination to shock, offend and force-feed their loyal fans the unexpected. The key difference in touring then and touring now is youth and the lack of it. There are no dreams, no projections of world domination. There is no time for ambition. Yet rather than have us imploding in a mire of hopelessness, the tenuous situation brings with it an electricity, a vitality to each performance. No-one is thinking of their future. Today it is about use-by dates. It is merely a matter of time. This is a countdown. And D.A.A.S are up for it.

I had not performed in Darwin for two decades. The immensity of the Australian continent proves costly when it comes to touring, and unless there is a strong guarantee that enough locals will turn out to see you there is no point in making the effort. The D.A.A.S. net is cast wide, and enough interest had been spiked for them to make the journey to the Top End.

The five-hour flight from Sydney had me, as usual, in the rear of the cabin, while ensconced in the pointy end with the D.A.A.S. leading cast were the national showbiz phenomenon known as The Wiggles, booked for two shows in the same venue as D.A.A.S. the following night. No doubt it was an unusual day for the Darwin Entertainment Centre, with families and children flocking to morning shows and matinees by The Wiggles before the descent into the dark night of the ageing, death-defying D.A.A.S.

D.A.A.S. successfully soiled the wholesome Wiggle-saturated atmosphere of the Darwin Entertainment Centre in front of an enthusiastic crowd. Darwin had evolved since the group were last there, and the locals seemed to approve of the evolution of D.A.A.S. from three strikingly cute, boundlessly energetic youths into this creaking trio of living fossils, an unnatural selection of Hominini a long way from phenome.

On departure, when I casually mentioned the curious nature of returning to our old Australian haunts to Paul McDermott in the air-conditioned luxury of the Darwin airport lounge, he didn't turn to face me; he kept staring at an expanse of wallpaper in front of him. 'Can you see the join?' he said. 'Where the pattern repeats itself? I don't like patterns that don't repeat themselves . . .' He was right, the pattern didn't repeat. Unlike the rebooted All-Stars, heading out of the slow-heated haze of the Top End en route to the upper hemisphere, where London and Edinburgh lay in wait for the return of D.A.A.S. after a hiatus of twenty-odd years.

CODA

On a grey day the larkspur looks like fallen
heaven . . . and when there is grey weather in
our hills or grey hairs in our heads, perhaps
they may still remind us of the morning.

G.K. CHESTERTON, 'THE GLORY OF GREY'

In my diary of August 1989, I noted the first thing that struck
me on setting foot in the United Kingdom was the oppressively
low grey sky. In my youth I couldn't wait to get back to the
vast open blue canopy over Australia. A country with no lid.
A young nation with a future, unbound by the past. In August
2016, I felt a cosy snugness beneath this low ceiling of soft
grey on arrival in the Old Dart. Perhaps age had something
to do with it. This time around I had my own long history. I
was something of a relic, with a lot of future behind me. I had
much in common with Britain.

True to form, I boarded our flight to London nursing an impressive head cold. Here's a tip: if you are going to be ill on a twenty-three-hour flight, business class is the way to travel. From the limousine pick-up to the upper deck of the Qantas Airbus A380-800, I was addressed by name, fed, pyjamaed and tucked into my private pod. As I reclined in all the comforts of someone else's home, I was fully aware that it was twenty-seven years to the day since I boarded that Thai Airways flight on 31 July 1989 en route to London with Mark Trevorrow on our mission to support the Doug Anthony All-Stars, where we suffered through our own little hell of shared influenza and chain-smoking bogans. This time I was travelling bogan-free. Tim Ferguson, Cameron P. Mellor and Paul McDermott were further towards the business end of business class, but I was not complaining; I had never felt less harried while feeling so abysmally ill.

My affliction also deflected my mind from a feeling of dread that had been building for some time. What on earth were we doing? Returning to a festival once owned and conquered by the Doug Anthony All-Stars for almost a decade, yes – but that decade was decades ago. And from all reports the festival had moved on and grown to epic proportions. The 2015 Edinburgh Festival Fringe boasted 50,459 performances of 3,314 shows in 313 venues.

More than twenty years had passed. Memories are short, as are most comedy careers, and while D.A.A.S. had made their mark at the time, their continued individual success and careers in Australia were all but invisible to the Brits. The All-Stars were about to appear out of the blue – or the grey, to be more precise.

Frank Woodley recalls his attempted glorious return to Edinburgh in 2001, almost a decade after winning the coveted Perrier Award.

> I remember giving out free tickets on the Royal Mile and saying to this girl, 'Look, they're free tickets, we must at least be alright, because we did win the Perrier Award once,' and she said, 'Oh? When did you win it?' And I said 1994 and she laughed in my face. She just went, 'Oh right, like in ancient times.'

Tim Ferguson had no doubt the former D.A.A.S. army of supporters would emerge from the woodwork and that this current incarnation would attract a new audience. I had my reservations. It's what I do best. I envisaged D.A.A.S. disappearing into a mire of performers half their age, hungrier for fame and much less physically repugnant than the current line-up. To my mind we were taking a used Holden Camira to a Formula One Grand Prix, or a penny farthing to the Tour de France.

Our business-class status came crashing down on arrival at Heathrow, where, after twenty-three hours travelling with luxury all over our laps, we were to catch a domestic flight directly to Edinburgh. A packet of Corkers Crisps and a cup of tepid tea with milk squeezed from a plastic tube was offered, and an inability to connect the fuselage to the terminal on landing had us held on board for longer than the flight. Eventually a set of stairs was procured, but this was of no use to Tim, of course. (Our production manager, Samantha Kelly, arrived twenty-four hours later with a similar tale. In this case the pilot waited forty minutes on the tarmac before opening the cockpit window and yelling to ground staff, 'Will some bastard please get us some stairs?!') Our heads were no longer in the clouds and our feet were firmly on Scottish ground.

They needed to be, as many of the streets of Edinburgh are cobbled, especially in the Old Town, where we were staying. Cobblestones, while quaint, are nothing more than an excuse for replacing a perfectly paved road with an uneven brick wall, and in no way suited Tim Ferguson's state-of-the-art set of wheels. It was clear a heavy-duty wheelchair would need to be acquired if Tim were ever to leave the hotel and make the journey to The Pleasance, the venue where D.A.A.S. had made their first big splash, a mere few hundred metres by cobbled road.

But this was not The Pleasance of 1987. In those days it was hardly more than a courtyard surrounded by a couple of small theatre spaces. It has somewhat enlarged in the intervening years and is now home to a hive of venues, from the fifty-seater Pleasance Cellar to the seven-hundred-and-fifty-seat Pleasance Grand, the entire complex delivering over two hundred performances per day.

The All-Stars' venue was the Pleasance Forth, with a seating capacity of two hundred and fifty.

In the past, venues such as The Pleasance and the Gilded Balloon were the Fringe favourites for up-and-comers; nowadays many of the acts in these prime venues are corporate-sponsored, and an unknown kid from the backwaters of Australia – i.e. Richard Fidler – would have a much harder time landing a gig sight unseen. Many first-timers now debut their efforts at what has become known as the Free Fringe Festival, the Fringe within the Fringe. Beginning around 2004, small rooms, pubs and the like were opened to performers with no venue hire charge and no admission price. The audience members are free to make a donation following the show if they wish.

This scenario was perhaps inevitable in view of the prohibitive costs of performing in Edinburgh for an unknown entity. I've known performers who have mortgaged their homes to follow the dream of Edinburgh Fringe success. These free venues have taken over from traditional busking. Working the street was not only bread and butter for performers like D.A.A.S. in the eighties and nineties, but a sure-fire way to win fans and sell tickets. As in most parts of the globe, in Edinburgh busking has been formalised, legalised and amplified. A visit to The Mound in the centre of Edinburgh, where the Dougs once attracted large crowds – along with various other young hopefuls, like Eddie Izzard – has now become a space for 'professional' busking acts. You know the type: the tricycle-riding, fire-eating cat jugglers with deafening sound systems and microphones. To busk on The Mound these days you need to audition, be granted a licence, then book in a time. Hence the growth and popularity of the Free Fringe.

Having once secured a venue, drawing attention to your show is the next hurdle. Posters cover the city walls. Smaller acts with A4 flyers appear as postage stamps next to the bill-boards of the big-name acts. Thanks to Al Murray and Avalon Promotions, sizable D.A.A.S. posters were spread across town. Al is a true believer in the D.A.A.S. cause, and I have no doubt it meant as much to him to have the boys appearing at the Fringe again as it did to Tim Ferguson and Paul McDermott.

I earlier warned that performing at the Edinburgh Fringe after 10 pm can be lethal for an act without song, dance or the ability to intimidate and dominate.

D.A.A.S. were to go up at 9 pm sharp, the cusp of the late-night horror zone. As in the past, there was no dressing-room as such, simply a brightly lit corridor between a stairwell, an elevator and the door to the stage. And, more pressingly, there was no toilet within easy access. Bear in mind that I am a senior citizen who would normally be in bed by 9 pm, and at sixty, the spirit may be willing, but the bladder is weak. There was no way out, I had a job to fulfil. I was hired to present a short introduction and then play the few guitar chords required while pretending to be a dithering old performer well past his peak. Since I actually was a dithering old performer well past his peak, I was the natural choice for the gig.

As night fell, generally around 9 pm in Edinburgh this time of year, my flu symptoms descended. That first night the house was close to full. I sensed McDermott's tension. He was pacing more frequently than usual. Or it could simply be the case that there was not a chair in sight. Not one without wheels, in any case.

Even if Tim had the ability to pace, he wouldn't have bothered. He sat scribbling and chatting to whoever passed by that stair-well-cum-dressing-room. News from front of house that Al Murray and Jon Thoday were in attendance saw McDermott lift his pace and my bladder shudder. Tim was overjoyed.

A completely blocked left ear meant my foldback speaker was set to deafening. At one stage during the set the ear moment-arily cleared. The guitar was too loud, and the tempo a little too fast. I pitied McDermott beside me, trying to sing above my twelve-string rabble. The ear soon blocked again and, while I couldn't hear too well, I could clearly see Al Murray at the back of the room, beaming like a proud father as the All-Stars did their worst, which is always their best: shock, awe, filth and insult instigating a smattering of mid-show walkouts before a standing ovation to end the evening.

One down, nine to go. I did not stay for after-show drinks that first night in the Bunker Bar beneath the venue, as my viral sputum was best shared alone in my hotel room.

The morning after I sat by myself in a Greek cafe not far from The Pleasance. One of the most outstanding changes I noticed was the food. From past experience the definition of a meal in Scotland was something vaguely organic rolled in batter and deep-fried. This time the choice was wide, fresh and edible. I sat quietly enjoying my tiropita, reading former Bishop of Edinburgh Richard Holloway's *Looking in the Distance: The Human Search for Meaning*. As I glanced up into the distance I had a clear view of Arthur's Seat, the main peak of a group of mountains surrounding Edinburgh. I'd climbed it last time; this time I had no intention of climbing peaks of any type. Edinburgh was overrun with young hopefuls flushed with the self-importance of youth, thousands of them, a city full of butterflies, all hatching in the stomachs of these young performers. Youthful ambition had long abandoned me, I think mainly in frustration. I lacked drive, I followed in other people's wakes (these days I go to them). I was quietly overcome with gratitude to be in Edinburgh again, exploring familiar ground, but with no onus upon me; I was onus-free. I had nothing to prove. Just a single role: to serve the Doug Anthony All-Stars and those who made it possible for this dream of theirs to play out.

One of the All-Stars' first promotional duties was to perform three songs as part of a BBC radio program. *An Audience with Al Murray* was to be recorded before a live audience and broadcast to a mere four million listeners. The BBC venue, a massive complex rivalling Cirque du Soleil in scale, had been set up in the grounds of George Heriot's School, where I first supported D.A.A.S. in 1989. The most difficult part of this exercise was to find three D.A.A.S. songs suitable for the BBC audience – a near impossible task. 'World's Best Kisser' seemed harmless enough, until the verse:

> I've only kissed one girl before,
> My grandma on the kitchen floor,
> She dribbled and grinned and said,
> 'Hey, kid, you taught me things your grandpa never did.'

Not particularly BBC-friendly. 'Krishna Riding Shotgun' was quickly dismissed due to the final stanza:

> And when Irish eyes are trying,
> To make the Pommies pay,
> We'll get Krishna and his shotgun
> To join the I.R.A. Hari Ha Hooray!

No luck there. 'Broad Lic Nic' made the cut, even with its finale:

> I pray that when I die
> There'll be someone else around
> To kiss my arse goodbye.

'Arse' was a no-no, but 'ass' was okay. A second number, the Irish ballad 'The Auld Triangle', was perfect for the BBC with its sweet harmonies and sight gags. Sight gags can work a treat on radio: the listening audience are induced to attend the show to see what all the fuss in the studio was about. The third choice was 'The Sailor's Arms', a rollicking sea shanty about cross-dressing and gender ambiguity. The Brits love that stuff, even though a few producers on the studio floor turned a bit pale when it came to the chorus:

> Love is where you find it
> Wherever that may be
> For me it was in the Sailor's Arms
> With a better man than me
> Her husky voice seduced me
> My heart was in a mess

As I sat upon her knee
And something twitched beneath her dress
There was something more than knees beneath her dress . . .

These appearances no doubt lured a certain audience to the D.A.A.S. shows. What they didn't expect when they turned up was that this ever-so-slightly-bawdy bunch of elder gents had a lot more powder in the gun than just asses and cross-dressers. The Beeb crowd was not quite ready for songs glorifying bestiality and internet porn. Hence, each night at around the same point, a fair chunk of the audience stood up and left. There is a line late in the show where Paul McDermott shakes his head and mutters, 'I think you people may have forgotten what we were really like.' It garners one of the biggest laughs of the night, and often comes after one of the most offensive new entries in the D.A.A.S. songbook. At the beginning of this book I quoted a few lines from that early All-Stars anthem 'Broad Lic Nic'. These lyrics read like a nursery rhyme compared to this new tune, 'Self-Pollution', a stern warning on the dangers of onanism. I shall here quote from those lyrics (and I expect induce quite a few walkouts from this book):

Bikini-clad she-male dwarves on crack
Squirting female bondage slaves get turkey-slapped
German bi-sex romps with drunk teen amateurs
While big-boned chicks from Brazil peg homo nerds.

Some who stayed in their seats for the duration included critics and reviewers. Within days D.A.A.S. had made the top-twenty must-see shows in *The List*. The reviews rolled in. None was less than four-star and all were eloquently written; these reviewers had seen through the filth and muck floating on the surface of the show to the hairier underbelly, which spoke of loss, decay, death and love. It seems no matter how brutally McDermott ridicules, chastises and mistreats his companion All-Star in the wheelchair, what seeps through the horror is an indefinable but undeniable love between these men. And the critics agreed.

> The reunited and rambunctious musical trio provide proper, from-the-gut, I-can't-believe-they-just-said-that laughs. Do you catch your breath sometimes, wondering if McDermott has gone too far? You bet you do. Yet because Ferguson licenses all this disrespect, because this nastiness is done with such palpable love, instead it's life-affirming, liberating.
>
> ★ ★ ★ ★
>
> Dominic Maxwell, *The Sunday Times*, 9 August 2016

> So, did the profanity match the quality of their previous era? Well, hell yes . . . In an era when Fringe comebacks largely fall horrendously flat, DAAS can take pride in having produced a return with as much life in it as the offerings from their halcyon days. Clearly there's less venue-trashing and more medication-swallowing among the gang, but hats off to the Dougs for making a wholly unsentimental return to the Fringe fray.
>
> ★ ★ ★ ★
>
> Brian Donaldson, *The List*, 8 August 2016

It's been well worth the wait, as this show had tears of laughter running down faces all across the venue . . . the group has retained its dark-as-hell humour, its comic timing, and its ability to send themselves up continually . . . it's a breath of wonderfully filthy air on an otherwise dull day.

Graeme Strachan, *British Theatre Guide*, 8 August 2016

But these glowing reviews of the first week were not enough for the All-Stars. Only four out of a possible five? It didn't seem to matter that *The Times* never gave more than four. The four-star All-Stars were not amused. Eventually the first five-star review came. It was from *Chortle*. They were not initially impressed. *Chortle*? What kind of low-level drivel was this? But soon the boys were enjoying much reverence and backslapping for the rating.

There's an audaciousness to the bad taste that draws gasps among the guffaws from an audience more used to pussy-footing around disability. Outrageous it may be, but it's cathartic to be given licence to laugh at the taboo topic. And they get away with it because of the palpable love between Ferguson and McDermott.

Steve Bennett, *Chortle*, 13 August 2016

A five-star review from Bennett is a rare and envied occurrence. So rare that at this festival it was only D.A.A.S. and Louis C.K.

who made the five-star cut. Disdain turned to gloat. The boys were living their dream. Again. I was mercifully left out of these reviews for the most part. One reviewer, however, did mention that the show was introduced by the 'iconic' Flacco. Personally, I would have preferred 'funny' but I'll settle for 'iconic'. After all, it's a step up from 'unsexiest comedian alive'.

As the season progressed it became obvious that many of the audience were much like the Australian fans: having been affected and infected by the All-Stars of thirty years ago, they had come to pay homage. From all corners of Great Britain they came bearing gifts, old posters, memorabilia and, above all, gratitude. Over the course of the season a new audience began to emerge, D.A.A.S. virgins, and, in a sign of genuine respect, there was the increasing presence of other comedians, young and old.

The logistics of getting Tim Ferguson on- and offstage for the promotional appearances was daunting, but Tim was there to work, and was intent on answering all calls to duty. Cameron P. Mellor and Samantha Kelly bore the brunt of organising this exercise, constantly planning and carving a path for Tim's wheels. Two spots were secured within the bustling Gilded Balloon: the first was on the top floor, the second on the ground floor.

Mervyn Stutter's *Pick of the Fringe* has been running for twenty-five years. A now-legendary showcase, it features seven acts a day from 1 pm to 2.30. Getting Tim to the top of the Gilded Balloon was the easy part. Getting our man onstage was a completely different matter. The room features a classic proscenium arch with an elevated stage. The only option was manpower. A collection of the Gilded Balloon's heaviest gents was assembled to lift performer and chair onto the stage. An otherwise awkward moment was saved by the sublime skills of Paul McDermott, harassing and haranguing from the stage. This was McDermott at his best: the overzealous supervisor, commandeering and chastising crew and audience; the ringleader, offering no physical support but bursting with blame and bluster. Once Tim was onstage, the short set went down a treat and he was manhandled from the stage to the ground floor for a spot on Stephen K. Amos's *Talk Show*. Again, McDermott saved the day as Tim was hefted onto the stage. Once hefted, McDermott and Ferguson did what they do best, insulting the host, the audience and each other. Another triumph.

The day ended with complimentary tickets to Al Murray's show, *Let's Go Backwards Together*, in a Spiegeltent in the Assembly George Square Gardens. Murray owned the room from the moment he appeared in the guise of his alter ego the Pub Landlord, who wasted no time weaving a dozen punters unfortunate enough to inhabit the first few rows into his set, brilliantly improvising a plot around them. Al made it all feel seamless, the sign of a performer at the top of his game. The high point for me was a relentless barrage of a setpiece, a tour de force on the subject of xenophobia and misplaced nationalism. Never once didactic, any underlying 'message' it had was delivered as a sustained diatribe in the voice of this comically pontifical pub landlord – the crux of the piece being a massive whinge regarding the influx of foreigners to 'our' shores, moving backwards in time from the present to Scotland circa 500 BC. It was a performance of immense skill, depth, attack and endurance but, most importantly, it was take-your-breath-away funny. It was Al's ability to shun the moral high ground by wallowing unashamedly in immoral low filth that impressed me most, and I'm sure Al wouldn't mind me saying I sensed there was at times more than a touch of the All-Stars influence permeating his performance. I gave it ★ ★ ★ ★ ★.

I could barely speak to Al post show. I was reliving my Lily Tomlin moment. Remarkably, the D.A.A.S. stench still lingers in this town, but it's not their clothes this time – the potency of their scent is the material itself. I knew of no other comedians on the Fringe who were delivering performances of that calibre. Except Al Murray.

To the delight of Tim and Paul, Christopher Richardson appeared in the audience at The Pleasance, the venue this seventy-seven-year-old gentleman had managed until 2005. Here was the person Richard Fidler had contacted almost thirty years earlier to beg for a spot in the venue, and here I was, sharing a drink with the man himself. In that single move, Richard had changed not only D.A.A.S.'s trajectory but also the fortunes of The Pleasance. According to Richardson, the Dougs played a formidable role in rebooting its status in the 1980s. Christopher not only adored the new D.A.A.S. show, he was moved to tears. And it's not often you see the Little Black Cornflake of Hate respond with anything approaching empathy, but as he chatted to this man who gave D.A.A.S. their first real crack at the Fringe in 1987, I definitely detected moisture accruing in McDermott's eyes. Mind you, it could just have been those contact lenses playing up again.

Come the second week of the festival, D.A.A.S. were invited back to the BBC complex to appear on *The Janice Forsyth Show*. The Dougs performed another safe set free of filth but delivered with lashings of gusto. Then it was time to hit the streets. I had been dreading this moment. Any attempt at legal busking was not on the minds of Tim or Paul. They decided to hit the cobbled streets wherever they liked. A spot outside the Gilded Balloon was chosen, and then the rains came. The boys made a bold attempt, but it's hard to get a crowd to gather under a deluge of Scottish summer rain.

Another D.A.A.S. must-do was to revisit Late'n'Live, to return to the pit and throw themselves to the lions one last time. The date was set. On their second-last night of the Fringe, D.A.A.S. were booked to appear at Late'n'Live upstairs at the Gilded Balloon. Our call time? 1.30 am. I was horrified. The boys were more than up for it. After coming down from our show at The Pleasance, we headed for the Balloon. The venue was awash with patrons in various stages of intoxication. Tim would need assistance to scale the steps leading up to the stage once more. This time the venue staff hired a troupe of professional wrestlers to do the job. As a tag team of masked marvels lifted Tim to the stage, Paul McDermott was primed and champing at the bit, ready to attack – no doubt spurred on by memories of flying pints and glass ashtrays.

Whether it be the sight of a guy in a wheelchair or simply a D.A.A.S.-savvy audience, McDermott soon had to change his blustering tune. For all his bellowing insults, all this lot gave back was respect, attention and consideration. McDermott was not at all used to that. Not at 1.30 am in the toughest room of the Edinburgh Fringe. This mob was barely more offensive than the BBC audience. They listened, they laughed, they showed their appreciation. I was relieved, McDermott was disgusted, Tim was having the time of his life hitching a ride offstage in his human harness of pro wrestlers.

The final night of the All-Stars' festival run was a Sunday. The boys were in fine form. Although they'd toured Australia for the past two years, they had never before attempted ten consecutive performances. The show was tight, in a rambling ramshackle sort of way, and ended with yet another standing ovation. D.A.A.S. prepared for the encore tune, a crowd favourite for thirty years. Paul had barely begun the intro when, to the surprise of everyone in the theatre, a figure in a bright pink suit leapt out from side stage and grabbed a microphone. It was Mervyn Stutter. He had an unexpected announcement to make: the Doug Anthony All-Stars were the recipients of a Spirit of the Fringe award, one of 'The Merv's', as they are affectionately known. After Mervyn's kind words a trophy was handed to Tim. Mervyn then promptly left the stage and the boys ripped into a roaring rendition of 'I Fuck Dogs'. Thank you, Edinburgh, and goodnight.

With my influenza on the wane, I stayed around for some of the post-performance celebrations. I met one person whose life was changed by the Dougs at the Prince Patrick Hotel in the 1980s, and there were new, younger fans who had never seen anything like D.A.A.S. There was much adoration and love shared around, and some tearful goodbyes from the dauntingly professional staff and crew at The Pleasance. The Fringe has always been a twenty-four-hour party for those with the stamina and 2016 was no different. The concept of 'letting loose' was beyond me. After all, we were flying to London the following day for a season of shows at the Soho Theatre. But it didn't stop McDermott or Ferguson, the latter allegedly spending the final night of the festival venue hopping (or rolling) until 5 am.

The Soho season was virtually sold out on our arrival in London.

Opening night saw D.A.A.S. deliver one of their best shows of the tour. They were performance fit and, with a batch of rave reviews under their belts, cocky and keen. The Soho Theatre in Dean Street has an atmosphere reminiscent of the old Bear Pit in Edinburgh – steep raked seating surrounded by an upstairs balcony.

Some very special guests turned up in the audience for the Soho gigs. Among them were veteran comedy comrades John Moloney and D.A.A.S. mentor Jerry Sadowitz. In an extraordinary admission, Sadowitz confessed to being moved to tears and unsure as to whether he should be laughing at certain points. This from the only act that has ever intimidated D.A.A.S.

Every performance drew standing ovations. Even after one show in which I completely forgot the chords to the first number, Tim forgot his opening lines and McDermott forgot the final ten minutes of the show and had to be dragged from the comfort of the dressing-room (complete with toilet) back onstage to complete the gig. It seemed the more cracks revealed, the more poignant the result. What a treat to be involved in a show where lack of stagecraft, memory or comic timing is all part and parcel of the charm. The tour brought into focus for me what the heart of this show truly is. It is the tale of a pensioner, a cripple and a cocksure silver fox dicing with death, decay and ageing. And it offers an antidote: laughter. This unexpected adventure at the age of sixty provides a stark contrast to the young man on his first overseas tour. This time around I held no dreams of world domination; gone was any callow vainglorious swagger. Nor was there any sign of that youthful symbol of hope, a wallet full of condoms.

Al Murray's daunting tour schedule had him say his good-byes before the end of the season. Cameron P. Mellor attempted a speech but there were truly no words to convey the extent of our gratitude to this man who had made the triumphant return of D.A.A.S. to the northern hemisphere a reality. Clearly Al Murray loves these men. And that love is reciprocated. D.A.A.S. came, were seen, and conquered. Again.

Tim and I flew home the day after the final show. Unlike some in the group, Tim and I had work to return to: the Larkspur was about to premier his debut feature film, and I had a book to complete. It rained on the last day. I felt comforted by that low grey London lid. It was a breeze getting through

Heathrow, and the comforts of business class had me sleeping intermittently during the twenty-hour flight to Australia. Each time I awoke I looked over to see Tim Ferguson, bathed in the light of his laptop, typing away at yet another script, a new project. The man is unstoppable.

Through a cosy in-flight haze of fine pinot noir and half a Valium, I pondered this past month. How D.A.A.S. were described as cathartic, unsentimental, wonderfully filthy, life-affirming and liberating by the British press. Can there really be some purpose to this absurd profession? Are comedians akin to Richard Holloway's small and forgotten souls who are able to 'bear witness against injustice and cruelty . . . recording angels whose words stand defiantly against those evils they protest . . . the voices of the universe's victims'?

A reviewer writing for *The Scotsman* seemed to hint as much:

The All Stars came back to the Edinburgh Fringe this year and their show was one of the greatest things I have ever witnessed . . . Life is a hell of a business and we endlessly seek some meaning or at least some understanding of what it's all about. And great comics – truly great comics – help us in this quest just as much as the most celebrated writers and philosophers do . . . Comedy, at its finest, is as serious as any art and the tendency of some to dismiss it as somehow lesser than other forms continues to frustrate me . . . Tim Ferguson, I salute you. Thanks for reminding me of those three important words: Tick f***ing tock.

Euan McColm, *The Scotsman*, 30 August 2016

Was it true? Could my youthful remonstrations at being dragged from high art to lowbrow prove to be the reverse? And all the while I've actually been plummeting upwards? Or perhaps I was just overtired, overthinking and overcome by the extraordinary response the Dougs garnered from an audience half a world away. Perhaps it's enough to be simply funny, like Spike Milligan, Victor Borge or Eric Morecambe. For Al Murray, the whole game is a dance, an experience to be shared.

> Performance occupies this ritualised thing, which is why I also think . . . you know, comics who are 'edgy comics' aren't edgy to their audience, they are just giving them what they want. I mean, if my mum and dad went to see the Dougs that would be edgy for them, but to the Dougs' audience they are not. So what you've got – it's this overused expression – the theatre is like a safe space, it's literally somewhere we can play together and you are doing a dance with the audience, you're on a date with them, or whatever: it's like that.

On our arrival at Sydney airport at 5 am it was straight through customs, as Tim instantly recognised the stern-faced border security guard; the pair had gone to primary school together. It's not often you see a customs official welcome you with a broad grin. (The only low point on the return journey was when our wheelchair assistant in Dubai mistook me for Tim's father.) I arrived home at 6 am. I took a stroll around the harbour foreshore, scanning the immense clear blue sky for at least one comforting grey cloud.

If someone had told me thirty years ago that I would still be performing as Flacco in my dotage, I would have shuddered in my Doc Martens. Yet I have Flacco to thank for introducing me to the Larkspur, the Little Black Cornflake of Hate and the nationally treasured Boab. Looking back now I can almost laugh. Almost.

And so the D.A.A.S. army rolls on. At a snail's pace. But at least they can stop and smell the dirt. Filth has always been a key ingredient in the D.A.A.S. armoury. Filth, mirth and after-birth – now there's a title for a D.A.A.S. show, should there still be three men left standing to deliver. Correction: two guys standing and one sitting very pretty. D.A.A.S. won't be burning out this time. Life's too clement these days. Tempers don't flare, they simmer, and egos are bruised, not battered.

As for this Naked Mole Rat, just as I stood in the wings watching D.A.A.S. in the eighties, these days I continue to be amazed and moved by the extraordinary connection these men have with their audience. It has been an unexpected privilege to carry my spear beside these distinguished but not quite extinguished gentlemen.

ACKNOWLEDGEMENTS

Whenever I think of the past, it
brings back so many memories.
STEVEN WRIGHT

I am forever indebted to those instrumental in getting *D.A.A.S.:
Their Part in My Downfall* off the ground, on the road and onto
the page.

THE PLAYERS

Lead vocals

Janet A. McLeod, Rod Quantock, Frank Woodley, Greg
Fleet, Sue-Ann Post, Mandy Jones, Patrick Stokes, Michael
Petroni, Eddie Izzard, Steve Abbott and Mark Trevorrow

Key boards

Jane Palfreyman, Sarah Baker, Ali Lavau, Louise Cornegé
and the Allen & Unwin ensemble
Edwina Stewart and the HLA Management combo

The highly strung quartet

Paul McDermott – on wobble board and strumpet

Richard Fidler – on ear drum and horn of plenty

Tim Ferguson – on medication and old triangle

Flacco – on before D.A.A.S.

The Avalon management top brass section

Al Murray – on percussion and purse strings

Jon Thoday – on repercussions

Richard Allen-Turner – on status cymbals

Backed by Bjorn Wentlandt, Adam Booker, Karl 'Special K' Wustrau, Rhys Thomas, Victoria Wedderburn and Charlotte James

Dynamic duet

Samantha Kelly and Anne-Sophie Marion – second fiddlers

Work experience guy

Cameron P. Mellor – frugal horn and ill wind section

The maestro

Ted Robinson – conductor and insulator

Choir of angels

Di Star, Brian Livingston, Marlene Zwickler, Frehd Southern-Starr, Shane Rozario, Marc Urbanski, Graeme Petrie, Mat Govoni, Geoff Kelso, Bridie Mayfield, Pammy Swain, Marty Coombes, Joel, Jordan, Ilter, Ally, Tor, Kristy, Claire, Tommy, Rachel, Shelley, Sa and Jess

Composers

Lyrics from the following songs are reproduced with the permission of the Doug Anthony All-Stars: 'Broad Lic Nic', 'I Fuck Dogs', 'Krishna Riding Shotgun', 'The Sailor's Arms', 'War Song' and 'World's Best Kisser'.

Decomposer

Some lyrics from 'Self-Pollution' are reproduced with the permission of Paul McDermott.

The audience

Chortlers, cheerers, applauders and supporters of D.A.A.S., from the streets of Canberra to the cobbled roads of Scotland and beyond